From Our Springtime

Judaic Traditions in Literature, Music, and Arts
Harold Bloom and Ken Frieden, *Series Editors*

פון אונזער פרילינג

ליטערארישע זכרונות
און פארטרעטן

פון
ראובן אייזלאנד

ארויסגעגעבן פון ה. אייזלאנד
יובל קאמיטעט מיאמי ביטש.
פלארידא ...
אין פארלאג אינזל נויארק
1954

Title page of the original edition of *Fun unzer friling,*
drawn by B. Kopman.

From Our Springtime

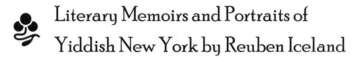

Literary Memoirs and Portraits of
Yiddish New York by Reuben Iceland

Translated by Gerald Marcus

SYRACUSE UNIVERSITY PRESS

Copyright © 2013 by Syracuse University Press
Syracuse, New York 13244-5290

First English Edition 2013
13 14 15 16 17 18   6 5 4 3 2 1

This work originally appeared as Part I of *Fun unzer friling,* by Reuben Iceland (New York: Inzl, 1954).

All photographs are courtesy of Judith Meiselman, except where noted.

Parts of the chapter on Zishe Landau appeared previously in slightly different form in *Pakntreger* (Fall 2010). The chapter on Anna Margolin appeared previously in slightly different form in *Yiddish, Modern Jewish Studies* (Fall 2011).

The paper used in this publication meets the minimum requirements of the American National Standard for Information Sciences—Permanence of Paper for Printed Library Materials, ANSI Z39.48-1992.

For a listing of books published and distributed by Syracuse University Press, visit our website at SyracuseUniversityPress.syr.edu.

ISBN: 978-0-8156-3303-7

Library of Congress Cataloging-in-Publication Data
Iceland, Reuben, 1884–1955.
    [Fun unzer friling. English]
    From our springtime : literary memoirs and portraits of Yiddish New York / by Reuben Iceland ; translated by Gerald Marcus. — 1st English edition
        pages cm — (Judaic traditions in literature, music, and art)
    Includes index.
    "This work originally appeared as Part I of Fun unzer friling (New York: Inzl, 1954)"—ECIP title page.
    ISBN 978-0-8156-3303-7 (cloth : alk. paper) 1. Iceland, Reuben, 1884–1955. 2. Poets, Yiddish—New York (State)—New York—Biography. I. Marcus, Gerald. II. Title.
    PJ5111.5.I24A3 2013
    839'.18303—dc23
    [B]   2012045872

Manufactured in the United States of America

In cherished memory of David Kazanski

Contents

Illustrations

⚘ Acknowledgments

I AM DEEPLY INDEBTED to the many people who responded generously to my requests for information and help, and without whom this translation would not have been possible. I want to thank first of all Jules Chametzky, who read an early version of the manuscript and gave me much needed encouragement and advice. Throughout the course of this project, Itzik Gottesman gave me the benefit of his great knowledge of Yiddish and the world of Yiddish. Ben Sadock was extraordinarily generous with his time and expertise and helped solve many linguistic riddles. I am indebted to Ruth Wisse, who suggested a solution to the mystery of "the sweet singer in Israel" (chapter 6, note 1). Ben Feldman's close reading of the manuscript and advice were extremely helpful. Sheva Zucker and Binyuman Schaechter helped greatly with linguistic questions. I thank Naomi Tannen and Joe Mahay for their help and support. I thank my dear friend Isidore Haiblum, whose rich knowledge and love of Yiddish have been an inspiration for many years.

I thank the librarians and archivists at YIVO Institute as well as the librarians at the Dorot Jewish division of the New York Public Library. The help and advice of Ilana Abramovitch, Joel Shatzky, and Jeffrey Shandler has been very much appreciated. I thank Ben Kraus for his insights into religious questions and terminology and for giving me the benefit of his profound knowledge of Rabbinic and biblical Hebrew. I thank Robert Stevens for giving me access to recorded interviews with Reuben Iceland's children and for answering my many questions; much of the information that appears in the introduction came from him and those interviews. I thank my editor Mathew Kudelka and the editors at Syracuse University Press, in particular Ken Frieden, for his erudite afterword and for his support of this translation; and Jennika Baines and Kay Steinmetz, who patiently and expertly guided the manuscript through the complex process of becoming a book; and I thank Mary Petrusewicz for her fine copyediting. I especially want to thank my wife Frances, who believed in this translation from the very beginning, for her patience and support. And last, I thank Judith Meiselman for entrusting me with this project.

This translation is dedicated to Judith Meiselman and her late mother, Rebecca Iceland Halpern.

❧ Introduction

IN THE EARLY YEARS of the twentieth century, a number of young Jewish poets immigrated to the United States from Eastern Europe. They came together in New York City and formed one of the most important groups in Yiddish literary history. Reuben Iceland, who was a central member of the group, tells us the intimate stories of these poets' lives. He writes of their struggle to find their voices as poets and how they sought to formulate their revolutionary approach to Yiddish poetry. He tells us of their loves, their friendships and their feuds, and how they struggled to survive and provide for their families.

Most of them had grown up in traditional, religious Jewish communities where secular culture was discouraged and people lived according to long-established rules and customs. Although they had different reasons for leaving their homes to come to America, they all found themselves in the same environment where they were no longer bound by the old rules, where competing ideas were passionately held, challenged, and defended, and where differences of opinion could lead quickly to personal and intellectual rivalries.

Reuben Iceland arrived at Ellis Island on September 15, 1903 at the age of nineteen. He came from the small town of Radomysl in Galicia, which at that time was part of the Austro–Hungarian Empire and is now in Poland. Although he was brought up in a traditional Hasidic family, he became interested in secular culture while still a teenager, a tendency that met with disapproval from his parents and the townspeople; and when he began to introduce other young people to his secular books, the animosity became more intense. He had already begun to write poetry when he left the constrained life of his provincial town and immigrated to the United States.

Five years after his arrival, he married Minne Gottfurcht, who lived in the same tenement as he. They had three children, two sons and a daughter. In their early years together, they lived in small, crowded apartments in rundown neighborhoods in the Bronx, Brooklyn, and the Lower East Side of Manhattan. Like most of his contemporaries, Iceland was forced to take jobs in factories or engage in other forms of manual labor in order to support himself and his family. During much of this early period, he worked as a packer in a hat factory. He describes the heavy toll this took on him:

> In the corner where I worked there were constant clouds of uncoiling steam, hissing from huge four-cornered copper vats and from monstrous hydraulic machines. With the eternal gloom, the eternal choking stench, the constant pain in my back, and the burning in my feet from standing every day for ten or more hours, my mood was always bleak. (p. 2)

One year, having been laid off his job at the hat factory and having no other prospects, he opened a small delicatessen in Brooklyn with financial backing from his brother, but he could not make a go of it. Giving away food to his hungry friends also did not help his bottom line, and he was, much to his own relief, forced to close. In a later period of unemployment he worked in a large delicatessen owned by his brother on the Lower East Side. Because of the very long hours he had to work, he moved his family into an apartment near the store to avoid commuting to his job. The contrast between his intellectual and literary aspirations and his physical struggle for survival was summed up succinctly by his wife, who, seeing him one day from their window carrying a heavy barrel, said to their daughter, "Look at the poet, carrying pickles on his back."

The poets of that time had to have tremendous energy and resilience to withstand the punishing work they did, find the strength to raise their families, stay out late at night discussing literature, and still find time and stamina to write their poetry. These difficult circumstances were reflected in their poetry:

> [Zishe] Landau held that by poeticizing the mundane, poetry would show that joy exists and can be everywhere in all kinds of circumstances. I preached the poetry of the mundane in order to show how

gray, how impoverished, and how dull the atmosphere was in which we were sentenced to live. Mani Leyb did not want to hear of bringing into poetry what he hated so much in life. In his opinion, poetry should concern itself only with the inner life of the individual, who throws off his gray, mundane surroundings and dreams of a more beautiful and brilliant life. (p. 70)

Eventually, Reuben Iceland was able to give up physical labor and support himself and his family by writing for the daily newspaper *Der tog* (The day).

In 1907 Iceland and his friends formed the group that revolutionized Yiddish poetry in America; it came to be called Di Yunge (The young ones). They met every evening in cafes and restaurants, where they held long, heated discussions, gossiped, and read their latest works to one another. The group provided the camaraderie and artistic stimulation that were essential to their development as poets as well as a refuge from the brutal reality of their daily lives in the shops and tenements.

In the anthologies and journals they published, Di Yunge established—for the first time in the history of Yiddish literature—a credo based on aesthetic rather than ideological or religious considerations.

We proclaimed [poetry's] freedom and its right to an independent life. We maintained that poetry should not exist by reason of whatever ideas it has, because it lives for its own sake. It has its own place and its own function in life. Therefore it is not obliged to—no, it must not take upon itself—other functions, because then it would not be true to itself. (pp. 6–7)

This was a radical innovation in Jewish literature. Aestheticism was contrary to the traditional values of Jewish communal life, which stressed the religious, ethical, and practical value of ideas. Literature, to be acceptable, was expected to serve those values. The doctrine of art for art's sake was repugnant also to politically radical Jews because they considered it effete and bourgeois. And most ordinary immigrants were indifferent to the poetry of Di Yunge because, in avoiding themes they considered parochial or nostalgic, the poets rejected the very ingredients the immigrants expected and yearned for:

> For the new immigrants, . . . we, the new generation of writers and especially the poets, were even more alien than the older writers. We didn't follow the spirit and taste of their favorites on the other side of the ocean, and we didn't concern ourselves in our poems with the themes that would be close to them, because they could only be themes that reminded them of the Old Country. They had fled from the Old Country because it was for them so confining and distasteful; yet once they arrived here, they missed it. The things they missed were *shabosyontevdik*, and they wanted to find it in the things they read in Yiddish. In our lyrical poems, we couldn't and didn't want to give them that. We didn't want to be like the poor aunt who visits the rich uncle sometimes on a Friday night to eat a little gefilte fish. (p. 79)

As a result, the readership of Di Yunge was small.

A central concern of Di Yunge was the state of the Yiddish language itself. If it was to serve pure artistic goals, then the language, too, had to be pure. It must be ridded of clichés, *daytshmerish,* and other foreign influences. Iceland writes that Di Yunge "enriched" Yiddish by "impoverishing it." That is, by depriving it of foreign influences, writers were forced to search for equivalent words in Yiddish.

> If we didn't find available words for everything we needed, we would surely find words that could evolve, bend, be rebuilt and re-created so that they would serve our goals while retaining the spirit and sound of our language. (p. 8)

The purification of Yiddish was one of Di Yunge's major accomplishments and contributions to Yiddish literature: "More than anything, we purified the language. We protected it, we nurtured it, we made of it a wonderful, poetic instrument." (p. 54)

American culture was foreign to Di Yunge and even disdained by its poets, but they were deeply affected by it. It was an influence that helped determine the direction and many of the qualities of their poetry. Iceland notes that the poetry of Di Yunge could not have been written anywhere else but in America. The poets wanted very much to be Americans. But they dreamed of being Americans who retained and treasured their Yiddish culture. Indeed, they dreamed of the day that Yiddish literature would be considered part of American literature, on an equal footing with English.

The most important publication by Di Yunge was *Shriftn* (Writings), a series of anthologies of poems and prose that first appeared in 1912. The anthologies were important because they "brought a new message to the whole of Yiddish literature" and "began to crystallize a collective artistic will, and because a school would later emerge from them—the first literary school among us." (p. 54) The books were beautifully and tastefully designed, thanks to David Ignatoff, who served as editor. He spent a great deal of time and money on them and included reproductions and illustrations by contemporary Jewish artists.

The third volume of *Shriftn* was the most important for Reuben Iceland personally because it included his most mature poems and was therefore a landmark in his life's work. At that point the group was beginning to break up, each poet going his own way while remaining true to the fundamental ideals of Di Yunge. The breakup of Di Yunge was, in Iceland's opinion, quite natural, inevitable, and ultimately beneficial to the writing of the poets of that circle. A school is merely an "exit," he believed, through which the poets must leave in order to mature and develop individually. Only "followers and imitators" remain behind.

In 1919 Iceland began a relationship with Roza Lebensboym, who came to be known by her pen name, Anna Margolin. She was one of the most gifted Yiddish poets in New York and was, by most accounts, a beautiful and passionate woman. Their relationship, though stormy, was fruitful artistically, for they encouraged and inspired each other. He waited several years until his children were teenagers, then left his family to move in with Margolin. They remained together until her death over thirty years later.

Margolin had a strong impact on Iceland's life and poetry, as he did on hers:

> In the fall of 1919, I came into her life. In the first few years there was great intensity and struggle between us. Many of the poems in my book *Fun mayn zumer* (From my summer), which came out in Vienna in 1922, and a very great part of her book of poems, which came out in New York in 1929, describe in different ways that intensity and that struggle. (p. 149)

Anna Margolin's book *Lider* (Poems) was received enthusiastically in Europe, but in New York it did not receive the notice she felt it deserved. Prejudice against women writers may have been part of the reason, but she also had alienated many of her and Iceland's friends by speaking dismissively of their work. The lukewarm reception of her book was, no doubt, one of the reasons she withdrew from literary life. She never again published a book of poetry, although she continued to write regular articles for *Der tog*. She was in a continuous state of emotional upheaval that made social and professional relationships very difficult. In time she became a complete recluse, emotionally unable to accept visits even from friends and poets whom she longed to see. She left her apartment very rarely.

Iceland continued to support his children until they were grown and his wife Minne until her death. He remained close to his children until the end.

When he was fifty-five, Iceland had his first heart attack; there were to be several more. As his health deteriorated, so did Anna Margolin's, who suffered from extremely high blood pressure. She died in 1952 at the age of sixty-five. That same year, Iceland moved to Miami Beach, where he spent his last years. There he met Ida Kay and they were married in March 1953. Reuben Iceland died on June 18, 1955. His daughter arranged for his remains to be brought to New York.

The memoir closes with an elegiac chapter about Abraham Liessin, a highly prominent poet who was older than Iceland. The chapter takes place in a summer colony where Liessin, Iceland, Margolin, and other Yiddish poets and writers were staying, creating a kind of *Magic Mountain* ambience that intensified the intimacy, friendships, and conflicts among the colony residents. The outside world intruded in the form of daily newspapers, which introduced the terrible foreboding that the onset of the Hitler years and anti-Jewish riots in Palestine were causing.

Although he disagreed with Liessin's approach to poetry, Iceland had great respect for him nonetheless and took great pleasure in joining the other writers who gathered every day on Liessin's porch to take part in intellectual discussions. Liessin had a daughter who was very intelligent but severely handicapped physically and deformed. He was very proud of her intelligence and her ability to contribute original ideas to the discussions that he had with the poets who came to visit him, but she required constant care for all of her physical needs. This burden fell mainly on his sister-in-law, who, over the years, was being slowly worn out by the weight of the responsibility. Liessin's personal tragedy and the impending tragedy of the Jews in Europe, with its dire implications for Yiddish culture in the United States, intertwine in this intensely poignant chapter.

The poets who formed Di Yunge came to America filled with youthful fervor and a mission to transform Yiddish literature. They found a chaotic environment that allowed them to search and experiment, but only if they were willing to live on the edge, only if they had the stamina to withstand brutal physical conditions and the grind of poverty. Despite the toll these conditions took on them, the poets of Di Yunge created a superb and unique body of work. They wrought a revolution that enabled Yiddish to become the vehicle for poetry that was on a par with American and world literature.

A Note on the Translation

One summer evening about ten years ago, in a restaurant in the Adirondacks, my wife and I had dinner with our friend Judith Meiselman and her mother, Rebecca Iceland Halpern, Reuben's daughter. She talked about her father at length and with great love, speaking about his devotion to his family and to poetry. She also talked about his close friendships with members of Di Yunge and how, when she was still a young girl, he would sometimes take her on a Sunday to join his friends in their favorite restaurants. She cast quite a spell on us that night, and we left feeling as if we had actually met Reuben Iceland. A few years later, after her mother's death, Judith asked me to translate his memoir, *Fun unzer friling*.

As often happens with translations, some of the most interesting and expressive aspects of Iceland's writing were the most difficult to translate. For example, Iceland writes long, complex, even Proustian sentences, interspersed with short staccato ones, that are sometimes grammatically incomplete but create a beautiful, poetic rhythm. Occasionally I had to join some of the shorter sentences together or simplify some of the longer ones in order to make them intelligible in English. I did this as seldom as possible. In translating the poetry that is cited throughout the book, I did not attempt to re-create rhymes or keep to the original rhythm. Rather, I tried to convey the mood and imagery of the poems. Transliterations are provided so that the reader will be able to experience the poems' rhythms and sound patterns.

I transliterated Hebrew terms and names to reflect the pronunciation that was used by Yiddish speakers; for example, *Sukes*, not Succoth, and Dvoyre Leye, not Dvorah Leah. In the case of names of well-known people, I followed the spelling that is commonly used in order to avoid confusion.

Fun unzer friling has two parts. I have translated the first part, in which Iceland describes his life and the revolution in poetry that he and his friends set in motion. Here he analyzes their poetry in great detail, describing it with exquisite nuance. Part 2, which is entirely distinct from Part 1, consists of reviews and essays about Yiddish and German writers, as well as essays concerning Iceland's ideas about various aspects of Yiddish and German literature. I feel that these essays would be better served as part of an anthology of Iceland's collected works.

Fun unzer friling was published in 1954 when Iceland was gravely ill. It is the most extensive history of Di Yunge written by a core member of the group. It is also, by virtue of the beautiful and poetic quality of the writing, an important part of American Jewish literature. Except for some few excerpts, it has not been translated before. I hope this translation will, in some measure, provide the audience that was denied to Reuben Iceland in his lifetime, as well as to the other poets of Di Yunge, albeit in a language that was foreign to them.

1. Reuben Iceland, ca. 1927.

2. Reuben's father, Jehuda Leybish Iceland, in Poland.

3. Reuben's sister Khane in Poland;
murdered by the Nazis.

4. Reuben's younger brother Isaac in
uniform, ca. 1914. Killed in Word War I.

5. Reuben's first wife, Minne, ca. 1908.

6. Reuben and his daughter Rebecca Iceland Halpern, ca. 1948.

7. Reuben's granddaughters Judy and Joan, Rebecca's husband David Halpern, Rebecca, Reuben, ca. 1948.

 Foreword

WITH ELEVEN OF THE TWELVE ARTICLES, longer and shorter, that make up the first part of this book, I simply want to give my intimate impressions of the life and work of these poets and writers of my generation who were personally close and dear to me. Of course, in writing about them, their time, their activities, their disputes, their outlook on life, and their approach to word art, I will also have to mention other poets and writers who arrived with us during those same years, from 1905 to 1915. That was truly the springtime of the new Yiddish literature in America, with the fragrant buds, the colorful blossoms, the restlessness, the pain, the dreams, the longing, the expectations, and the hopefulness of young growth that one feels every spring.

If only certain names are mentioned, that doesn't mean that others were deliberately omitted. Nor does it mean that only the ones I mention are important enough to include. I will be writing only about those with whom I was intimate and whom I knew well enough that I could do right by them and their writing. If I was not close to someone during those years, I must not write about him, no matter who it was. I regret that in this book there will be no accounts about David Kazanski, A. Raboy, and—long years to him—Joseph Rolnik. For that I blame lack of strength and time.

Finally, I want to express my deep thanks to my friend the painter B. Kopman for drawing the title page for this book; to the Reuben Iceland Anniversary Committee, its chairman Dr. A. Mukduni, and his secretary David Friedman, who made it possible for this book to be published; and to my friend Herman Felzen, my brothers Khaym Pesakh and Moyshe Yankev, my sister-in-law Molly Iceland, and my fellow countrywoman and old friend, Rokhl Bernknopf. Without their help, this book could not have been published.

R. I.

From Our Springtime

❀ With Zishe Landau

WE WERE FOUR. Three wrote poetry and one, novels. Almost thirty years knit together. In literature and personally. We spent a lot of time together, dreamed together, together published journals and anthologies, quarreled and argued, sometimes over foolish whims, sometimes over wounded vanity, sometimes over serious personal matters and theoretical fine points. But we never parted. We always reconciled and again became one, as before. Now that Zishe Landau is gone, there is emptiness and grief in my heart. Yet when I sit writing about him, grief becomes mixed with joy—with the joy of a friend who wants to speak of a friend. Somehow his image floats before me as I saw him at different times, at different moments, and on different occasions. Somehow, I will speak of him.

Our First Meeting

I don't remember what year it was when I met Zishe Landau. Nor do I remember if it was late in autumn or early in spring. But I remember clearly that it was in the evening on Canal Street in front of the old Drukerman's bookstore, that the evening was cold, misty, and muddy, and that I wore a heavy winter coat. All the passersby wore heavy winter coats, as did everyone in the little group of young writers who were standing in front of the shop waiting for a new periodical that was supposed to be brought from the printers that very night. All of us, that is, except the thin blond boy with the big blue eyes, who was introduced to me as Zishe Landau—he wore a light, slim-fitting, leather-colored summer topcoat buttoned tight over a prominent belly.

Those who knew Landau later on, when he was broad and hefty, will find it hard to imagine that in his nineteenth or twentieth year he was thin, almost sickly, just as they will not, perhaps, imagine that he was a dandy back then who favored tight clothes, a stiff collar, and a derby. Though I should note that when it came to the derby, he was not an "only child." All of us in those years had rings notched into our foreheads from the hard, round hats we wore.

"Zishe Landau!" I exclaimed. "Are you really Zishe Landau?" I sized him up from head to toe. "And where is your mustache?"

"With your gold!"

My question referred to a bad poem of his that had been published under Pinski's editorship in *Arbeter* (Worker) in which *vontses* (mustache) became *vontsn* so that he could use it as a bad rhyme with *tantsn* (dance). For that time, though, and especially for a beginner, it was an interesting and heartfelt poem. His answer was an allusion to a number of poems I had recently written, which were just as bad as his and not at all as heart-felt and all of which glittered with gold. For that gold in my poems, I had my hard life to thank, and this is why:

Like most of the young Yiddish writers in America at the time, I was a factory worker—a packer in a hat factory. When I met Landau, I was already a married man, the father of a child, and life was very hard. The eternal yoke and the eternal worries stressed and depressed me. The fac-tory where I worked was one of the biggest in that trade and at the time also one of the cleanest. But still, in the corner where I worked there were constant clouds of uncoiling steam, hissing from huge four-corned copper vats and from monstrous hydraulic machines. With the eternal gloom, the eternal choking stench, the constant pain in my back, and the burning in my feet from standing every day for ten or more hours, my mood was always bleak. For me there was a single beacon in that gloomy life—the golden crown on the tip of a new skyscraper. On fine days, at a certain moment every afternoon, that crown would reflect the rays of the sun and itself became a sun—a golden, glowing sun. In my dreary corner in the factory, the sun would appear like a miracle. And though the miracle occurred almost every day, nonetheless, I always waited for it with a flut-ter in my heart, as you wait for a woman you love. And what did that sun not set ablaze in and around me! Wonderful landscapes blossomed before my eyes in the midst of the mountains of caps and stacks of hats and even bigger stacks of four-cornered and round boxes among which I stood as if walled in. In those moments, I fell in love with every girl in the shop; sunny fields floated through my dreams; thousands of memories from my childhood turned suddenly to gold and sought expression in my poems. Sought, but did not find. That is, I did not find the expression, and I wrote only bad poems.

Like a lot of beginners who have not yet found their own voice, I sang—perhaps without realizing it—with an alien voice, using poetic expressions that others before me had coined. I did not yet realize that even the strongest experiences and the deepest feelings do not in themselves make good poems. Only later, when one becomes richer artistically, often after great pain, does one uncover the secret that much more than *impression*—that is, experience and sensitivity—one has to have *expression*. The best words in the best order is what Coleridge demanded. That means rhythm and form, both valid only for a given poem and not for any other.

For Landau and me there was no love at first sight. We immediately began to speak the truth, and the truth hurts, especially when you are young. Landau was five years younger, but in my eyes I was the younger, with all the possibilities and hopes that shine on the youngest, but also all the pain and self-doubts that hurl you down one precipice and then another. To be young is to hope, for if a young poet has not achieved everything he dreams of today, he will certainly achieve it tomorrow, next year, or years later. What difference does it make? To be young, though, also means to be morbidly sensitive, and I was certainly that. At the time, the slightest unkind word or blow to my honor wounded me deeply. On our first meeting, Landau told me a lot of unkind things, and I, for my part, did not spare him. Perhaps what I told him also struck its mark. Yet in hindsight, Landau was more skillful and always remained so. To use words like knives thrust in each other's ribs—no one else could do it.

That night I tossed and turned. I felt so deeply wounded by my first meeting with Landau that I could not sleep. I spent all of the next day standing at work, empty inside, and when I got home I could not eat a bite. At the time, I was writing all of my unpublished poems in a clean notebook, then pasting the published poems into a second one. A few days after meeting Landau, I took both notebooks, tore them in half, and threw them into a burning stove. That was neither the first nor the last time that I tore up my poems, and it was always curative.

That particular trait—of telling the truth, especially about poetry and in such a biting way, so that it would penetrate deep into the bones—is one that Landau kept his whole life. The closer someone was to him, the more did Landau permit himself that openness. Very often he did it to learn whether it was possible to form a friendship with another poet. The moment Landau felt that a poet could not hear the truth about himself or his poetry, he became a stranger. He could still meet with him, play cards with him, brag about the preserves he had made or what a connoisseur of drinks he was, but he could no longer discuss poetry with that man.

Landau was not always correct in his judgments. No matter—who is always right? Unfortunately—and this was Landau's greatest fault—in his own eyes, he could never be wrong. Moreover, he often redeemed false-hoods with even greater falsehoods. It seems to me that this trait, just like telling someone the bare truth to his face, was something he inherited from the Hasidic court of his grandfather the Strickover Rebbe,[1] which is where he grew up. The progeny of rebbes learn from childhood to speak bluntly. In the households of rebbes, as in all households that constantly play politics, one is never wrong. It's always the other side that's wrong, the party with which one is having an open or hidden quarrel. The quarrels may be for the sake of heaven—because of one or another wrinkle in worship. The methods, though, aren't always heavenly. Even deceit is justified if it is necessary, or if one thinks it is necessary. Landau's quarrels were always for the sake of heaven. Even his unfairness or malice—as his targets called it—did not come from a wanton desire to cause pain, but from the fact that, like every poet, he could not always be an objective critic. Hippolyte Taine once remarked that every true poet who has his own method must by nature be one-sided and even believe fanatically that only his way is the correct one. Naturally, a person like that cannot

---

1. Rabbi Fischel Shapira of Strickov (1743–1822) was a disciple of the Magid of Mez-ritch, Rebbe Elimelech, and the Seer of Lublin. He was known for his extreme modesty and humility.

appreciate the value of anther poet, especially one who is going in a different direction.

Brotherhood

A closer acquaintance between Landau and me began at the meetings of the group Literatur, which published the two anthologies also called *Literatur*. We grew even closer in the summer of 1910, when we were preparing the second *Literatur* anthology. At those meetings, I got to know Ignatoff, Lapin, and Moyshe Warshaw, most of whom were included at one time or another in the group called Di Yunge, as were Rolnik, Schwartz, Halpern, Khaymovitch, Opatoshu, and Dilon, whom I had known earlier. I only met Raboy later. Kazanski and Leivick also came later. I knew Mani Leyb longer than any of them. Zeldin had introduced me to him in 1905, though we didn't become close friends until the summer of 1910.

The Literatur meetings were attended by sixty or seventy young people who, from time to time, published a poem or a sketch in one of the daily or weekly newspapers of that era. Most of them did not remain writers. Some of them, after a while, went to work for newspapers. Others became union leaders, doctors, dentists, pharmacists, or businessmen. At the meetings, from the start, the group began to emerge that would later make history with the *Shriftn* anthologies. Later, that group too split into smaller ones, and the smallest of these—Mani Leyb, Landau, and I—over time inherited the name "Yunge." Later, David Kazanski became one of us. Because of their approach to literature and their poetic nature, we also had to include Rolnik and Raboy, but they never completely identified themselves with us.

The name "Yunge" began as a derisory word for a group of young writers who in 1907 had the chutzpah to declare that one must free the little bit of Yiddish literary strength that existed from the influence of the newspapers, and who tried to create their own literary corner in the slender volumes of the monthly journal *Di yugend*. Later, the name came to mean all young writers who claimed to be different, though artistically they really had no relation to us. Only with the crystallization of our group did the name take on a definite meaning. Now it became the name of a unified school—the first literary school among Jews. A school that never wrote down its credo yet had recognizable traits that distinguished it from its surroundings and that put such a stamp on Yiddish poetry that to continue to write in the same manner as before was no longer possible.

Three people, different in temperament and character; different also in those vital (for a poet) childhood impressions of home, landscape, and environment, of melody, song, and story; different in education, adventures, dreams, aspirations, and formative influences (ethical, aesthetic, literary); different in their literary styles; nonetheless created a unified school with a clear method, a clear view, and clear artistic criteria. How this happened is a mystery to me to this very day. I explain it partly by the fact that, for all our differences, we had one trait in common: acuteness of the senses.

This is a trait that all artists have. If we were not the first artists, we were the first deliberately formed artist group in Yiddish poetry. Our outlook, our world view, our approach to humanity was artistic. The demands we placed on all Jewish poets—most of all on ourselves—were purely artistic. One of our cardinal requirements was not to be satisfied with what we knew simply because it was accepted, because we had heard it, or because we had "read it in books," but to approach every phenomenon with open eyes and an open mind and try to know it anew, to know it in our own way. Not so much with our intelligence as through the senses. Not logically but intuitively, psychologically.

This requirement was itself the result of a discovery. A discovery to which we came gradually, after much searching, reading, and comparing; after long days and nights spent deep in conversation about one thing— poetry, which was dearer to us than everything else and for which we would sacrifice everything, even the vanity that is for poets just as sharp as, if not sharper than, for women. We never spared one another. All the defects we saw in one another, we pointed out. And not with silk gloves, God forbid, but in the sharpest and most biting ways possible. We flogged one another until it hurt, until blood flowed. But it had the necessary effect.

When we appeared, Yiddish poetry was at the service of ideas and movements, social and national. The poets stood tall and took an honored place. But that poetry was, as always in such circumstances, dead and buried. We proclaimed the freedom of poetry and its right to an independent life. We maintained that poetry should not exist by reason of whatever ideas it has, because it lives for its own sake. It has its own place and

8. Members of Di Yunge, ca. 1907. Sitting from left: Menakhem Boraisha, Avrahm Reisen, Moyshe Leyb Halpern; standing from left: A. M. Dilon, H. Leivick, Zishe Landau, Reuben Iceland, A. Raboy. Pictures on the wall: on top, Joseph Rolnik; from left, Sholem Asch, I. J. Schwartz, Perets Hirshbeyn, Joseph Opatoshu. Courtesy of the YIVO Institute for Jewish Research.

its own function in life. Therefore it is not obliged to—no, it must not take upon itself—other functions, because then it would not be true to itself. And our literature sounded foreign then and sounds even more foreign today, when parties and movements rule life more than ever and place their dictatorial paws on everything and everything must serve them.

When we arrived, our poetry, especially here in America, was grating—shouting—bombastic and melodramatic when it dealt with social themes; soaked in Jewishness with an aroma of *tsholnt* and *mikve* when it involved itself with national themes; and scattered with spangles of poetic Germanisms when it wanted to express individual, lyric experiences. The poets of the past wrote their satiric poems in good, authentic Yiddish only when they wanted to laugh at something. Because nothing in their eyes was as ridiculous as authentic Yiddish. In retrospect, they were the ridiculous blood brothers of the authors of our old trashy (*shund*) novels. In those novels too, only the funny characters spoke good Yiddish. It was the heroes and heroines who had the authors' fullest sympathies because they were modern, up-to-date people who knew such modern things as love and who spoke with a poetic Germanized Yiddish.

As a reaction to all this and to all the clichés that our poetry was then full of, we Di Yunge impoverished it both in themes and language. So that we would not become tempted to fall into bombast, we threw out social themes; to protect ourselves from sweet, flowery language, we avoided national motifs. We realized that to properly express intimate, lyrical feelings, we must do two things: search within ourselves for understanding in order to understand the world; and at the same time, clean out all the garbage, all the absurd words that minor poets and half-baked newspaper writers had gathered in various alien places and from which that flowery gushing that passed for poetry had spread.

Having been impoverished of trite themes, our poetry became richer because we, in striving to know ourselves, opened so many gates and doors to the inner, individual life. Once we had pruned out all the foreign absurdities, Yiddish began to sound different—richer and more natural. This in itself was a great achievement. But we did not stop there. Our artistic instincts told us that our language did not lack words for the deepest experiences and finest moods. One need only look for them in the right places. If we didn't find available words for everything we needed, we would surely find words that could serve our goals while retaining the spirit and sound of our language. Mani Leyb found what he was seeking in the mouths of the folk. Landau and I found it in folklore: in the *Tsenerene*, the *tkhines*, the folksongs, the storybooks, and the Hasidic stories.

Landau and I went even further. We preached that one must throw out all poetic motifs and instead try to poeticize one's own life. Mani Leyb did not like this tendency. To his last day, he believed that this was all the result of a shameful influence that Kolya Teper had—especially on Landau. He forgot that I brought out the commonplace theme with my poems *Fun ale teg* (From every day) in 1914, when I hardly knew Teper. I think that in approaching the commonplace, we arrived, perhaps, at the most important contribution of Di Yunge—simplicity. Because only then was it possible for Yiddish to become a fine, poetic instrument.

But I don't mean to write here the history of Di Yunge. Even less, to do what we never did—set forth the program of Di Yunge.

An artistic school is no more than an exit, at which the artists who belong to it go their separate ways, in search of their own multifaceted experience and perfection. Only the followers and imitators remain stuck in the doorway. Along the way, every artist arrives through experience and maturity at new realizations, in the light of which the school and most of what it stands for become insignificant, often even comical or completely false. Through the years, all the poets of Di Yunge went through a series of transformations each in his own way, according to his character and to his new experiences in life and art. There were times when the nearest of the near felt estranged from one another—to the point of revulsion. It happened more often between Mani Leyb and Landau, less between them and me. Landau became sick to death of Mani Leyb's "musicality"; Mani Leyb came to loathe Landau's excessive cleverness; and those two did not conceal from each other what they thought. Both wanted to strike to the quick, and they did. Each was sure they would no longer speak to the other. But very quickly, they met again and embraced as if nothing had happened. However much we changed over the years, in essence we remained the same. Only the branches had gone in different directions. The trunk remained rooted in the same artistic convictions.

Zishe Landau

They say about Avreml Tshechanover[2] that when he was told about the invention of the horseless wagon, he asked why it was needed. When they answered, "Because it goes faster than a horse and wagon," he was, in his great naïveté, surprised: "Why don't they have any time?"

His great-grandson, Zishe Landau, drove an automobile, and if he never flew in an airplane, it was merely by chance. Instead of naïveté, he

---

2. Rabbi Avraham Landau of Tchechenov (1784–1875) was a revered and renowned scholar and rabbinical judge.

had cleverness, perhaps too much of it; but in essence, he was not far from his great-great-grandfather, the *gaon* and founder of the Tshechanover line. Also, Zishe Landau more than once asked with astonishment: "Why don't they have any time?" His surprise, though, was not directed at the inventor of a new means of transportation and the speeding up of the old, but at writers who pushed themselves forward with their elbows and brought to bear all kinds of means in order to arrive more quickly in the land of glory.

Above all, we could not stand literary *alrightniks*. These were the people who, justifiably or not, prospered with their literary merchandise. And like all parvenus, they jingled the little bit of change in their pockets and made a lot of noise about their success. I don't remember whether Landau, I, or someone else created the term "literary alrightnik." But none of us Yunge ever distanced himself more proudly, pursing his lips and buttoning up his jacket when a literary alrightnik began to puff himself up, than did Landau.

Landau also could not stand it when poets wanted to conquer the world by nonpoetic means.

When one of the now very famous Yiddish poets appeared among us, no one befriended him as enthusiastically as did Zishe Landau. But Landau was also the first of Di Yunge to distance himself from him, because it seemed to him that he noticed in the very talented new poet a tendency to obscure and mystify his poems in order to be more of a success with our uncultured, nonartistic audience, for whom "deep" was merely that which was vague, unclear, and therefore not understandable. Landau once said of one of these poets: "He has just gotten up on his feet when, already, he begins to prepare a state funeral for himself."

Once, when we were about to put together one of the first *Shriftn* anthologies, one of the big shots came running, beaming with joy. What was the big deal? Dr. Zhitlovski[3] had promised to contribute a piece for the next anthology.

---

3. Khaym Zhitlovski (1865–1943) was one of the most important and influential Jewish intellectuals of his time, a founding member of the Socialist Revolutionary Party in Russia, an advocate of Yiddish language and culture in Europe and the United States.

"Really! You've had a stroke of luck," Landau cried out. "On his coattails, you'll be able to slip more quickly into posterity." Never had I seen Landau look so disgusted.

Among the small circle of Di Yunge, there came to be an unwritten code concerning how a poet should conduct himself. We were especially insistent about what a poet should not do. Among the mortal sins were these: hanging out with celebrities to pass for a celebrity himself, flattering critics and editors, displaying lust for glory, and all cheap and underhanded ways of publicizing himself. Whatever one was ashamed to do publicly, one must not do privately.

The precept of a certain cynic, that laws are made to be broken, applied naturally also to the unwritten laws of a group as tightly knit as ours. With time, one grows apart from such precepts just as one grows apart from other childish things. But even in our youth, we used to laugh at the bidden and forbidden that we voluntarily took upon ourselves. It is only human that a writer should want to be popular; and if it doesn't come by itself, it is perhaps not pretty but no more than human to want to hasten it a little. Many successful writers have succeeded thanks not to their literary talent but to their talent for letting the world know they have talent. In other words, a lot of writers have succeeded mainly because of their sharp elbows.

I once pointed this out to Landau, who replied that this was certainly true, but what did it prove? Was it more acceptable because it was true? Besides, we weren't in a position to follow the lead of other literatures. For the others, it was worthwhile. In other literatures, if one became a successful writer, it meant money, honor, and sometimes even power, be it political or social. But for us? For us, if God helped and one became famous, one could sometimes earn a permanent corner in a newspaper with a salary of ten to, let's say, sixty, seventy dollars a week. But any newspaper writer who had nothing but a nimble pen, and who could write long columns on any theme and at every opportunity, could attain that glory.

When attacking an opponent, Landau would destroy him without pity. But not everyone was deserving of destruction at his hands. In that sense, too, he was the son of a rebbe's court: not with everyone was it worth quarreling. He chose his opponents very carefully.

Before we published our monthly journal *Inzl*, we worked out several guidelines for it. Landau didn't want any polemics in *Inzl*. He felt that one can persuade more quickly with laughter than with logic. Besides, he noted, most big shots and speechifiers were simply comic when they started to argue about literature, so one must laugh at them, not argue with them or about them. We, the others, tried to stand against him, but it was Landau who won. There were attacks in all sixteen issues of *Inzl*, but never polemics. Landau himself enlivened every issue of the journal with articles and notices in which he slashed away with irony as if with knives, but he did not resort to polemics.

All of which perhaps suggests that Landau was an elitist. Nothing could be further from the truth. On the contrary, he was the most democratic person I have ever known. No one was too lowly or too common for him. He could and did befriend people of every kind, and he never acted the great man or made a show of being a poet. He expressed contempt, scorn, and even disgust only to the literati who always and everywhere made you feel: "Make way, a writer is coming!"

Since I'm on the topic of *Inzl*, I want to recall an episode that shows how pure Landau could be concerning literary matters.

From the very beginning, it was understood that the editor of *Inzl* would be me and that no one else need interfere. Of course, I had to run the editorial office according to the line set forth by the *Inzl* group: Mani Leyb, Landau, Kazanski, and me. Once, Landau asked me if a certain poet had brought me some poems for *Inzl*. For convenience we'll call the poet "L." Then Landau told me that "L" had come to him with a series of poems, but he didn't even want to glance at them because I was the editor and only I could decide what would or would not be accepted by the journal. That same day, "L" came to see me. I liked his poems and immediately accepted them. The next day, when I told Landau, there appeared on his face a smile that was both pleased and guilty; he confessed that when he had spoken to me a day earlier about "L," he had already read the poems and liked them. But he had not wanted to tell me for fear that if he influenced me, he would never forgive himself. And this is the reason why:

"L" had first come to him declaring that he could easily get an advertisement for *Inzl* worth fifty dollars, and that if Landau just gave him the word, he would do it. Usually, we had enough money to continue the journal. As it happened, though, at that time we were in a tight spot and the printer had threatened not to run the journal if we did not pay at least a part of the debt, which had reached several hundred dollars. At such a time, fifty dollars was like a gift from heaven. Just after Landau asked him to indeed go ahead and get the advertisement, "L" showed him the poems. Landau never thought much of "L" as a poet, and when he saw that this time "L" had brought a series of good poems, it seemed to him a miracle. Since Landau did not believe in miracles, he thought that the prospect of the fifty dollars had blinded him. There was no way he would ever forgive himself for this. Now that I, who didn't know anything at all about the ad, had told him that I too liked the poems, he could breathe easier.

Zishe Landau Reads a Poem

His blond head rocks
his head rocks back,
and under heavy eyelids
his gaze becomes misty.

His lips murmur knowingly
and twitch slightly, like
a boy in love speaking
trembling to a woman.

Two fingers locked together,
a round link.
The link twists in the air
whispers and sings.

His blue eyes smile
shining mischievously:
a sharp word is lost
and wisdom hangs on it.

Now a line of teeth
bites his lip;
his tongue tastes the words
and samples them like wine.

His blond head rocks,
his head rocks back.
The word, searched for,
is here and shines in his gaze.

His blond head rocks
his head rocks back:
"Oh, rock me, rock me, rock me,
oh my absent joy."

A vig dem kop dem blondn,
a vig dem kop tsurik.
Un hinter shvere viyes,
farneplt zikh der blik.

Di lipn zinlekh murmlen,
un tsukn laykht azoy.
Vi s'redt farlibt a yingl,
mit tsiter tsu a froy.

Tsvey finger zikh farshlisn—
a kaylekhdiker ring.
A drey dem ring in luftn,
a sheptshe un a zing.

Di bloye oygn shmeykhln,
un laykhtn shkotsish oyf:
a vort a sharfs farlirt zikh,
un khokhme hengt deroyf.

Ot bayst a shure tseyne
zikh in a lip arayn;
di tsung farzukht di verter
un pruft zey oys vi vayn.

A vig dem kop dem blondn,
a vig dem kop tsurik.
Dos vort dos oysgezukhte,
iz do un laykht in blik.

A vig dem kop dem blondn,
a vig dem kop tsurik;
"O vig mikh, vig mikh, vig mikh,
O mayn nit-doik glik."

Unconnected Episodes

Some unconnected episodes that will reveal, a little, Landau's gestalt.

During his bachelor days, Landau lived for a time with Dr. Yekhiel Kling. It was on Bathgate Avenue, in a house with an empty garden in front and a larger garden with two or three thin trees and weeds in back. Landau lived in the attic, where the walls were sloped and came to a point over the window of the front wall. This gave the attic the appearance of a shrine, which was appropriate for Landau because of his interest in Christianity at that time. This interest was inspired by Kolya Teper and by Moyshe Warshaw, who was then his closest friend and who shared the attic with him. (Teper and Warshaw, and the influence—for good and for bad—that they had on his development, demand a separate treatment.) Landau at that time worked as a house painter and, as with everything he did, he showed himself to be a good and skillful worker. But for all his skill, he had very little work. Warshaw had no job at all, and quite often both of them went hungry. This in no way affected Landau's spirit. He was then, as always, happy and lively. In public, at least.

One summer Saturday night, Landau and I went out strolling in Claremont Park. We called on Warshaw, but he didn't want to go. On the street, we came across a girl we knew. A naïve, slim child with full, red lips and doe's eyes. In the park, on the hill, we looked for the familiar tree that used to be the meeting place for most of the young writers then living in the Bronx. The three of us stretched out on the grass, belly down. Landau took the girl by both her hands and paid her some lighthearted compliments—and eyes sank into eyes. The flirting became teasing. The teasing charmed the girl all the more, and with a long, outstretched neck, she swallowed every word he spoke.

Suddenly, Avrahm Moyshe Dilon appeared, with gossip as always. Whether it was a greeting from the "mysterious madam" who lived on

Riverside Drive and was in love with everyone from Di Yunge, though she had never seen any of us, or about something else, I no longer remember. I remember though, that Avrahm Moyshe's gossip shattered the idyll that had developed before my eyes. A long, deep conversation about a literary matter took place, and it was as if the girl had been erased. Our literary conversation, apparently, bored her terribly because she suddenly stood up and said, "Come! Now!" Her voice sounded so peremptory and was so unexpected that we all three obeyed and rose from the grass. Landau, with a loving smile, went over to the girl, wanting to take her by the chin with two fingers, but she angrily turned away from him and took Dilon and me by the arm. Like an arrow, we dashed down the hill and didn't stop until we were on the other side of Webster Avenue in the middle of Claremont Parkway, which was then still called Vandover Avenue. Landau, who had bad feet, lagged behind. Only after ten minutes did he catch up to us, or more accurately, did he catch up to me, because the girl and Dilon had disappeared.

"A nice kosher goat!" Landau said, laughing when he came up to me. "Where did she go?" And when I told him that she had gone home with Dilon, Landau again burst out laughing. Just amazing. But his eyes, which usually were laughing, were this time quite dreary and sad. We wandered around a while, trying to nurture a conversation, but it didn't work. As was his nature when he was preoccupied or depressed, he began to rock his head back and forth. Suddenly he said: "I am terribly hurt." "Hurt? From what?" I pretended not to understand. This exasperated Landau. "Did you really not notice that I'm not indifferent to the kosher calf?" I smiled. Landau gestured with his hand, as if to say, "You're impossible and will never understand." He muttered "Good night," and went home.

That was one of the few moments when Landau said a word to a friend about an intimate feeling. He locked away his intimate life even from his closest friends. He used to be proud that he didn't have the character of a Slav, with a "repulsive, open soul," who pours out his feelings for everyone. The typical Slav was, in his eyes, Mani Leyb—in moments of anger, of course—but such moments were not rare, especially in his younger years.

A Second Episode from That Time

As I have already said, Landau and Warshaw often went hungry. But if one lived with the Klings, one did not have to go hungry. The good Berta Kling wisely and tactfully looked after us, and when she called us to tea, there was always a cookie, a tart, or a pastry, and very often, on the table, there was simple bread with butter and a herring or some sausage. "And perhaps you will taste a fine piece of meat or a piece of chicken that is left over from lunch?" It was impossible to leave the table hungry. But it was possible not to go to the table. Landau and Warshaw suddenly stopped coming down from their attic when they were called to tea, precisely because they looked forward to being called.

Once, after a long summer fast, Landau, late at night, succeeded in getting a nickel from someone. At the bakery on Washington Avenue, he bought six big, fresh, warm rolls and with joy ran home to share them with his friend, who was surely just as hungry as he. But Warshaw was already asleep when Landau came home. Landau though to himself: never mind, he would eat his share and leave the rest until Warshaw woke up. After he had eaten his three rolls, he was still hungry and Warshaw was still sleeping. Landau could not prevent himself from eating a fourth roll. Soon, he had gobbled up the fifth and he wanted to pounce on the sixth, too. At the last moment, though, he overcame his lust and rescued the last roll. To avoid temptation, he put it in a paper bag, took it out to the corridor, and stuck it under a rafter.

When he woke the next morning, Warshaw was already sitting at the table bent over a book. Landau leapt out of bed, went out to the corridor, and in triumph brought Warshaw the hidden roll. And as Warshaw was chewing, Landau told him the whole story. Warshaw listened quietly. Suddenly his pale cheeks reddened and he said, "I'm embarrassed to tell you that I in your place would not have held myself back. I would have eaten all six rolls."

Landau told me this after Moyshe Warshaw, a few months later, took his own life.

Moyshe Warshaw, the weakling, the intellectual, the homebody who felt at home only with a book, and who early in life had the distinguished appearance of an elderly man or a monk—this man, in the last weeks of his life, became a night watchman in an apartment house that was being built. One night, he went to an upper floor of the unfinished building and threw himself off. He was found dead on the sidewalk.

End of Summer, 1915

We were preparing to revive the journal *Literatur un lebn* (Literature and life). All the plans had been worked out. We even had half the material for the first number. We were only waiting for Landau, who any day now would be returning from the country, where he had spent the summer with his wife, somewhere in New Jersey.

One day we heard that Landau was back. He was staying with Sotshe Dilon until he found an apartment. Mani Leyb and I were then neighbors in Boro Park. The next afternoon, a Saturday, Mani Leyb met me and we rode downtown. We met Landau in L. Shapiro's restaurant on East Broadway. We kissed, we asked about each other, we read poetry to each other. Right in the middle, we remembered we had to be at a certain Dr. Wexel's, who had prepared an article for our journal (which would have to be translated from English) about the latest trends in painting. Landau suddenly became distant; he kept sitting with us, but he wasn't really with us. This enraged Mani Leyb, who for a while controlled himself. But finally:

"What is it, Landau?"

"It's nothing," Landau replied calmly, but becoming even more withdrawn.

"Yes, there is something," Mani Leyb shot back, "and don't play hide-and-seek with us. If there's something you don't like, tell us."

"Itsy bitsy pictures," Landau said finally, with as much contempt as he could muster.

He didn't like our using Dr. Wexel's article. Painting is a very fine and lofty thing. It just wasn't our subject. Did we go to exhibitions? Yes. Could we sometimes stand for a long time staring at a picture? Fine, yes. Did a chill sometimes run up our spines because of a painting? Of course. But what did we *know* about painting? Certainly not more than we did about poetry, or more than our readers. Our journal needed to concern itself only with that in which we were immersed—only with word art. Everything else was *shatnez*, no more than pretension.

Even so, the three of us went to the Bronx to Dr. Wexel, a nice and interesting man. We also met a young architect whom Dr. Wexel believed in very strongly and who dreamed about Jewish buildings in New York that would be a synthesis of ancient synagogues and modern New York buildings. We spent hours with these two fascinating people, who, to our shame, we never saw again. From there we went to the Klings, where that night there was a party, and where all the rooms were already packed with guests.

About twelve o'clock we left. But not alone. There were two sisters, one of whom—and not even the prettier one—was everyone's darling, and whom we had to escort home. There were other people who lived in that neighborhood, but farther down, and we had to accompany them home also. One girl lived in Harlem. How could we let her go home all by herself so late at night? We crossed one of the bridges over the Harlem River and escorted her to the door of her building. Now only Avrahm Moyshe Dilon remained with us. Dawn was breaking, and it was not far from Central Park, over which there hung a veil of dew, so we went to the park.

But we did not enter the park. Landau saw a bench outside, against the stone wall, and he refused to go further. Not even one more step! We had hardly sat down when Avrahm Moyshe Dilon threw his head back and fell asleep. We let him sleep, and then, an hour later, we got up and went looking for something to eat. His broad, boney face had in sleep something so movingly childish that we didn't want to wake him.

Sated, rested, and refreshed by the sharp morning air, we again started walking. And it was a walk that you don't forget your whole life. Our senses were alert as they seldom are, and every encounter and everything our eyes fell upon excited us artistically. Our brains toyed with us: every word suggested something, and a conversation began in which ideas, expressions, lines, and verses from poems became entwined with memories, dreams, and artistic plans. We became so absorbed in our conversation that we didn't notice that we weren't going in the right direction but in a zigzag; sometimes we even circled around the block. Finally, we came to an El station on Third Avenue. Here we stopped. Landau intended to climb the steps on one side and go uptown. The rest of us would climb the other side and go downtown and, from there, home to Boro Park. But one of us said, "Let's walk to one more station." And the same thing was repeated at almost every station, so hard was it to part. It was around eleven in the morning when we came to Fourteenth Street. Here we decided it would be a great idea to hop over to Raboy, who lived not far from there, and collect the story he had promised for our journal. We had just begun walking when Landau gave a start as if he had been bitten by something sharp. His face turned pale and he cried out: "Oy! Reyzl may be giving birth in a strange apartment and I'm dragging myself around with you for almost twenty-four hours." We couldn't say another word to him. He was gone.

Another Trifle from Those Days

We were at Mani Leyb's in a small room, he and I, the editors of the revived *Literatur un lebn*, sitting one evening, writing a program article for the first issue. It sounded so "written." It was not writing, but rather a long struggle that lasted several hours, for every paragraph, for every sentence, and even for single words. Something didn't please him *here*; something didn't please me *there*. One paragraph rang false and pretentious to *him*; one sentence was loose and flabby to *me*. Here it seemed that we weren't saying what we wanted; there it seemed that we ourselves didn't *know* what we wanted. And when everything was in good shape, Mani Leyb sprang up in protest: Just *who* were we and *what* were we that we should set out programs and rules for poetry?

Also in the room with us was a young poet, one of our followers and admirers. The whole time we were struggling, he sat gaping, and we were sure he was simply captivated by the spiritual performance taking place before his eyes. Suddenly we heard snoring as if from a saw. We took a look—the boy was lying across the bed on which he had been sitting, with one leg stretched out halfway across the room, sleeping sweetly as drool ran from the corner of his mouth.

Mani Leyb pressed his lips together, slowly picked up the sheets of paper from the table, gathered them together, and began to rip them from top to bottom: o-one, t-two, th-three, f-four! An agenda article wasn't needed, he said. If he, our heir—and he pointed to the young poet—could snore at a time like this, not one of us needed a program.

Later, when Landau heard about it, he slapped his knee and began to shake with tears of laughter.

A Leap Over Many Years

I was then well past forty. At that time, Landau had two jobs, neither of which overtaxed him, though they paid well. He had a nice house, a smart wife, and two pretty daughters. He was heavily involved with silverware that had been sent to him from Poland: family heirlooms from his grandfathers. From the silverware, precious stones, and jewelry, he "lived like a prince" and enjoyed life. Poetry? Bah! Something for young people and sentimental women. He had quit the union a long time ago.

Yet here we both are, walking on East Broadway. In the distance, Avrahm Moyshe Dilon and Abba Stolzenberg are approaching us. Avrahm Moyshe is striding on long feet, his hat tipped to one side, his hands waving in the air, and his round, pockmarked face is one broad smile, the smile of someone who is enjoying something tremendously. Near him, rolling quickly with his round belly leading the way, is the young, plump Stolzenberg. Likewise, his round, impudent face is one broad, satisfied smile. His nose is pointing up, and a lock of hair separates itself from his smooth, combed head, which for many years has not felt a hat on it.

"Oh, a pearl! Oh, a poem! Oh, a wonder," cries out Avrahm Moyshe when he comes up to us. Quite some time goes by before we discover that he means to say that Stolzenberg has written a poem that is a pearl and a wonder. He insists. We simply must hear the poem.

"Read it to them, Stolzenberg! It's really a beautiful thing!"

While Stolzenberg prepares to read, Landau waves for him to stop. Excuse us! Then, noticing that Stolzenberg's face is changing color, he adds, "Not now, we're both busy," and pulls me by the sleeve. We continue on our way.

Landau believed deeply in Stolzenberg. Of all the up-and-coming poets, he thought he was the only one whose poetry created that wonderful joy that only poetry and love can give. "A beautiful youth and full of talent!" Landau remarked about Stolzenberg. "But I'm afraid that nothing will come of him. How old is he? Twenty-four or five? The best years. Poems should shoot out of his sleeve, and he squeezes out one in half a year. And already a big shot, with a belly, with a wife and child, and, I wouldn't be surprised, even a bankbook. That holy fool, the imbecile Avrahm Moyshe, I'm envious of him. Older than me, older than you, older than all of us, yet a lot younger than Stolzenberg, the only poet among us. What, never wrote one decent poem? Bah, so what? Dressed in rags? What does he care? But is he free? Is he constantly in ecstasy? And who is as constantly immersed in poetry as he? Ay, we wasted our lives away! I, you, Mani Leyb, the Brooklyn guy. Do you ever see him? Still hasn't finished the five-volume novel?[4] Honest characters, wonderfully moody situations and images. But why does he fuss over them?"

There he meant Kazanski, with whom he was, at the time, very angry. It was an anger that lasted many years.

From the Same Period

Landau worked in the publicity department of the New York Charity Federation. One year, when the federation was conducting a big campaign, Landau couldn't manage all of the Jewish publicity work by himself and asked me to help him. I worked with him for three weeks and was simply astonished at the ability, inventiveness, and energy that he showed at work. Some tens of articles had to be prepared, as well as untold notices for all the Jewish newspapers. There was very little material for the work; only some meager, unreadable paragraphs about the institution and even less substantial information about another. Yet the articles had to be weighty and important, and the notices written in such a way that they would be newsworthy so that the news editors would not throw them out. Landau was adept at these things. He also knew how to

---

4. David Kazanski, *Arum un arum* (Around and around) (New York: Inzl). Only three volumes were ever published: *Treyfene blut* (Unclean blood), 1930; *Blinder mazl* (Blind luck), 1930; *In yokh* (In the yoke), 1935.

convince newspaper editors to give plenty of space to the campaign, and that editorials should be written, and that news editors should treat the notices from the Charity Federation differently than the packs of other publicity with which newspapers are usually inundated.

One day, we had to prepare two full pages of articles for the *Forverts* and *Morgen zhurnal*. The office was full of reporters from all the English newspapers; the telephones didn't stop ringing; Landau had quarreled with me several times because I did the work as I understood it; I was seated at one typewriter, he nearby at another; our hands burned with work. Suddenly, I heard Landau's machine begin to click more and more slowly while he hummed under his breath. I lifted my eyes, took a look, and lo, Landau was sitting with his tongue between his teeth and writing—a poem.

Sundays with Landau

Every Sunday night there was a "literary table" at Landau's. A lot of people used to come. Besides writers, there were painters and just ordinary people.

It was like a rebbe's table—not, however, the intense, ecstatic rebbe's table that is about worship and divinity, but rather what in our circle was called "the second table," after *bentshing*. The formality is gone and the rebbe is pulling the strings no longer by himself but in partnership with his chosen ones: those close to him, scholars, sharp tongues, jokers, storytellers, gossips, and politicians; sharp words, deep thoughts, and repeated stories mix with jokes, gossip, and even political intrigues.

There was always something on the table, and whoever came in could without ceremony sit down and have a bite to eat. After some time, the "table" would end with, heaven forbid, a game of cards. The card games were ended partly by Landau's depression and his illness.

In public, Landau liked to pretend that he read nothing. It seems to me, though, that in our circle, no one read as much as he did, and he followed everything that came out in Yiddish. One Yiddish bookseller had a standing order to send him every book of Yiddish poetry, no matter where it came from. He also bought a lot of English, German, and Russian books. Every Sunday night, you always found "new merchandise" on the table, on the dresser, on the bookshelves, or even at the typewriter. Whoever wanted to could choose a corner and read to himself.

Very often a quiet, individual reading became a reading for the whole group—when the book greatly pleased the reader, of course. And if it was a good reader, who could properly emphasize the best passages and who could smother the weakest, it was like a holiday in the apartment. No one read their own poems, except quietly in a corner. Landau also did not.

Those Sundays made a lot of reputations and ruined a lot. There were also plenty of literary discoveries. One Sunday night, Landau introduced Reuben Ludwig to us. Another time, I "took the crowd by storm" for [Melekh] Ravitch. We had an equal part in discovering Stolzenberg, around the same time as [Meyer] Stiker, when they published their first things in *Union Square*. Both things that they published there were horrible. But in the overblown and florid language, plagiarized from [Peretz] Markish, their own specks of gold shone out. The very next day, Landau went looking for the two young men who had shown such accomplishment. He wanted to cheer himself up at their expense, but they also fascinated him.

Landau liked to rummage through old pages of prayer books. Very often, he would buy entire boxes of assorted booksellers' literature, such as *khumoshim*, prayer books in Yiddish, storybooks, and Hasidic stories.

One Sunday night, Landau announced that he would show us a trick. He had just bought a whole box of *tkhines* printed in various places. One of us would shuffle them and read whichever he wanted; Landau would immediately recognize where it had been published. I took upon myself the task of reading. It seemed, however, that Landau succeeded only in part. For example, he always recognized a prayer that was published in Vilna. He also partly recognized which prayers came from Warsaw. But it was hard for him to recognize the differences among the Lemberg, Pietrokov, and Lublin prayers. We soon realized why. The Galician and Polish prayers were almost all in the style of wonderful, ancient, literary Yiddish; The Vilna prayers, however, had been rewritten in a "modern" Yiddish. The Warsaw style was mixed: some of the prayers they stole word for word from the Galician and Polish styles, others from the Vilna style. Landau was enthralled with the Polish-Galician prayers. The Vilna prayers, however, he could not stomach. The Polish-Galician prayers were for him (as they were for me) examples of purity, delicacy, intimacy, and beauty of speech. The Vilna prayers were the opposite—they lacked style and were harsh in expression, without a drop of feeling for language. The Polish-Galician prayers had been written by simple people with faith and full of love and reverence for their work. The Vilna prayers, by contrast, sounded like abominable merchandise sold for three or four bucks by a freethinker, a heretic, who never had God in his heart and who didn't have a feel for language. How could he have, when everything that was old Yiddish was, in his eyes, withered and moldy? The more authentic and fine the Yiddish, the more comical it sounded to his ears.

Landau one day noticed something interesting. The Vilna prayers always embellished when calculating the attributes of God. Where other prayers would have a woman turn to the "Lord of all Worlds," the Vilna women had to turn to the "Great" Lord of all Worlds. "Great God in Heaven" became, in the Vilna prayers, "Almighty." God in the other prayers was both great and almighty; in the Vilna prayers, He became "awesome." And so on.

In reading the prayers, Landau wanted to demonstrate how right we Yunge were in our opinion that good, beautiful, and mellifluous Yiddish is found only among the Polish, Galician, and Ukrainian Jews, whereas the Lithuanians were deaf to sound, harsh in expression, and generally lacking a feel for language. One day, though, in paging through the prayers, I came across a "Prayer for Livelihood" in a Vilna prayerbook that destroyed Landau's theory. Here one could not recognize the freethinker and heretic who does not believe a word he writes. Here stood a poor Jew who poured out his bitter heart; who complained about his luck and the luck of all the poor, the repressed, the insulted; who reproached God and showed Him how bad it was when a man didn't get his just deserts, and when his wife and children went hungry; and who declared that poverty and need must bring a man to sinful temptation that is hard to overcome. And all of this in such wonderful, rich Yiddish, like ringing crystal, that by comparison the Polish-Galician prayers sounded hollow and empty.

"Ay, we have suffered a defeat, Iceland!" Landau called out, and I completely agreed with him. We had suffered a defeat, and a well-deserved one. But we held to our original opinion, nonetheless. Even now, I am still not sure if it was prejudice from which we couldn't free ourselves, or whether the "Prayer for Livelihood" was merely one of those exceptions that proves the rule.

Last Days

I, a sick man, spent two winters in Florida. One evening I had an attack. A doctor came and gave me the necessary injection, and I sank into sleep. When I woke up, it was late at night. My first thought was—Landau. I must write to him, I thought, tell him about my own situation and ask about his health. But instead of a letter, I wrote, in my thoughts, a poem. By morning, it was finished. As soon as the doctor allowed me out of bed, I wrote it down, and though it was still rough, I sent it to Landau that same day. Because it was essentially a letter to him, I titled it "To Zishe Landau." It read this way:

> There is still a brightness that calls,
> a tree that blossoms, a path that leads
> and the joy of walking.
>
> There is still a book, a newspaper in my hand
> a chair, a sofa and a bed
> and the joy of rest.
>
> And when the palmetto gleams steel-green
> and it scrambles up the white and pearl-grey walls,
> the climbing plant;
>
> And when the roofs glow red and the hibiscus blazes
> among dark pines and the green palm—
> my heart blossoms.
>
> But when the enemy gets a hold of me unexpectedly
> and treads with heavy elephant-paws on my breast,
>
> (The oleander at the window still smells almond sweet,
> bougainvilleas still caress with cool violet red)

Suddenly, my tongue becomes like parchment and my eye like glass,
and all my limbs cry out, stiff and cold from fear:
"Already?"

Es iz nokh do a likhtekeyt vos ruft,
a boym vos blit, a veg vos firt
un freyd fun geyn.

Es iz nokh do a bukh, a tsaytung tsu der hant,
a shtul, a zofe un a bet
un freyd fun ru.

Un az es blankt in shtolik grin di palmeto
un se drapet zikh af vays un perl-groy fun vent
di kleter-flants;

un az es gliyen dekher royt un der hibiscus flamt
tsvishn tunkele sosnes un der griner palm—
blit oyf dos harts.

Nor az der soyne pakt mikh umgerikhterheyt
un tret mit shvere helfant lape af der brust,

(der oleander farn fenster shmekt nokh alts vi mandlen zis,
bogenvileas gletn nokh mit kiln lila royt),

vert mit amol di tsung vi parmet un vi gloz dos oyg,
un ale glider shrayen oyf farshteyft un kalt fun shrek:
"Shoyn?"

We Di Yunge always had an aversion to the exotic. I was, therefore, afraid that the exotic names of tropical plants and flowers would invalidate the poem in Landau's eyes. In the letter I sent with the poem, I pointed this out to him and explained that for me, these tropical plants and flowers were no longer exotic, but had become familiar, constant companions that one's eyes meet wherever one turns.

Several days later, I received from Landau *this* answer:

Dear Iceland:

I am here (in New York) and in Lakewood, and so, I have lately lost all contact with you. The couple of days that I have been in New York have slipped through my fingers, and I can't always find out about you from Sheliubski[5] by telephone. It was very good of you to send me a few words. I gave up Lakewood entirely but will, perhaps, return in a couple of weeks when the bitter cold lets up.

I am completely all right. And the days when I feel a little under the weather, it's my own fault. Drink and eat too much. Am lately bothered from too much sugar that is in me and makes me thirsty all the time.

What unpleasantly surprised me a little in your poem were not the tropical plants, but something else. Namely, that you use the exotic word for a real, existing situation. In the years when we spoke about the "exotic word," we thought that one must use it when it is a question of something that doesn't exist . . . you write naturalistic phrases; that is very bad and unpleasant for a friend to read.

I don't know whether or not you have reason to be so uneasy. But it's not good that you have such a feeling. Lakewood is in my bones and despite the doctors not knowing why it should be better for me there than in New York, it really is better for me and the whole time that I am there, I feel very good.

Your,

Landau

I don't remember when it was that we were supposed to have said that one must use an exotic word only "when it is a question of something that doesn't exist." It wasn't even clear to me what Landau wanted to say, unless he meant that we were always against taking a factual, existing situation as a subject for a poem. If that is what he meant, then he forgot a piece of his own history when he, together with me, preached and practiced poetry from *factual*, everyday, ordinary life. As I have already said, this was a reaction to the clichéd "poetry" that we found when we arrived. Even later, when the "ordinary" theory was thrown out, because the reason it had been formulated was no longer fundamentally important, because the remedy for clichés had itself become a cliché, Landau still taught that "only that which exists is beautiful."

5. Moyshe Yudl Sheliubski (1893–1974) was a publisher and Yiddish writer; he was the business manager of *Der tog*.

Incidentally, there was an earlier time when Landau had made a point of celebrating the "nonexistent." Another indication of how inconsistent artists are.

The letter is dated February 14, 1936. Eleven months after that, almost to the day, Landau was dead.

During the time that I spent in Florida, we wrote to each other only once. And when I returned to New York in the spring, and he came downtown to see me, my heart sank. That's how bad he looked. How he felt when he saw me, I don't know. After that we seldom saw each other. No more than three or four times, it seems. It was hard for me to go to him and it was hard for him to come to me. When I was told that Landau was no longer alive, I was not surprised. We knew, those last few years, that he was fatally ill, that every day he was with us was literally a miracle, and that by his not taking care of himself, he could any minute fall down in the middle of the street and never rise again. And that's how it actually happened. Not a surprise. But the pain was tremendous. A piece of my own life had been torn from me, and I will continue to miss it as long as my eyes are open.

🎔 Twenty-Five Years Later

THIS IS THE TWENTY-FIFTH SPRING since the publication of the third volume of *Shriftn*, the first series of our anthologies. It's an important date for Yiddish literature because, with those three books, a period began and ended in that poetic movement that brought a new message to the whole of Yiddish literature, a message that today is still known under the general, meaningless name "Di Yunge." Among sophisticated people, those three anthologies would come to be seen as rarities, sought out by professional collectors, cherished as treasures by booksellers and book lovers. But among us: I saw one of those books not long ago, lying on a bargain table in a bookstore, marked fifty cents. True, the "bargain" did not lie there for long. It soon found a taker. I wasn't sure, though, if anyone would have been interested had it not been fifty cents, but rather let's say a few dollars or even one dollar. My doubt was based on a sad experience. Some years ago, when the twenty-fifth anniversary of one of our most famous poets was celebrated in New York, his closest colleagues published a number of his best poems in a beautiful, deluxe edition, with fine type and the best paper that one could find, bound in Morocco leather. The entire edition was only thirty-seven copies. In the non-Jewish world, one would have paid a hundred dollars for such a book and a hundred people would have chased after it. Among us, the book was priced at only ten dollars. And though the book was publicized far and wide, and though some two thousand people came to the celebration, and though the newspapers wrote about the event and also about the rare book that the poet's colleagues brought to the celebration as a gift, still, in all of America and in all the world, not one single person was found who wanted a copy.

Others would have celebrated the twenty-fifth anniversary of *Shriftn*. Not, God forbid, with committees, with a fuss in the newspapers and halls, as one is wont to do all the time for this or that big shot, but with memoirs, critiques, and treatises; with revisions, appraisals, and evaluations; with reverence, but also with biting irony; with indications of the good and positive that Di Yunge brought to Yiddish poetry, along with the negative and destructive. Among us, such a date goes by quietly. No one writes, no one celebrates a holiday, no one gets excited, not even with sheepish enthusiasm about those "good old days," and no one mocks. Such a thing can be imagined to exist only among an uncultured people. And perhaps that is why we speak so much about culture. If there is no whisky, let's at least *talk* about whisky! So dear and beloved is our Yiddish culture that no fewer than two large central organizations fight for the honor of which should busy itself with—a big corpse. Almost symbolically.

The anthology on the bargain table induced in me a sentimental feeling. Because, if the first three books of *Shriftn* were an important moment in the history of Yiddish poetry, the third and last was no less important in my own life. Because my series of poems, *Fun ale teg* (From every day), was printed in that book and was, in its time, rather well received. And because—what was for me, personally, a lot more important—for the first time I found myself as a poet with my own expressive identity, my own voice, and my own poetic path. I'm not ashamed to say that my heart throbbed when I saw the long book with the thick, leather-colored cover and the long, green, snakelike writing on top, and the two thin green trees on the crest of the round hill in the middle. I approached, as one goes to a former lover whom one meets suddenly, not having seen her in many years and whom one had long since forgotten. With a little of the past warmth, a little curiosity and a little fear, because the eye is, against one's own will, pitilessly objective. There is a grey streak in her hair, a row of wrinkles on her face, besides a lot of organic imperfections that were always there, but one had shut one's eyes, not wishing to see them. How do my poems seem today—twenty-five years after they were published? Have they aged, or do they still have the freshness they once had? What about their organic shortcomings, which I saw then but pretended not to? It was in those poems, as I have already said, that I found my poetic path. Am I still on the same path, or have I long since taken other paths and detours? And what about the whole anthology, which had at the time made such an impression in the Yiddish literary world? How will these poems sound in my ears now, and the cadence of their stories? How far has my path run parallel with theirs, and where have they diverged? What has happened to them in the course of these twenty-five years? How many of them are still the same, and how many have become estranged? If estranged, what led to the estrangement? What, during those twenty-five years, happened to Yiddish literature in general? How many new people have arrived, and how many of them have brought their own identities?

These and a lot of other questions ran through my mind as I stood at the bargain table and paged through the anthology. But instead of an answer, the pages radiated with sunlight and plants, and with hours of love spent in parks and on long walks over the half-built streets of the Bronx. With talk and smoke at tables in a stale cellar restaurant and between the cozy walls of a bachelor's narrow room; with pain, longing, sorrow, and joy; with long since disappeared faces, voices, laughter, sighs, and the tears of women in love and whom we loved; with the biting words of colleagues that poisoned days and nights, not letting us sleep; and with poems and lines of poems from the same colleagues, which, like wine, made us drunk and rang for weeks in our ears; in those springs, summers, and winters, when we were young and hopeful and lively and feisty and sure that there was only one artistic truth and that we were the only prophets—oh, no! Has it really been twenty-five years since then?

Ten people took part in the anthology. Three of them are already in the next world. Three of them we no longer hear from. Of the remaining four, only two have remained close. The other two, one seldom meets. Those who died were Moyshe Leyb Halpern, Avrahm Moyshe Dilon, and Zishe Landau. Those who remained were Mani Leyb, David Ignatoff, I. Raboy, and I. Mani Leyb and I remained close, as before. Both of us were estranged from Ignatoff, and Raboy distanced himself from us. He became a writer for the *Morgen frayhayt*, and when he was ordered to part from us, he piously obeyed. He declared that he repudiated all that he had written until then. And he really meant it.

He meant it because the things that he began to publish in the *Frayhayt* no longer had a trace of that Raboy who had been so dear to us since his first mature pieces appeared in *Shriftn*, and since we met him personally at Ignatoff's bachelor room on Washington Avenue where we used to meet every Sunday. Everything in him seemed black and big and healthy when we met him the first time. And his movements were village-slow and broad and a bit strange for us city people. The dark face was lit up with a smile full of big, healthy horse teeth when we were introduced and he extended us a big, healthy, workman's hand.

From the first minute, we were pained by his genuine modesty and freshness, which we were not used to. In contrast to all of us, he did not speak about literature at our first meeting, but about a farm somewhere in Connecticut where he then lived. He didn't like it there on the farm, and sooner or later he would leave it. But if I'm not mistaken, that Sunday afternoon at Ignatoff's in the small room made him give up the farm sooner. All of us were, at the time, filled with literary ideas and plans, like ripe, juicy fruit, and when we met, the membrane burst and the ideas came spilling out in speech. The long hours every Sunday at Ignatoff's in his room, from afternoon until late at night, were so rich in thoughts and ideas, so stimulating and mutually fruitful, that three days later, there remained with us the life that we had taken from there; and the other three days of the week, we lived in happy anticipation of what was to come. Sundays, very often, were literally a joy. One can, moreover, imagine that after such a Sunday, in the warm company of friends whom one longed for before one had even known them, Raboy could stay no longer on his lonely farm. Soon afterward, he came to the city and became citified and was a frequent guest at Ignatoff's, though not nearly as often a visitor as I and the others. I don't know if this was because he worked in the same shop where Ignatoff worked and had enough of him after a whole week, or if he didn't feel comfortable with so much talk about literature. Like the characters in his stories and novels, he was not much of a talker. He didn't take part in our theoretical conversations.

Back then he used to think a lot and speak little. Speech was for him—I am speaking about the days of *Shriftn*—not connected to thought but was its complement. Very often, when we got excited about a theoretical matter, he would suddenly jump in with an anecdote that he had to tell. In the beginning, it seemed that what he was telling us had no connection to the matter we were dealing with, but as one listened—and one *had* to listen, because what he was saying was so interesting—one felt that, somehow, what he was saying was indeed connected to the matter that was being discussed. One had the joyous feeling about Raboy's stories and novels that one was reading the work of someone who, in his whole life perhaps, had never read a book; as if before him there had never been a story; as if literature, in general, began with him. Raboy was also this way during literary discussions: his coincidental remarks gave the impression that he had never read a literary treatise. The things he said were crude and inept, but they also had charm and even weight. The later Raboy had repudiated the earlier one even before he fell in with the *Morgen frayhayt*, though he himself, perhaps, didn't know it. In his *Gekumen a yid keyn Amerike* (A Jew comes to America), one can already see a change. But in essence, there remained something of the former healthy honesty, which here and there would get the upper hand and overcome the falseness that he allowed to lead him astray. Even after his open break with himself and with everything and everyone that had been connected to his former "I," he still could not repudiate his fundamental "I." Raboy remained Raboy.

The break with Ignatoff began much earlier, as long ago as the completion of the third book of *Shriftn*. But the final break came later. In my heart, there remained a warmth and closeness to him and to Raboy, and perhaps they also felt that way toward us. I miss them very often. And when, for example, I hear Ignatoff's voice on the telephone (I haven't heard Raboy's voice for years), my heart races. Scarcely do I meet him than I feel that I care about his health and the welfare of his family. But to speak with him about what matters most to a writer—writing—that I can't do. In the course of those twenty-five years, there grew between us a distance that is greater than the distance of years. We speak two different languages, so different that we no longer understand each other. Did we ever understand each other? Yes and no. But more about that in the next chapter.

We Remained Four

All three issues of *Shriftn* had something important and worthwhile, and not just for their time. In every one of the issues there was one contribution that overshadowed everything else. In the first it was Opatoshu's *A roman fun a ferd ganev* (A novel about a horse thief). In the second, the same Opatoshu's *Moris un zayn zun Filip* (Morris and his son Philip). In the third, Mani Leyb's *Yingl tsingl khvat*. I'm speaking of both the literary and the broad audience. In the narrow circle of poets, though, there was a completely different opinion. Among the *faynshmekers*, as Opatoshu angrily called them, the first issue's existence was justified only by Mani Leyb's and Zishe Landau's poems, M. L. Halpern's *In der fremd* (In a foreign land), and Ignatoff's *Der giber* (The hero). For them, everything else could have been left out. In the second issue, the people in that circle found something worthwhile for themselves in I. Raboy's fragment, *Der laykht turem* (The lighthouse), Mani Leyb's and Landau's poems, and parts of Ignatoff's *In keslgrub* (In the whirlwind). In the third issue, one didn't know what to accent first: almost everything pleased everyone, except the poem that pleased the general audience the most—none other that Mani Leyb's *Yingl tsingl khvat*. It became an instant classic, yet Zishe Landau, for one, could literally not stomach it. And when he couldn't stomach something, especially by someone close to him whom he liked, he could punch so hard that the target could see his great-grandmother. In Landau's eyes, Mani Leyb had fallen from high poetic grace with *Yingl tsingl kvat*. I thought so, too. Mani Leyb's lyrical poems impressed us with their rich imagery, nuances, delicate feeling and the melodiousness of the line, which was almost always filled with hidden energy. And here he suddenly comes out with a story in rhyme, in which the four-footed trochees chase one another around melodically in an artificial childishness. That was then. But now when I read that children's story, I realize how wrong we were in our judgment. With all of its shortcomings—and it has quite a few—and besides the fact that it has become banal because of a hundred imitations, *Yingl tsingl khvat* was and remains a masterpiece: with its purity, its fine, quiet humor, its fluency and deft rhymes, and mainly with its countless images, scenes, and situations, which are piled up so lightly and playfully—often no more than a feature or two—that it will always have an honored place, and not only in our children's literature.

In our eyes, Mani Leyb's short lyrical poem "Shtiler, shtiler" (Silent, silent), with which the third issue of *Shriftn* opened, stood, artistically, a lot higher than *Yingl tsingl khvat*. But now I see that we were mistaken about that, too. True, the short, lyrical poem has four wonderful stanzas. But for that very reason it has a superfluous encumbrance—a stanza that repeats itself like a refrain, no less than three times, though one could do without it even once.

It occurs to me that we, the aesthetes, the preachers of "art for art's sake," did not understand the short, lyrical poem's artistic value and the fact that it, for the first time, poetically brought out our moral view of life. A point of view, by the way, that must in the present turbulent revolutionary time appear reactionary. On our way to artistic truth, we came to realizations that had to lead to a certain moral view of life. One of the realizations was that no one can rise to pure art as long as he tries to go beyond the strength that is marked in his character, in his blood. In order not to raise oneself too high, the first and most important thing is to know oneself. The path to such knowledge must lead to humility. When one recognizes the limits of one's own strength, one feels, as a consequence, strengths greater than one's own that one will never be able to achieve, never mind exceed. One no longer wants what one cannot achieve. Perhaps only a child wants pie in the sky. In other words: in order to achieve perfection in whatever one does, one must not exceed the limits of one's own capacity. As for the rest, one must resign oneself. Once one has come to this realization, one must take it as a rule not only in art but also in life. When we Yunge set aesthetic goals, we undertook ethical tasks through which we could achieve our goals. One of them was *resignation*. Mani Leyb was the first to poeticize this resignation motif in "Shtiler, shtiler" (and, by the way, he was the first American poet to touch on this subject). This poem is about the longing for the Messiah that has lived in us for thousands of years. A hope because of which we refused the most precious things and for which we carry the heaviest burdens in life. He will come, if not today, then tomorrow; if not tomorrow, then the day after and,

From his radiant face
and his pure, white robe
joy will cast itself upon us,
upon us, his light will fall.

But what if he doesn't come? What if the entire hope is no more than a trick, a swindle, a mockery of our somber destiny? The sorrow will be great and deep, but the stubbornness to carry on, greater still.

If we've been tricked
and we've been mocked
and the whole night long
we have waited in vain,

We will, in our affliction
bow down to the hard floor,
and we will be silent
more silent and still more silent.

Fun zayn loytern gezikht
un zayn klorn, vaysn kleyd
veyen vet af undz di freyd,
faln vet af undz zayn glik.

Oyb men hot undz opgenart . . .
un men hot undz oysgelakht,
un di gantse lange nakht
hobn mir umzist gevart

Veln mir in unzer brokh
boygn zikh tsum hartn dil,
un mir veln shvaygn shtil,
shtiler nokh un shtiler nokh.

Resignation gives rise to heroism. This, I think, impressed us back then more than anything else, and, moreover, we overlooked or pretended not to see that in Mani Leyb's poem, the Messiah *must* come on the banal "white horse" and he *must* wear a "pure white robe." We also overlooked the fact that the key word, "silent," which sets the tone for the poem, is repeated so often that it begins, in fact, to shout.

In my younger years, when I read a book once or twice, it remained in my memory. With time, everything has been erased. But the tone and the taste of the poem remain. I even remember whether the sun shone or whether it was raining and what kind of smell was in the air. From hearing a poem read, I also remembered the voice and the tone of the reader, the faces and voices of the people around me, and the whole atmosphere. When now I reread the five poems that Zishe Landau published in the third issue of *Shriftn*, he stands before me as if alive. Thin, blond, with big blue eyes and sensitive lips that were always twitching while he read. His voice, like Halpern's, became completely different when he read a poem. Halpern was utterly hypnotizing with his slow, long, rolling reading, and had I not known that he had a lot of students and followers abroad, I would have said that a large part of his success as a poet was thanks to his reading. Landau could not bewitch an audience with his reading, but no one who heard him read individually ever forgot the experience. His voice became a different voice that had, it seems, an unpleasant effect yet was very rich. And what he couldn't do with a poem by reading it! With a mere nuance, he could kill a poem forever or he could bring out the most beautiful things in it and plant them forever in the hearts of his listeners. This with others' poems just as with his own. It is interesting, though, that when reading others' poems he could sometimes trick you, but when reading his own, never. I read his five poems now and find that those that didn't please me then, when he read them for me, also don't please me today; and that those that struck me then have over the years lost nothing of their beauty. His poems "Negerins" (Negro women), "Dinstik" (Tuesday), and "In yugend" (In youth), a motif reworked from *taytsh khumesh*, created an uproar then. He was accused of trying merely to shock. That he wanted to shock was indeed true. But that didn't in the least diminish the beautiful image that he painted in "Negerins," or the indifference he wanted to express in "Dinstik," or the lovely form that he gave a naïve, ancient, Jewish look at the difference between men and women.

Ignatoff was also accused of wanting to shock, in his short introduction to *Fibi*, when he declared himself to be in love with snakes. But that was not true. He didn't want to shock, but rather to perplex his audience with his strange declaration of love. It was, in essence, supposed to be no more than a symbol, so to speak, an indication, a wink that the story that he was getting ready to tell was about a girl, a snake, who poisoned with its flirting more than with its venom. But he used the opportunity to show off his fearlessness, individuality, and uniqueness. Everyone is afraid of snakes? Everyone is disgusted by snakes? Then I will show them that not only am I not afraid and not only am I not disgusted, but I can get down and gaze so calmly at snakes that I can perceive how beautiful they are and love them for their beauty. Because of this desire to prove himself, to make a point of being original—and very often not in a smart way—Ignatoff destroyed his chance to become the fine artist he could have been. Because of this character trait, we weren't always able to understand each other, even when we were close. That trait showed itself not only in his writing but also when he was editing *Shriftn*. The anthologies he published had to be the most beautiful, even outwardly. And he spent a lot of money and energy on them. Naturally, none of us could be against that. And if Landau spoke, even then, in an unkind way about Ignatoff's "itsy bitsy pictures," the unkindness did not have to do with the outer appearance of the books, but rather with the illustrations with which Ignatoff, from the beginning, adorned *Shriftn*.

I remarked earlier that according to Landau, we Di Yunge had to concern ourselves only with word art in our publications. All the other arts, in his opinion, had to be excluded, because for all our love of other arts—as much as we had—we were no more than ignoramuses. Moreover, to give space in our publications to painting or music, for example, would be pretentious. Mani Leyb and I both agreed and disagreed with him: we could have done without the pictures in the anthologies, but it didn't bother us when they were there. But all three of us were strongly opposed to more "weight and respectability" that Ignatoff wanted to give *Shriftn* by working with older, more important writers. We didn't want existing "celebrities" to lend beauty and more "weight and respectability" to our anthologies. We wanted to achieve our own respectability through our own works. In placing ourselves in the shadow of celebrities, we would surely not attain it.

This trait of needing to add more than he was capable of did Ignatoff a lot of harm. He was without question one of the finest talents among us. No one among us wrote prose as wonderfully as he could. And had he been content with this great gift that was his, he would have achieved a lot. But he wasn't satisfied; he always needed something more. That would not have been a problem, except that the "something more" didn't come from within him but had been selected artificially. In such cases, the "something more" is usually quite trivial but also becomes so dominant that it makes the author look ridiculous and causes readers to overlook the fact that, in the end, the superfluities can simply be skipped over. The superfluities do not render the whole unfit; they only render unfit the places where they have been placed. Thus, the short introduction to *Fibi* made readers overlook the fantastic virtues of that work—one of the most beautiful and accomplished novels we have in Yiddish. With its language, tone, and cadence, with the way in which he directs the characters and the moods that grow out of their encounters, with the speech and the silences and the drama that hangs over everyone, there is almost nothing else like it in our literature. As in *Fibi*, so in Ignatoff's other, earlier works. There is so much talent everywhere, and everywhere there is also a lot of superfluity and false wisdom, both of which hide the good and the essential.

Raboy's *Her Goldenbarg*, over the years, has become a little threadbare, like all of our works from that time. Yet the magical grace of its simplicity remains. It is somewhat contrived, but that doesn't matter. At most, the contrivances provoke a smile, never laughter. And even the contrivances are full of grace—that special, Raboyic grace—and you can never understand where he gets it from. When you read about the joy that begins to blossom in the cowboy when the Jewish farmer, Mr. Goldenbarg, brings his sister's daughter Dvoyre to the farm in the Far West, you sense here and there a superfluous word or even a contrived line, but the joy flows to you as if from a fine poem.

Like his hero, Raboy in his prose is not a big talker. When he decides to "say" something, he perhaps does not always find the most appropriate word. He detects, though, almost always, the tone and the manner of whatever his senses discern. There were very few writers whose senses were as acute as Raboy's. Especially that Raboy we delighted in, in our youth.

Growing Hurts

When Mani Leyb was about to celebrate his birthday,[1] he saw his heirs, the youngest generation of poets, in this way:

The poets that come after us—wild young horses
in the joyful valleys. Their tails soaring in the blue,
blood and milk in their eyes, their hoofs across the sky,
and the dust glittering brightly like diamonds beneath their hoofs.

Di poetn vos kumen nokh unz—yunge ferdlekh on tsoymen
af di freylekhe toln. Di ekn farshartst in di bloyen,
blut un milkh in di oygn, di kloyen ariber di roymen,
un der shtoyb vi der diment blitst hel unter zeyere kloyen.

Were we, in our time, also "wild young horses . . . tails soaring in the blue?" Perhaps. But not always in joyful valleys. Along with our hopefulness, our frivolousness, and our impudent self-assurance, which is so typical of most young poets, there was also a lot of pain and sadness as well as whole periods of disappointment in ourselves—strange, unacknowledged self-doubts that nagged and grieved us.

I began to publish poems in 1905. But only in 1912 did I feel that my poetry had matured. Almost every poet loses his way in his youth, and I, with my friends, was in this regard no exception. It took me longer than everyone else to arrive at my own poetic way. Perhaps this was because I had heavy ballast to cast aside. My pious-Hasidic, childish world was a very old one. I didn't go through a revolutionary period that would clear a way for me to a free worldview. And my first poetic influences—from which it is the hardest to free oneself—were dated and, for me, especially harmful. My first poets were from the German Romantics; my favorites were Eichendorf and Merke. Two very fine poets, but their motifs and methods were like poison for the lyrical-dreamy boy that I was. The line between lyricism and sentimentality is very thin, and in my wayward years I was constantly straddling that line. I wrote a lot then, but I published very little. My writing afforded me little joy. I was always my own

1. It is not clear how old Mani Leyb was at the time.

strictest critic, and what didn't please me I tore up and burned. Unfavorable criticism is very painful for every young poet. My own unfavorable criticism was no less painful.

My friends arrived, some a year earlier and some a year later, but we met between 1905 and 1910. Those were the years of blossoming in Yiddish literature. In Vilna there was David Einhorn and the *Literarishe monat-shriftn* (Literary monthly writings). In Warsaw there arose a third generation after Peretz: Menakhem, A. M. Weisenberg, Jonah Rosenfeld, Moyshe Stavski, and others. In Lemberg, there were Shmuel Jacob Imber, Jacob Mestel, Moyshe Leyb Halpern (under the pseudonym Freda Halpern), David Konigsberg, and later also A. M. Fuchs and Melekh Ravitch. Here in New York there was a group of young writers who were the first to try to free literature from the guardianship of the press and create a separate corner for it. The most important of these enterprises were the monthly journal *Di yugend*, published and edited by Yoyl Entin, M. Y. Khaymovitch, Jedidiah Margolies, and B. Senter; and the two issues of the anthology *Literatur*, published by the society Literatur, where all the young writers of that time were gathered. That group gave birth to a small literary circle, the first in New York. We used to gather every Sunday afternoon, and at those meetings the group developed that became Di Yunge and founded *Shriftn*.

Every true poet has his own style; in just the same way, every time has its own style and its own clichés. These clichés lead the true poet astray before he finds his own path. That is where the struggle between young and old begins, with such hopefulness on youth's part. From that, also, comes the phenomenon whereby every new artistic school is stronger in its negative criticism of its predecessors than in its positive program for itself. The newer generation finds it easy to discern the weaknesses of the earlier one; to find one's own way is harder. When we, Di Yunge, sensed what was rotten in American Yiddish literature, we didn't yet know what we ourselves wanted. At that time we were still not a cohesive group; we only knew what we *didn't* want. That was the first thing that unified us. The rest came from within us.

Even then, as fledglings, we were grown enough to understand what many still do not understand today: foreign essence does not make a poem, but every good poem creates essence—original, weighty, and precious poetic essence.

Those were wonderful years for us. Especially the years between 1907 and 1910. True, they were years of confusion and pain; but they were also years of discovery and realization. Every day brought something new— at least, new for us—from foreign literature and from our own Yiddish literature, from across the sea. We swallowed everything with the same thirst, and we learned something from everything—even when it was how *not* to write. True, we liked only the foreign literature with which we were then acquainted: the Russians, the Germans, the Poles, and the French, from whom all modern writers learned. Baudelaire, Verlaine, and Rambeau, whom we knew only from translations, were our daily poetic bread, no less than Sologub, Bryusov, Balmont, and Bloch, or Lilienkroen, Dehmel, Rilke, and Hoffmanstal. Later we became acquainted with Stefan George and Theodore Storm, though Storm belonged to an earlier generation of German poets. Thus, we had a lot for which to thank the Russian and Scandinavian novelists. Especially the latter. We learned from them the secret of the wink, the pause, the unexpected psychological turn of speech, and how to bring out the maximum poetic mood with just a few simple words.

Of the Yiddish poets in Europe, we quickly seized on David Einhorn's first book *Shtile gezangen* (Quiet songs). An immediate surprise for us was Menakhem's contemporary, exotic poems, such as "Tfiles" (Prayers), "Shvartse royzn" (Black roses), "Kadosh, kadosh" (Holy, holy), and others of that sort. More than by all the others, we were delighted by S. J. Imber, one of our finest lyrical poets, who would have had a respected place in a rich literature, and who of course, in a poor literature such as ours, has been ignored for the past twenty years. From cover to cover, his *Velt ayn, velt oys*[2] (World in, world out) is full of poems of the rarest, most thoughtful beauty; yet not even one review of it has been published. His first small book, *Vos ikh zing un zog* (What I sing and say), remained in all our hearts

2. This is actually the title of an anthology compiled by David Ignatoff published by Farlag Amerike (New York, 1916).

for a long time. His poetry was the most European and most purely lyrical that we had found until then in Yiddish poetry. Lines from that book were on our lips for a long time. M. L. Halpern, a sentimental person, used to break into tears when he sang out these lines as if counting pearls:

> When the forest is chopped down
> every tree weeps;
> and very quietly, very quietly
> the ax weeps with them.
>
> Do you believe me when I say:
> I, the ax, I weep?
>
> Az men hakt dem vald
> veynt ayeder boym;
> un gor shtil, gor shtil
> veynt mit zey di hak.
>
> Gloybt ir ven ikh zog:
> ikh, di hak, ikh veyn?

Today those lines sound sentimental, romantic in an old-fashioned way. The allegorical weeping of the trees did not attract us. But that the ax weeps—that struck us like lightning. It was the lightning that grasped us, though logically such a thing is hard to imagine. From Imber's lines that were then on everyone's lips, the only ones I remember are these: "About quiet ones, like old men" and "a golden star, a branch with a rose." That reminds one of a Japanese drawing. Forever sealed in my memory is the following drama-laden verse:

> The red apple lies cut—
> half for me, half for you;
> the sharp knife gleams in the middle
> and winks to me and winks to me.
>
> Der royter epl ligt tseshnitn—
> A helft far mir, a helft far dir;
> Dos sharfe meser blankt in mitn,
> Un vinkt tsu mir un vinkt tsu mir.

But I don't remember whether the stanza is also from that first book or whether I read it somewhere else.

Poets, especially when young, are narrow-minded, intolerant, and impatient. Disappointments come to them even more quickly than enthusiasms, and when they are disappointed, they become brutal. Yesterday's idol becomes tomorrow's laughingstock. Very often there doesn't even need to be disappointment: it is enough for a new idol to cast darkness on the preceding one. What yesterday was "wonderful" the next day is "dreadful." Menakhem, for us, eliminated Einhorn. Imber quickly drove both of them out of favor and then was pushed aside by Konigsberg. Why Konigsberg was worthy of this is now a mystery to me, though at the time, I was one of his chief followers.

The strength of a poet is in his words, and Konigsberg was and remains dumb. Indeed, we called him "the silent poet," and he made a remarkable impression on us. His little book with some twenty sonnets was stuffed in our pockets along with countless poems of our own. We carried it around for a long time. We knew that he stuttered, but it seemed to us that behind the stutterer lay an unusual poet. Five or six of his sonnets simply astonished us. But when I reread them not long ago, I shrugged my shoulders.

What did we see in him? It occurs to me now that Konigsberg impressed us because he came to us with simple, everyday subjects, while we were stuffed with romanticism.

In my memory there remains a false impression of a rare silence in his poems. I had a grandmother named Matele, whose voice rang like a bell. When she spoke quietly in her store, you could hear her on the other side of the market. My mother used to turn pale when she heard her mother-in-law's voice. When my grandmother went out walking on a Saturday in summer, there was a commotion because she always went out with daughters, daughter-in-law, and grandchildren; their procession took up the entire width of the road. When my mother went for a walk, she went by herself. She took with her only a child, small enough to need a guardian but not too small to spoil her walk. And she would turn off the road onto a path in a field and without speaking walk and walk, from time to time bending down to look at a blade of grass, an herb, or a bush. The same quietness was in her reading the *taytsh khumesh* and in her praying, and in her getting dressed when she was in a good mood. I was striving for quietness in my poems, and it seemed to me that I found it in Konigsberg.

One of the masters of the quiet poem was, in our opinion, Joseph Rolnik. Especially in the landscape poems of his childhood. He impressed me for the first time with "A shikkhe in feld" (A *shikkhe* in the field), in which he compared himself to a cut stalk that the reaper had forgotten in the field. From a simile is born a complete transformation. Man becomes shrunken and small and thin, like straw, and his desolation becomes almost physical, not the desolation of a man, but that of a stalk, soaked by the rain and blown about by the wind. This is one of the first demands on every poet, but rarely achieved.

Mani Leyb found himself as a poet around 1910, in the series *Toybn shtile* (Silent doves), which was in the second *Literatur* anthology; Zishe Landau found himself a year later, in the series of poems that was published in Avrahm Reisen's annual, *Dos naye land* (The new land). I knew what I wanted, but it was as if I was shackled and couldn't attain my wish. "The days are rooted in stone, / and growing hurts." So wrote Anna Margolin many years later—the best expression of what I went through during that time.

The Warshaw-Teper Legend

On a sunny but cool spring afternoon, a few young writers brought a simple wooden coffin, covered with a black cloth from the burial society, out of a Bronx morgue. In the courtyard of Fordham Hospital where the morgue was, ten other young people whom I didn't know stood waiting. When the coffin was carried through the courtyard, those who were outside followed. Some lent a helping shoulder, and others leant a hand for appearance's sake. In the entrance to the hospital courtyard, the hearse stood waiting with two open doors. In front of the open doors stood a small man with a gray, curly beard that hugged a filthy, smiling face. That was the cemetery caretaker for the burial society. He showed us how to lift the coffin carefully from our shoulders and slide it into the hearse. Then, with a cheerful, hoarse voice, he asked if we wanted to form a line.

When we nodded yes, he said "All right," and ordered us to do it quickly, because the day would not stand still and the way was long. While we got in line, he crawled up to the seat beside the driver and the hearse began to move.

The wagon went slowly, a thin ribbon of mourners stretching behind it. We went down a street to a corner of Bronx Park, where everything glittered in various shades of new green. We went along Fordham Road to a long, empty block. Here, among gray, naked rocks on both sides of the road, the sun hid behind a cloud and a sharp wind cut our faces, carrying something of autumn and bitterness. A lump was in our throats, but no one cried. Only three people, who followed close behind the coffin, seemed truly grief-stricken. One of them was Zishe Landau. The second was a short, thin man with deep black eyes and a long mustache that hung down as if sprained. "Kolye Teper!" one of the mourners whispered in my ear when I asked who he was. Between those two walked a girl, almost as small as a child, with her head cast down. "A sister?" I asked. "No, a friend. A very close friend. Reyzl." Later, Reyzl Landau. After we went down a long, empty block, the hearse stopped. The man on the seat near the driver bent down a little from his place, turned his dirty face to us, and said: "Enough!" Before we had properly heard him, the hearse began to go faster, leaving us standing in the middle of the street, confused and bewildered. For a while, we watched the hearse recede into the distance. Soon it completely disappeared from our view, and with it, also gone forever, was Moyshe Warshaw.

The name Moyshe Warshaw, like the name Kolye Teper, would follow Di Yunge like a legend. In Hasidic stories, almost every *tsadik* has a mentor, the soul of another *tsadik* who lived hundreds and thousands of years earlier. That soul revealed hidden secrets to the *tsadik*. That soul also helped the *tsadik* rise from one spiritual level to the next. Something similar took place between us and Warshaw and Teper. Like holy patrons, they stood by Di Yunge, revealed for us the secrets of word art, and helped us become what we became. Like every legend, this one had a kernel of truth. We will soon see how big that kernel was.

Let's take a look at Moyshe Warshaw. The first impression is the strongest, though not always—and, perhaps most of the time, not the correct one. This is how I saw him for the first time: small, weak, and flabby, with white, almost feminine hands. With a gentle, milk-white face. With near-sighted, gloomy blue eyes that squinted behind thick glasses when they looked at you, and with thin, arrogantly tight lips. Someone with an appearance like that could not arouse love when you first met him. Warshaw was not someone you could easily get close to. He moved in a narrow circle. And in that narrow circle he was not much loved. Only a few were close to him and only three or four stuck with him. And when the man with that face frowned when he heard a poem read that he didn't like—not to mention when his thin lips shot out a poisonous word that wounded you deeply—it sowed in your heart a hatred from which it was hard to free yourself, even after you came to know him better and saw that he was not as poisonous and as arrogant as you had thought. In essence Warshaw was a modest man, at times even abject. But he was also quite arrogant. He was considered erudite, and he often used to play the erudite, looking down on others and speaking of them contemptuously. So Warshaw couldn't have had a great influence even if he had had something with which to be influential. Because there cannot be any influence without closeness, and you cannot be close with someone who scorns you. One pays for scorn with scorn and even with hatred. And I could name a few of Di Yunge who hated him. His contemptuousness was all the more annoying because Warshaw himself wrote nothing, or if he did, we never knew about it. Because he never published anything and he never read us anything—not even (so I believe) to Zishe Landau, who was his closest friend from childhood on. After his death, we learned that he had indeed written poems, and bad ones at that. If we had known that while he was alive, we would have had a weapon with which to defend ourselves from his scorn, but since we didn't know, his scowls were all the more dismaying. Those who knew Warshaw better, respected him. I was certainly never close to him, but at the end of his life a friendship began between us. At the beginning of our acquaintance, I listened to those who did not like him. Later, I had true respect for him. But not for his knowledge—that, I still considered exaggerated. Today, when I leaf through his book, *Vegn fun a neshome* (Paths of a soul), which Teper and Landau published after his death, I see that I was right. He had read perhaps more than any of us, but we knew more than he. He liked what I would call creative knowledge, by which I mean the intuitive sense that goes straight to the very most important thing that he reads, that selects it and chews it over so that it becomes his own and different. He liked the creative kernel that draws from alien sources, just as the seed draws from the earth those chemical elements that help it become what it must become. Only healthy kernels that possess potential life become fruitful when they come in contact with foreign elements. Unhealthy ones become devoured by them.

Moyshe Warshaw was poisoned and devoured by the things that he read—things that in large measure contributed to his early, tragic death. Like a lot of other Russian Jewish intellectuals of his generation, he was also affected by the revolutionary movement and by the search for a god that came with the reaction to the failure of the first revolution. He chose Christianity. How much his own disposition and his own orientation brought him there and how much was because it was then the fashion, I don't know. What I do remember well, though, from frequent conversations I had with him in the last half year of his life, is that his way to Christianity went—however strange this may seem—by way of Nietzsche, Weininger, and Chamberlain, a few Russians, and the Polish revolutionary Stanislaw Brzozowski, whom he literally deified, mainly because Brzozowski, in his time, was an inspired revolutionary as well as a zealous Catholic. When Brzozowski was suspected of being a provocateur, it was, for Warshaw, practically a personal tragedy. Influenced by the opinions of most of the writers he admired, Warshaw, on his way to Christianity, was afflicted with anti-Semitism that turned into self-hatred. Like a pious Hasid, he, like Weininger, enumerated all the inferior qualities that brilliant convert saw in the Jewish character; and as we see in the pages of the diary that Warshaw left behind, all of the defects that Weininger ascribed to Jews, Warshaw saw in his own character. If before he took pride in his knowledge, at the end of his life, through that same knowledge, he saw himself as more insignificant and worthless than a worm. In his diary, he speaks constantly about "sin," but it seems that his only sin, in his eyes, was that such an inconsequential creature such as he should walk on God's earth.

He hated in himself his very Jewishness; he hated himself for his physical weakness. For his "unhealthy nerves, withered limbs, ugly habits, rotten thoughts," as he described himself in his sick, exaggerated way. He invented all kinds of sins and tortured himself with all kinds of immorality. But whoever knew him and later read his diary felt that all of the self-accusations were, for him, only a mask, behind which he hid the truth that troubled him. He was troubled by a feeling of inferiority that made him unable to enjoy life simply, like all the people around him. One saw this best in how helpless he used to feel in the presence of women. He was, perhaps, also troubled by what he knew: that while he could criticize very well what others wrote, he himself, with all his knowledge and understanding, was insignificant creatively compared to them. Only in one place in his diary does he reveal this. But even there, he attributes this not to his incapability, but to his "not wanting to." "I am weak," he writes in one place, "and my life is unnecessary, but I want to believe: work is waiting for me, black work, but—work for Yiddish culture . . . I will not be one of the creators—I don't want that. I am a nest of sicknesses, ugliness. Whatever is mine, my own personally, can only poison."

One mustn't take a writer literally when he speaks about himself, especially when he says negative things. Sometimes he does this only to make a dramatic impression; sometimes because it's useful; sometimes it's merely an affectation, and if he actually means it, it's still an exaggeration. Warshaw surely meant everything that he wrote about himself, although of course, he exaggerated terribly. But there was some truth in his self-criticism. Yes, Warshaw had a direct influence. One person, at least, his best and most intimate friend, Zishe Landau, he infected with his sickly Christianity. But it was exactly from that bit of sickly Christianity that he got from Warshaw that Landau produced the liveliness that sprouts from his best poetry. Warshaw had only an indirect ethical influence on others who came in contact with his personality. During the years he was among us, he changed several times. Out of the arrogance we once saw in him grew, by the end, the humility of a saint who had withdrawn completely from the world. And he remained that way. A conversation with him led to soul searching. One came away from such a conversation with, at the very least, a desire to become a better person.

It is well known that Warshaw committed suicide. In the last months of his life, he earned his living as a night watchman at a building site in the Bronx. On the night of April 22, 1912, he climbed to an upper floor of the unfinished building and threw himself out a window. When passersby found him, he was already dead. He was taken to the Bronx morgue. When I arrived there the next day, I saw him on ice, still in his clothes, just as they had found him on the street. One sleeve was torn; a broken, bloody hand and wrist could be seen. The upper part of his face was handsome—more handsome than in life. But his mouth and jaw were smeared with blood, like a slaughtered calf. I had seen corpses before, but this was the first time in my life that I had seen someone who had died in such a way, and I could not tear my eyes away. Again and again, I gazed at the broken hand, at the clotted blood in his wrist and around his mouth, and murmured to myself: "Warshaw . . . Warshaw. . . ."

It was impossible to believe that this slaughtered corpse (I could not erase the first impression of a slaughtered calf) was Moyshe Warshaw. I felt peaceful. I felt no grief. Even after the caretaker from the burial society cut away his clothing, and Warshaw was entirely naked, I still couldn't look away. I gave a start when the caretaker took the naked body by the head and someone else took him by the feet, and naked, without a shroud, laid him in the simple wooden coffin. I, Ignatoff, and the others protested: Just like that? Naked? Without even a shroud? But he calmed us down by saying that that would be done at the cemetery in the *tahores shtibl*. "Here in the morgue, it's not permitted." Only when we lifted the coffin to carry it from the morgue did I feel a lump in my throat. The hearse drove off with the coffin and left us feeling lost in the middle of the street. Some of us raced to a trolley, which would take us to a subway, which would carry us to the cemetery; others of us realized that we didn't even know in which cemetery Warshaw would be buried. When I came home that night, and was served meat for dinner, I felt nauseated. For several months, I couldn't stand the sight of meat—or even less, the smell—because Warshaw after his death had seemed like a slaughtered calf. For a long time after that, I didn't take a pen in hand; for several months, Warshaw pursued me. Wherever I looked, I saw him. At work in the shop, among friends, I would suddenly see him—not as a corpse, but as he looked in the last months of his life, bent over, wrapped up in himself, an introspective old monk though he was at his death no more than twenty-five years old. His death tormented me. In different ways, I tried to get inside him, in order to understand what could have driven him to suicide. The result was a story, "Der zaytiger" (The outsider), in which I tried to describe the last day of his life.

Sooner or later, the dead are forgotten. Warshaw stopped appearing before me. The revulsion for meat disappeared. And suddenly, once again, I heard rhythms humming in my ear. But they were much different rhythms than before, and the lines that emanated from them were fuller and heavier and of a completely different character. I could no longer write about distant, joyous things. Warshaw, in his death, had for the first time shown me the brutal, banal, naked truth of life. The romantic veils disappeared from my life and my poetry. A new song was born, ancient and entirely my own.

Kolya Teper deserves a chapter to himself. In connection with Di Yunge, he belongs to a later time, though he was older than us. I won't dwell on him long, except to remark that in almost every detail, he was the opposite of Warshaw. He was, perhaps, even shorter than Warshaw, and thinner. But he was also livelier, more manly, and, in contrast to Warshaw's passivity—quick. Quick in everything: In his walk and in his gestures. A quick mind and a quick fighter. When attacking and defending himself against an opponent, he was amazingly quick to strike the weakest spot. He was a great connoisseur, knowledgeable in several European literatures, and a wonderful conversationalist with polish, elegance, and sparkle—he could, at table, literally bewitch you. Magic stuck to his name. He was still a legend in Russia. In his early youth, almost in his boyhood, he had been a favorite of the Zionists, especially in the Akhad Ho'om[3] circle of Odessa. He was a wonderful orator—perhaps the greatest we had—and with the reputation he enjoyed among the Zionists, it was a

3. Pseudonym of Asher Ginzberg (1856–1927), Russian Zionist and founder of Cultural Zionism.

yontev for the Bundists[4] when he went over to them. The more intellectual of the Bundists viewed him literally as a god. When I traveled through the Midwest in 1915, people fell silent with awe when I mentioned his name. They considered it a great honor that they had been at a secret meeting in the woods at which Teper spoke. Others were tremendously proud that they had risked their lives to smuggle him out of prison when he had fallen into the hands of the tsarist police.

He, too, became a searcher for God and went over to Christianity—in the Soviet Union—to Christianity! Indirectly, he certainly was more of an inspiration and influence than Warshaw. But he could not have directly influenced the development of Di Yunge, because he had arrived among us when everyone already had his own poetic face, his own voice, and his own approach, and—most important—because for all his impressive virtues, and despite his wonderful style as a speaker and writer, and despite his great playfulness and capriciousness that is usually attributed to an artistic nature, he was not an artist; he was a great connoisseur and enjoyer of poetry, but his approach to poetry was definitely that of a stranger, not a poet. And only another poet or another artist can directly influence poets.

A Store Without Customers

Should any future historian come along and try to sum up the contribution of *Shriftn* to Yiddish literature, he will have to be objective. Who knows if anyone like that will ever appear? He will certainly have plenty to ridicule. The times and the pitiful state of Yiddish literature in America will certainly seem ludicrous to him, though the elemental, artistic truths with which *Shriftn* arrived must be considered a revolution. He will, perhaps, laugh also at the people who were associated with the anthology, just because they took their achievements and themselves so seriously.

---

4. Jewish Labor Bund founded as a Jewish Socialist party in Vilna (Vilnius) in 1897 and active throughout the Russian Empire and North and South America. It advocated secular Jewish nationalism with Yiddish as the national language; it was anti-Zionist.

But whatever his opinion, he will have to admit that the *Shriftn* anthologies were an important moment in Yiddish literature, and not only in America. Important, because the anthologies began to crystallize a collective artistic will and because a school would later emerge from them—the first literary school among us.

Studying that time, the future historian will come across frictions and rifts that developed within the group over the anthologies. Many of the frictions he will, perhaps—and rightly so—attribute to personal motives. He will give them more importance than they actually had. Even without personal motives, sooner or later there would have occurred a split between Ignatoff and Opatoshu, for example. They were so fundamentally different in their writing and in their character that it is astonishing that they worked peacefully together on two anthologies, until the third, when they finally went their separate ways. And the ideological and artistic rifts among Mani Leyb and Halpern and Landau and Halpern were just as unavoidable, though these never ended in personal breaks. Halpern was even represented by two of his own poems and some translations in the third issue of *Shriftn*. But even earlier, he had a "separate table" in the café because he felt that the distance between the other poets and him was becoming greater. In his poems, he gradually became noisier and "stronger"—while we were becoming more reticent and "quieter," traits that he characterized, more than once, as sickly. We accused him of writing journalism. He accused us of being effete. It is understandable that no great love can exist between two opposing poet-natures—between Halpern and Rolnik, for example. For the highly sensitive and easily distracted Rolnik, it was natural that he would perceive and react poetically to the smallest breath that touched him. For the healthy and not overly sensitive Halpern, Rolnik's slender and deeply felt poems had to sound like sickly complaints. It is interesting that when one opens Halpern's volume of poetry, one is amazed at the lamentation that gushed from him. We all poured out too many poetic tears.

More than anything though, we purified the language. We protected it, we nurtured it, we made of it a wonderful, poetic instrument. Halpern toiled over it, but almost nothing came of his labor. He had a rich vocabulary, but he didn't know what to do with it. We were, perhaps, poorer in words, but we were able to bend them, make them our own, wield them to our heart's desire. In his rich vocabulary, Halpern had no more than six or seven pairs of rhymes, which he used, indeed, only in pairs. He also used a lot of word combinations that we considered alien to the spirit of the Yiddish Language. He also lacked idioms. We nurtured ourselves with folk song, folk tales, the *Tsene-rene* and *tkhine*—all the things that give so much flavor and intimacy to the folk language. We did not find this in Halpern. Halpern was a great poet. There are poems of his that could be considered great in any type of poetry. But his shortcomings were great as well. One of his greatest faults was his lack of feeling for language. Feeling for language is, in the greatest measure, "home feeling"—that is, the longing for the intimate, childish, and boyish impressions of home and surroundings, the ones that everyone and especially the poet carries with him his whole life. Halpern never spoke of his childhood with love, and in his poems one finds not a spore of it. This is, perhaps, because he was torn too young from his hometown of Zlotshov and transplanted to Vienna; perhaps even more, it was because in Zlotshov his father had not been at home—he had been a stranger, a traveler from Russia, with little love for his adopted place, which, as one can tell from several of Halpern's poems, had not treated him in a very friendly way. Home feeling gives the language richness, intimacy, and elasticity, as well as a mass of localisms that can easily become abused. Indeed, many poets stumble— though less here in America than elsewhere, because in the local melting pot, where all Yiddish dialects are cooked together, the poet feels that he can use only those localisms that will not stick out from a poetic line. In language feeling, Halpern was exactly the opposite of his countryman and closest friend, Moyshe Nadir, the greatest language master among us. Moyshe Nadir's wealth of home feeling was clearest to see in the striking landscapes he could so wonderfully draw out from his narratives, as if by magic. I don't know anyone who can, in this gift for detail, be compared to him, though others, especially Rolnik, were also rich in landscapes from their childhood.

Rifts began to form even before the first edition of *Shriftn*. And even before the second edition was published, we knew that the break was unavoidable. By the third edition, half the group had already broken away; and while Ignatoff, Mani Leyb, Landau, and I prepared to publish the third edition of *Shriftn*, Opatoshu, I. J. Schwartz, J. Rolnik, M. I. Khaymovitz, Yoyl Slonim, and others were preparing the anthology *Di naye heym* (The new home). I don't know which of the two anthologies was better. I do know that ours was more consistent. There were stronger artistic connections among the poets in the *Shriftn* than among the poets in *Di naye heym*; and our poets, as a whole, were more closely related to *Shriftn's* prose writers, Ignatoff and Raboy, than the poets of *Di naye heym* were to its prose writers, Opatoshu and Khaymovitz.

But even the narrow, unified group of *Shriftn* writers could not, after that, "live together" for long. There occurred a break between the poets and the prose writers, or more precisely, between the poets and Ignatoff. I have already pointed out the reason for the rift. I will only add here that even before the third edition was published, Mani Leyb said it would be the last, and Landau and I agreed with him. Perhaps the *Shriftn* would have ended anyway, even if it had not come to a rift, for it had already served its purpose and was no longer needed.

The third edition of *Shriftn* came out in the spring of 1914, although it had been printed perhaps a year earlier. I have already mentioned that for me personally, the book meant a lot because it included a series of poems that was my most mature work, and so it was an important date in my life and a landmark in my life as a poet.

So one can imagine how impatiently I awaited that edition. I had to wait too long, and in the meantime there arose financial problems that made me forget the anthology.

I was laid off from the shop where I had worked for years and was left hanging with a wife and three small children. It was a bad time, and there was no chance of getting work in my occupation, with so many workers already going around with empty hands. So I had to look for another livelihood. Like a lot of unemployed Jewish shop workers, I had no choice but to open a store, so I became the proprietor of a delicatessen. Cutting sausage and constantly going around soiled with grease isn't agreeable, even for someone who writes poetry. But I had no other choice. I did not have any experience in business, and I didn't have a penny to my name. For experience and money I had to go to my brother. He was prepared to lend me several hundred dollars, but only for a business in which he had experience, and he had experience only in the sausage business. For six hundred dollars, he bought a store for me in Brooklyn, on Broadway near Van Buren Street, which at that time was a terrible neighborhood; it had a mixed population of Jewish merchants, Irish saloon keepers, poor people of all nationalities, and pimps, drug dealers, and prostitutes, also of all nationalities.

I could not make a living from the store. But I did get a lot of literary satisfaction and even joy. No customers came in, but fellow poets did, from near and far. During that time, the third edition of *Shriftn* was published. Friends and other poets came with their compliments. Zishe Landau brought Kolye Teper, whom I had seen only once before, at Moyshe Warshaw's funeral. Teper sent Leivick, who at that time had just appeared among us. One day, Mani Leyb came by with a tall young man who looked like a tramp. "This is Kanzanski!" Mani Leyb said when he saw that I couldn't take my eyes off this tall man with a stubbled face, shirtless, wearing only a threadbare jacket over a thin summer undershirt, bare feet in slippers. I offered the young man my hand. When I still didn't take my eyes off him, Mani Leyb said, "You know each other, don't you?" Yes, David Kanzanski I already knew. But was this really the same David Kazanski? The other time I saw him, in Ignatoff's bachelor room on Washington Avenue, he had been completely different. That Kazanski had been a well-dressed man with a straight, neatly combed beard and a fine leather briefcase that never left his hand. In the briefcase he had a novel that he had brought to Ignatoff for *Shriftn*. But at their first meeting, the two men disliked each other so much that Kanzanski, it seems to me, no longer wanted to leave his manuscript.

At Ignatoff's, Kazanski had not made a good impression on me. I no longer remember why. Perhaps it was his beard, perhaps it was the briefcase. We were accustomed to carrying our manuscripts in our pockets until they were well worn, and here comes someone all dressed up and with a beard and a briefcase. "No, not a man for me," I thought. But the "tramp" Kazanski pleased me so well after a chat of half an hour that I simply could not let him go. He, too, was by then a merchant—a laundryman. And Mani Leyb had torn him away in his work attire and brought him to me. Several days later, at the threshold of my store, I spotted a handsome young man, dressed like a prince. Who was this? It was a while before I realized that this was the same Kazanski. The transformation was so surprising that I couldn't believe my eyes. This time, Kazanski was no storekeeper. In just a few days he had got rid of his "business." I had to wait nine long months for the miracle to happen to me. Only a miracle could have released me from that business, and that miracle happened thanks to Kazanski. He brought me an agent, who brought me a client, who freed me from my affliction.

Mani Leyb knew Kazanski early on, and he introduced him to Landau. In a short time we four became close, in literature and personally. Like Mani Leyb, Kazanski and I lived in Brooklyn, so Kanzanski's apartment there became our center.

At the time, Landau was the only one of us who lived in the Bronx. He used to come to Brooklyn often. Usually he would first drop by and spend some time with me. But then he would go to Kazanski, with whom he spent hours and even whole nights. One morning, when I opened the store, I noticed a folded piece of paper lying on the floor that someone had slipped under the door. On the sheet was written in pencil a humorous poem that began like this:

> Sleep peacefully in your bed
> young merchant and poet.
> Tomorrow you will have to
> sharpen your knives
> and cut sausage
> so people will suffer pain
> in their bellies.

> Shlof zikh ruik in dayn bet
> yunger soykher un poet.
> Morgn vestu darfn
> dayne mesers sharfn
> un di vorshtn shnaydn
> mentshn zoln laydn
> afn mogn.

The handwriting looked like Landau's. The voice I recognized as Mani Leyb's. The friendly greeting brought me happiness and awakened a longing that held me the whole day as if intoxicated. Only when Kazanski visited me that night did I find out that Mani Leyb and Landau spent the whole previous night at his place. At dawn, they went to my store— perhaps it would already be open. When they found it shut, this poem was written extemporaneously, with paper pressed against the window of the locked door.

That poem freed me, as if by magic, not from the store (for I still had to wait a long time for that), but from slavery to the store. Because I envied my friends, who were not chained to anything but could move feely and spend time together whenever they wanted to, I suddenly threw off my yoke, and when I heard that Landau had come to Brooklyn and knew that they would again spend a night together, I abandoned everything and went to Kazanski's.

That summer brought the world war. Our ties with the Old Country began to fray. Dr. Karl Fornberg and Max N. Meyzel published a journal, *Literature un lebn* (Literature and life), which was linked to Niger's *Yidishe velt* (Yiddish world) from Vilna. A strange combination it was, and it made a humorous impression. The journal had two parts: the first edited and published in Vilna; the second, in New York. The part published here was made up chiefly of social-political articles by Isaac Hurwitz, Jacob Milk, Dr. Karl Fornberg, and others, and it was so different from the Vilna part that even the paper and the type were different. When the world war broke out and the *Yidishe velt* no longer arrived from Vilna, Fornberg had to fill the journal entirely with local material. That led to a marriage between the above-mentioned social-political publicists on one side, and Mani Leyb, Landau, Kazanski, and me on the other. We also brought in Menakhem, who had just arrived from Warsaw. We left the social-political side of the journal entirely in the hands of the publicists, while we took over the literary side. This is where the history of Di Yunge really began. But that is a completely different chapter. It no longer had any connection to *Shriftn*.

🎕 With Mani Leyb

Our First and Last Meetings

I got to know Mani Leyb during the winter of 1905/06. He had been in the country for only a few months, I for over two years. Alexander Zeldin, who came to America almost at the same time as Mani Leyb, introduced us. All three of us were then young, apprentice writers, and all of us had to do physical work to make a living: Mani Leyb, until he was in his fifties, in a shoe factory; Zeldin, in a carpenter's shop; and I, in a hat factory as a packer. Of the three, Zeldin was then the most important. In Russia he had already published a story in the Petersburg *Tog*, which Frishman cited as the most important thing that had been published in that newspaper. He published stories and monologues in the pages of the *Fraye arbeter shtime* (FAS; Free voice of labor) that made a name for him among other young writers. I remember the strong impression that his stories made on me then: "Ganovim" (Thieves) and "Erev khasene" (Before the wedding). To this day, it is a mystery to me why he did not become *the* writer that we all thought he would become. Mani Leyb had also made a name for himself, with his poems, which he, too, had published in *FAS*.

He was especially praised for his rich language. I think by the word "rich" they were alluding to its folksy tone and melodic phrasing—both traits that were, however, still at that time quite primitive and not at all original. I was then still almost completely unknown. I published stories in the little newspaper *Dos yidishe vokhenblat* (The Jewish weekly) when it was already going under and had no readers, and I published poems under a pseudonym in *Dos folk* (The people), which was the organ of the

60

Socialist-Territorialists[1] and was edited by the then anarchist M. Katz. His chief assistant and only paid worker was S. Kotler, a young poet for whom everyone had great hopes and who suddenly disappeared just when he was in his most beautiful flowering.

Only years later was it discovered that he had become a salesman of women's clothing in Detroit.

I was introduced to Mani Leyb by Zeldin in the club of the Socialist Revolutionaries, which was, that winter, the liveliest spot on East Broadway. It was not just members of the Socialist Revolutionary Party that went to the club. In Russia, the first revolution had already taken place. But in the club, searing debates still burned in every corner, among young men and women who, in Russia, had belonged to all the revolutionary groups and who were, that winter, arriving in New York by the hundreds on every ship. At the club, young writers met whose work was being published in *FAS*, the *Forverts*, and other weekly and daily newspapers. Many young writers from Russia were connected to revolutionary parties of all persuasions. Mani Leyb had been a Socialist Revolutionary in his hometown of Nieshzin. Then in London he had joined the anarchists; even so, in his first American years, he also was drawn to the Socialist Revolutionaries. Zeldin, who introduced me to Mani Leyb, was then a Labor-Zionist,[2] as was I, until the split in the American Labor-Zionist Party, after which, for a short time, I went over to the majority faction, the Socialist-Territorialists.

When Zeldin introduced us, it turned out that Mani Leyb had already seen me, in the home of the former anarchist and writer M. Tsipin, somewhere on Broome Street, but only in passing. That was at the first meeting—if I'm not mistaken, also the last—of the Yidishe Yugend, which had been organized by a group of writers who were still young, though

1. A Jewish Socialist-Territorialist political party active in Russia and Poland, founded in 1905. The party favored the idea of a Jewish autonomous territory outside of Palestine.

2. A major faction of the left wing of the Zionist movement; it believed that the immigration to Palestine of the Jewish working class was essential in order to establish a Jewish state. Theoreticians of the Labor Zionist movement included David Ben-Gurion and Golda Meir.

older than we were, and who had already made names for themselves. M. Tsipin, H. Rosenblat, Jacob Adler, Yoyl Slonim, M. Shmuelson, A. Voliner (who had already published poems under his real name, L. Landau), and I. L. Kahan all belonged to the group. At a literary evening, which that group had organized at the former Apollo Hall between Broome and Delancey streets, and at which most of these writers gave readings, it was announced that all young writers—or just lovers of literature in the hall— who wanted to join the society could pay twenty-five cents and give their names and addresses to a committee that would be standing by the door at the end of the evening. I signed up. Zeldin signed up. So did others. Soon, I received a card with an invitation to come on a certain Sunday afternoon to a meeting of the society at a certain address. I went. Mani Leyb also went. But he arrived too late, just as I and others were about to leave, and we passed each other near the door. I didn't notice him because, while leaving, I was involved in a conversation with I. L. Kahan, who was also just leaving. Mani Leyb, though, did notice me and remembered my face and how intensely I was conversing with Kahan.

What remains in my memory from that first meeting with Mani Leyb is the image of a tall, thin young man in a black coat to his knees, with a black woolen shirt buttoned to his chin without a tie, and a row of mother-of-pearl shirt buttons. That he wasn't wearing a tie did not seem remarkable to me; I imagined that in his eyes, a tie was too bourgeois, as it was in the eyes of many in the club, most of whom wore Russian *rubashkes*. But the length of his coat and the black shirt seemed unusual even in that circle. That, perhaps, was the main reason why my eyes go first to his coat and his shirt when I remember that meeting. I also remember an oval, olive-skinned face with piercing green-grey eyes and a serious yet impulsive gaze. When he smiled, it warmed your heart; when he wrinkled his nose, it could curdle your mother's milk.

I often think that the latter impression is, perhaps, only a generalization caused by my own sensitivity, because I remember the crinkle of his nose in connection with a poem of mine that I had mentioned to him and that he happened to have read without knowing I had written it. I was then twenty-two and had to my credit barely three published stories and exactly as many poems—the last of these under a pseudonym—besides tens of other things that were not yet published and that were wandering around with me in my pockets. And what it meant to me, that crinkling of the nose of a fellow poet who was my age but much better known than I, perhaps all apprentice poets of all cultures and languages know. Because no one is as sensitive as a young poet, and nothing can cut him to the quick more than a word or gesture of scorn at his expense. But when I call up the memory of the image that I carry in myself of Mani Leyb—not only of that first meeting of ours but also of different times and different occasions—it seems to me that the smile that warmed me and the crinkle of his nose, or another gesture that could chill the soul, were two of his very characteristic traits, especially when they were silent expressions regarding a poem that had been read to him.

I saw Mani Leyb for the last time a year before he was taken from us. It was a Monday, November 6, 1952, the day before I gave up my New York apartment and went to settle permanently in Miami Beach. That was only forty-eight years after our first meeting. He came to say goodbye to me. With him came Itzik Manger, Isaac Horovits, and N. B. Linder. From that last gathering, there are before me four photographs. In two of them he is with us in a group of five; in one, in a group of three; and in one, only he and Itzik Manger. In none of them is there a trace of that picture that is in my memory. The contrast is sharpest in the picture with Manger, in which he sits with the upper part of his body bent forward and his clothes rumpled, his throat wrinkled as if it were leather, his crooked mouth open as if it were hard for him to breathe. His eyes are two cloudy cracks behind a pair of glasses, and his forehead above them is drawn and pinched. His flesh and face belong to an old man who is obviously tired and who wants to be left alone. But even here, where he is so different, he is still the same. Because if you look longer at that picture, it seems that on the face of that tired old man, a smile will soon appear that will gladden you, and in his cloudy eyes there are two sparks that are watchful, critical, and provocative, and you expect to suddenly see exactly the same offensive expression that you saw the first time you met him.

None of us lit up the way he could when one read him something that pleased him, and no one showed such disgust when he didn't like something. Literally with physical revulsion, he would shake off a poem that rang false and pretentious. But he did not consider false and pretentious those things that he did not understand or that weren't to his taste. He realized that the fact that he did not understand something, or that it was not to his liking, certainly didn't mean it was false. In connection with this, I remember an encounter between I. L. Kahan and him. For several years, Kahan owned a silverware store on Graham Avenue in Brooklyn. Soon after the First World War, he decided that he wanted to be a publisher of Yiddish books. What he thought he would accomplish with this publishing house, I don't know. What I do know is that he put about twenty thousand dollars into the business and never got a penny back. Most of the books that he published were translations. And since Kahan paid well, and Yiddish writers always needed some extra money, there were enough of us who were willing to take a book from him to translate. I translated one for him; Mani Leyb, who was having a very hard time financially, also undertook to translate a book. Whether he finished it, I'm not sure. Kahan did not give advances. But if you had forty or fifty pages of a book ready, and brought them to him, he immediately paid for them. Kahan had made an exception for Mani Leyb and had given him an advance.

Once, when Mani Leyb heard that I was going to bring Kahan fifty pages of the book I was translating, he said he wanted to go with me. The reason was that he was very much behind with his translation and he wanted to apologize for his lateness. He hadn't the courage to go to Kahan by himself, but if I were there too, he said, it would be easier for him. When we went to Kahan, we found him, as always, sitting behind the cashier desk. I handed him the part of my translation that I had brought, and he paid me what I was owed. Mani Leyb stood near me looking guilty and could not find the words he wanted to say to Kahan. As always, when he found himself in an uncomfortable situation where he was guilty, he stood there meekly and became irritated by his own meekness. I was becoming concerned; he was so tense that I was afraid he might explode. But Kahan suddenly asked us if we had read a certain poem by a certain poet, whose work neither of us liked. What we answered is not important. What is important is that Kahan thought we liked the poem and began to rave that it was worth nothing and that it was false from beginning to end and that no one had ever seen such a landscape as the one the poet described in his poem.

Kahan, as I already mentioned, was sitting behind the cashier desk. We both were standing at the side of the desk. On our right, and on Kahan's left, stood a glass case inside of which were various pieces of jewelry. On top of the case stood a shiny silver lamp. An electric light was hanging from the ceiling, covered by a white lampshade. The burning light with its lampshade, and the wire from the ceiling from which the light hung, were reflected in the shiny base of the silver lamp. Right in the middle of everything, while Kahan was in the midst of holding forth about the poem that was false, and how no one had ever seen a landscape such as the poet describes in his poem, suddenly the expression of irritation on Mani Leyb's face vanished and he asked, "What do you see, Kahan? I mean right there in the base of the lamp?"

Kahan remained awhile with his mouth open because he had not expected the question and didn't know what Mani Leyb was getting at. When Mani Leyb repeated the question, Kahan answered with a laugh. "What do I see? I see a lamp; the reflection of the electric light that's hanging from the ceiling."

"Right," said Mani Leyb, "but what else do you see?"

Kahan looked carefully at the base of the lamp and shrugged his shoulders. "Nothing," he answered "except the shade and the electric wire and nothing more."

"And what would you think," Man Leyb asked, "if I were to tell you that I see in the base of the lamp, not an electric light but a lily? A water lily with a golden heart and white petals surrounding it that sway on a long, trembling stalk?"

Kahan's laughter became a mere smile. Then the smile itself disappeared.

"True," he said after he had looked again at the base of the lamp, "if you really want to say that the lamp with the shade and the wire it's hanging from appear to be a lily. But what are you trying to prove by that?"

"That the fact that no one has ever seen what a poet describes in one of his poems is not a sign that the poem is, therefore, false," Mani Leyb answered. "For the poet, the optical transformation of the lamp is just as real, and perhaps more real, than the lamp itself."

I. L. Kahan, after a pause, admitted that what Mani Leyb had said was true, and Mani Leyb became immersed in a long conversation in which he tried to show that there are artistic truths that don't necessarily have to correspond to factual truths—for example, the rising and setting of the sun. It's been hundreds of years since it was shown as a scientific truth that it is not the sun that revolves around the Earth, but the Earth around the sun; nonetheless, poets do not desist from celebrating the sunrise and the sunset. The optical illusion is so strong that it's like a factual truth for all of us, and we have to try hard to convince ourselves that what we see is not true. There were, though, other natural phenomena that only the acutely observant eye of an artist can see, and even then, only at certain moments and under certain conditions. And if he can make it possible for us to see them too, then we cannot say they are false.

Mani Leyb very much liked to theorize and immerse himself in all sorts of speculations about the nature of art and artists, especially the nature of word art and word artists. Very seldom did he succeed in explaining clearly what he meant. But when he did succeed, it was a joy to hear him. And it was no wonder that Kahan's face shone when Mani Leyb unfolded for him his point of view concerning when a poem is false. According to his definition, a poem was false when the poet knowingly brought in a foreign element that had nothing to do with the essence of the poem, but that the poet was using to "grab" the reader. Sometimes it was a highly moralistic turn of phrase in which the poet wrapped himself, as if in a prayer shawl, in order to use a "lofty" word through which he could show the breadth and depth of his knowledge and understanding. Sometimes it was a current, combative slogan; sometimes it was simply an irrelevancy. Sometimes it was a cliché, and often it was a mystification or a similar means through which the poet could seek to hide his weakness, in the same way that a cantor chants with tears in his throat when he is not in good voice.

This conformed to Mani Leyb's poetic essence. He was one of those lucky—or unlucky—poets whose poems do not need to be interpreted, and it was seldom that one *could* interpret them. One either understood or one didn't. This is, I think, the main reason—perhaps indeed the only one—why our criticism, which is essentially expository, concerned itself so rarely with him while he lived. But this is also, I think, the main reason why Mani Leyb was a favorite of poets and children, both of whom respond to a poem, each in his own way, without reservation. Like a stunning landscape, like a fruit whose juices shoot into you when you bite into it, like a glance that bewitches and sends a chill up your spine and simultaneously splashes your whole body with joy. Critics should, like poets and children, be able to be captivated by a poem, and only then try to analyze it in order to see where its strength lies. Mani Leyb's poetry can often be weak. He sometimes uses old-fashioned or anachronistic words and expressions. Sometimes his poem is inarticulate, and then, of course, it is worth absolutely nothing. Mani Leyb was the most melodic of all our poets, and at times he allowed himself to be led astray by his melodiousness, to use phrases that were no more than poetic exercises. But he was never false in his poems according to his own definition of falsehood. He never used foreign elements, irrelevant effects, or other means to make a poem grab or "be weighty." The closest Mani Leyb came to extraneous effects was when he resorted, for a time, to mere mannerisms. Fortunately, he quickly outgrew that.

Nights with Mani Leyb

The summer of 1915, I lived near Mani Leyb in Boro Park. I was then entirely without work and had a lot of free time. Mani Leyb did have work, and compared to other workers, even in his own trade, he was not doing badly. And he also had a lot of free time. Since coming to America, he had worked in a shoe factory. He had free time because he was a very good craftsman. His work involved making a small part of a shoe, a part for which he was a specialist and so skillful that in six hours he could, all by himself, make enough of those parts to serve for a whole day. His workday, therefore, ended around two or three o'clock in the afternoon, and since we were neighbors, and since we both had free time, we spent a lot of time together. That summer, Goodman and Levine's restaurant on East Broadway—and after that one shut down, Lamed Shapiro's restaurant—became the center for all Yiddish writers in New York, older as well as younger. We spent the nights by ourselves, just the two of us, mainly on the avenues of Boro Park and on those large and empty stretches within the triangle formed by Boro Park, Bensonhurst, and the hinterland of Coney Island.

I don't know how that part of Brooklyn looks today, because I have not been there more than three or four times since that long ago summer when I lived in Boro Park. But in my time, only some parts of Boro Park were built up. True, the other parts were already mapped out, but only the stretches of asphalt and the young trees planted along both sides indicated that some day there would be streets and avenues there. The blocks themselves were then still empty. Most of them were overgrown with high grass and weeds; some were worked as vegetable gardens. To this day I can smell the various aromas that surrounded Mani Leyb and me, that used to barge into our conversations during those long walks that lasted until one or two in the morning and sometimes even longer. And to this day, I remember well the eternal conversations that we had during those walks. I remember even the two musical phrases of Tchaikovsky's symphony that used to break into our conversations when we grew tired, or when the moment came that we felt like halting the conversation.

From the beginning of our long walks, we maintained a disagreement over the "static and dynamic" in poetry. Mani Leyb argued for dynamism in poetry. By that he meant, first, that the true poet must always be emotional and constantly restless and always in a state of wanting something; and second, that he must be able to put this state into his poetry so that it is as if the poet himself is always filled with excitement and vibrates with quivering emotions. I held that neither is necessary; that a poet need not be constantly emotional and constantly restless, and that in the course of things, his poetry need not always vibrate with emotions. A poet can see, hear, and recognize something wonderful, become so delighted—that is to say, so captivated by what he sees, hears, or recognizes—that all emotions at that moment become still. I went further, telling him that the deepest emotional experiences can be adequately brought out in a poem only when the poet objectifies them. In the course of things, that quivering of emotions in poetry is not at all the same as in actual life. I went still further, asserting that a good poem need not grow from a direct experience;

that a lot of what we believe is rooted in personal experience becomes an experience in a poem only during the process of writing, when the poetry is concerned with the pairing of words and the arrangement of lines. Mani Leyb agreed with the last assertion because, from his own experience, he knew that what we often accept as the expression of direct emotions is, in truth, not a personal experience of a given moment, but shadows of experiences that we had at different times in our life and have continued to dream about, for who knows how long; and that we evoke them in ourselves by writing for our own needs; and that even then, they go through various connections and transformations. He said he agreed with me, but he didn't really, because in the end, he still maintained that a good poem is the result of personal experience and that only the experiences of a dynamic poet can lead to a good poem.

Theories, like gods, are created in the image of the people who invent them. The demand for dynamism was, like the melodic, vibrating, and brilliant image, and the unexpected change in the direction of Mani Leyb's poetry, completely in keeping with his restless and impulsive character. And he was especially restless and impulsive in the first weeks of that summer. I don't remember whether this was before or after his series of snow, national, and "white joy" poems. From the conversations we had during those long walks, this happened to be, for him, the appropriate time for such a series of poems. Mani Leyb, Zishe Landau, David Kazanski, and I were at that time a closed group that represented a certain direction in literature. The truth is, we did not always see eye to eye even among ourselves. The winter before, when I found myself on a tour in the Midwest on behalf of the journal *Literatur un lebn*, of which I was the literary editor, I gave a lecture at the Moishe Hess Club in Chicago in which I, for the first time, formulated our group's program. That lecture appeared a year later in the form of an article in the anthology *Fun mentsh tsu mentsh* (From man to man), which was edited by Moyshe Leyb Halpern. That article began, as did the lecture on which it was built, with this sentence: "The new direction of Yiddish poetry is the direction to life, to the daily life of the individual with his sufferings and joys." There was a bit of a quarrel about that first sentence between Zishe Landau and me on one side, and Mani Leyb on the other. Mani Leyb agreed only with the first half of the sentence: that the new direction of Yiddish poetry must be concerned with the life of the individual. But in no way did he agree that the direction should be the "daily life" of the individual. Landau and I were in the midst of our realist period, while Mani Leyb was drawn to the celebratory, the romantic, and—as Landau later called it—the "otherworldly." We spoke about poeticizing the mundane for several reasons. One reason, shared by Landau and me, was purely formalistic: by poeticizing the mundane, we would be protected against hackneyed poetic clichés. The other reasons were ideological, so to speak. But for Landau and me, they were not the same. Landau held that in poeticizing the mundane, poetry would show that joy exists and can be everywhere in all kinds of circumstances. I preached the poetry of the mundane in order to show how gray, how impoverished, and how dull the atmosphere was in which we were sentenced to live. Mani Leyb did not want to hear of bringing into poetry what he hated so much in life. In his opinion, poetry should concern itself only with the inner life of the individual, who throws off his gray, mundane surroundings and dreams of a more beautiful and more brilliant life.

In his mundane surroundings, he always had before his eyes his weary, burdened wife and four tiny children, which she, like a good wife, regularly brought into the world every two years. He saw me and some other colleagues whom he knew, with only one exception, in the same circumstances. He once told me on one of our walks that we were surrounded entirely by mares. All they knew how to do was bring children into the world. For them it was enough if they had sustenance for the children and could lick their calves like cows. Of course, one had to pity them, but for us, it was a greater pity. What we should have had were *ladies*, with luster and comfort and well-being around them, who would understand us and make our lives more beautiful, more comfortable and worthwhile. He dreamed of such a lady in the series of poems, *Vayse freyd* (White joy). In that series, a lady comes to him wearing thirteen veils in a princely palace, where he himself is transformed into a stern, domineering, evil nobleman. Perhaps the only glorified nobleman in Yiddish poetry. Of course this was only a poetic invention, one that was repugnant to him his whole life long. But the fact that for one short period in his life he created for himself a dream like the *Vayse freyd* and transformed himself into such an unreal image, that fact alone shows to what extremes the gray, dull surroundings he hated so much could lead him.

Mani Leyb's poetic abandonment of his hated surroundings foreshadowed a literal separation that had begun for him that summer. Mani Leyb's first wife, Hasia, was it seems no beauty. But from what I heard about her from Mani Leyb, she had been quite charming as a girl and he loved her so much that when he left Niezhin, he missed her terribly, and during the time he spent in London, in his longing for her, she became a beautiful dream, so that as soon as he came to New York and had started to earn something, he immediately sent for her and she became his wife. How she looked in New York not long after her marriage, about that we had very little information except for the memoir of Joseph Rolnik, who relates that when he saw her for the first time, not long after he came to America for the second time in 1907, she was already the mother of a child and that she had then "a mouth like a sliced apple." What exactly he wanted to express with that comparison, I don't know. But from the tone in which he tells it, I gather that she made a nice impression on him when he saw her for the first time and that youth and freshness radiated from her. In 1910, Mani Leyb wrote her a poem that goes like this:

I hate you! . . . only when rocked, lulled to sleep and gently kissed
the little, pale child in quiet, smiling rest
opens its eyes a moment, a moment closes them.
With sleepy lips he draws your breast to him,

and from your eyes thin tears run quietly down
the childish face, wetting it with tears like dew.
Then I bend low to your feet, oh mother,
my sinful, my sinful, my unhappy head.

Ikh hob dikh faynt! . . . nor ven farvigt un tsertlekh ayngekusht
dos kleyne, blase kind in shtiler, shmeykhldiker ru
a rege efnt oyf di eygelekh, a rege makht zey tsu,
mit shlofndike liplekh tsit zikh tsu zikh tsu dayn brust,

un fun di oygn dayne trern dine rinen shtil arop
dos kindershe peneml batoyendik mit trern-toy.

Dan boyg ikh tif tsu dayne fis, o mame ot azoy
mayn zindikn, mayn zindikn, mayn umgliklekhn kop.

From then on, as I remember, it was seldom that Mani Leyb would put into any poem of his a direct memory. But also from then on, the word "sin" is often repeated in his poems, very often rhymed in a banal way with "child" (zind-kind), not because he couldn't find a better rhyme, but because this was, for him, the best expression of what he carried with him for a long time: guilt that grew out of his desire to leave his wife, whom he had at one time loved so much and who now had become more and more estranged from him, except for the fact that she gave him several children.

When I saw Hasia the first time—around 1911–1912—there was not a spoor left of her former charm. It was early evening when Mani Leyb took me to a small, narrow apartment on a squalid street in a densely populated neighborhood of Williamsburg. His children were already sleeping when I came into the dark-green kitchen that was lit, like a thousand similar kitchens, with a small gas burner that hissed on a wall not far from a large coal oven. From a side room in which, apparently, the children were sleeping, his wife came in with bare feet in slippers, small and plump in a loose sweater over a faded skirt, her round face, old before her time, tired and depressed. She lifted her large, black eyes first to me and then to Mani Leyb; to me with surprise, as if she were asking who the stranger was that her husband had brought home, and then with resentment toward her husband—why had he brought a stranger into the house? But her eyes revealed that Man Leyb as a young boy hadn't necessarily been someone who allowed himself to be ruled by momentary impulses when he fell in love with her. A boy who grew up with her in the same city—perhaps even on the same street—could have loved her when she was a young girl. Mani Leyb could also have loved her during the period when Rolnik saw her for the first time. But since then, until that early evening when I saw her for the first time, Mani Leyb in every detail was so far ahead of her—and she, also in every detail, remained so far behind him—that it would have been a miracle if he had not, by degrees, taken a dislike to her. In just a few years, Mani Leyb grew to be a famous poet. And in those same years, he also blossomed physically. He had always been the typical good-looking poet. But during the span of several years, he became even more so. His glory and his beauty got to the point that many women devoured him with their eyes wherever he appeared and others openly caressed him with their glances. He would have had to be more than human for this not to impress him, and an angel not to begin to compare all those women who showed him so much love and honor to his wife, who, for all her love for him, saw only her husband. And of course, in all the comparisons, Hasia came out the lesser. It was therefore no wonder that a large number of his poems were full of dissatisfaction and a tearing away of himself, not knowing where.

Tearing himself away somewhere. But he was bound to Hasia with untold threads of love and tenderness. Even when it is the kind of love for a woman that endures because one remembers the grace of her youth and because she is the mother of your children, still, it is love. In the years after I saw her for the first time, until the summer of 1915, Mani Leyb had some casual flirtations, but none of them lasted very long. And it was Hasia who always won in the end, because after each one, Mani Leyb would go back to her with even more love and gentleness. But while the flirtation lasted, he abandoned her and the children and felt guilty because of it, and this guilt found expression in a whole series of his poems of that time.

For a short while, Mani Leyb also had a purely platonic love for the wife of a close friend, to whom not one of us was, then, entirely indifferent. Now that both he and our friend are in the world to come, one can say openly that Mani Leyb was, for a time, platonically in love with Mini Ignatoff, David Ignatoff's wife. I am almost certain that if she were to read these lines, she would be astonished, because during the time that Mani Leyb was platonically in love with her, she did not even begin to realize it, just as she did not know that we, Ignatoff's other friends, who, during the same time, just after their wedding, used to come to them every Sunday afternoon, as years earlier we used to go every Sunday to Ignatoff in his bachelor room on Washington Avenue, that we were also, each in our own way, quietly in love with her. And not for nothing. Because that was the first time that a woman appeared among us who exuded difference. American born; brought up in a house in which her father, in his younger years, dreamed of becoming an opera singer, and later, for the rest of his life, was a cantor in one of the richest Reform temples in Brooklyn; and where her mother, in her younger years, was a member of a circle of Socialist and anarchist intellectuals, some of whom were prominent writers, and she, also, had literary aspirations; so it was no wonder that they tried, from her earliest years, to give her the best education possible. She had hardly begun to show an interest in and understanding of music when her parents searched for the best piano and music teacher, and she had such talent that before she met Ignatoff, her parents were sure that she would one day become a famous pianist, and all of us were no less certain after we got to know her. From that young woman, who was in our eyes a mature artist, there radiated a silken silence, an aristocratic simplicity, and an open naïveté that captivated us.

That quiet, platonic love made Mani Leyb, more than in any of his earlier flirtations, very uneasy, and in his uneasiness he saw his children more abandoned than before. Poems are not usually reliable biographical material because one cannot know exactly what made a poet write such poems in one particular period and not in another. But through certain expressions and certain tendencies, if the poems repeat themselves often during one period, one can tell to which biographical detail these or those poems belong. But here are two poems that I don't have to try to guess from which time they came, because Mani Leyb himself told me right after he had written them what their origins were. Both come from those Sunday afternoons in the first months after Ignatoff's wedding when Mini almost always played for us. Both poems begin with the short sentence: "She plays," and the first one goes like this:

> She plays: my joy has flown far away from me.
> My joy, will you come back?—of course . . . of course . . .
> and he turns out the light and falls to her feet
> and remains there, stretched out at the piano.
>
> But she, she plays for those who sit slouched
> silently in the corner. She stops:—enough!
> And in the dark, someone smiles wisely,
> And someone burns with gray, misty eyes.

Zi shpilt: mayn glik iz vayt fun mir farfloygn.
Mayn glik vest kumen ven tsurik? Gevis . . . gevis . . .
un er farlesht dos likht un falt far ire fis,
un blaybt azoy baym piane oysgetsoygn.

Nor zi, zi shpilt far di vos zitsn ayngeboygn
in vinkl shvaygndik. Zi shtelt zikh oyf:—genug!
Un fun der finster shmeykhlt eyner klug,
un eyner brent mit groye, nepldike oygn.

In that poem, Mani Leyb is simply relating a scene that happened on
a Sunday evening at Ignatoff's. Mini was not in the mood to play. But for
Ignatoff, that Sunday would have been empty and ordinary if his wife
had not played. He went over to her once, twice, and a third time until
she agreed and went to the piano. Ignatoff, who had always liked pomp,
turned out all the lights, as he always did when she played, and sat down
on the floor near his wife, his head leaning on the wall and his hand on his
chest. Suddenly, Mini interrupted her playing right in the middle and ran
from the living room and, for a time, locked herself in her room. Only she
knew what kind of feminine or artistic capriciousness had led her to inter-
rupt her playing and run out of the room, and she understood, perhaps,
only at that moment. But Mani Leyb explained her behavior according to
his own feelings, and of course, the one whose "gray misty eyes are burning," that was he. The second poem goes like this:

She plays, I weep. The long, trembling fingers
like pale, yearning caresses in the dark—
yearning, they search, lose, and find their way
and my children weep, weep, my children.

In the evening, I dressed them in white shirts
I put them to bed and turned out the light,
closed the door and held the key a long time in my hand
went down the stairs and came to this place.

Like pale, yearning caresses in the dark—
She plays, I weep. The long, trembling fingers
yearning, they search, lose, and find their way

and my little children, in their white shirts,
With sleepy eyes, my children weep.

Zi shpilt, ikh veyn. Di lange tsiterdike finger
vi bleykh landishn farbenkte in der finster,—
farbenkte zukhn zey un blondzshn un gefinen
un mayne kinder veynen, veynen, mayne kinder.

Ikh hob in ovnt ongeton zey vayse hemdlekh,
ikh hob geleygt zey shlofn, un dem lomp farloshn,
di tir farshpart, in hant gehaltn lang dem shlisl,
di trep arop un biz aher gekumen.

Vi bleykhe landishn farbenkte in der finster,—
zi shpilt, ikh veyn. Di lange tsiterdike finger
farbenkte zukhn zey un blondzshn un gefinen.
Un mayne kinder kleyne, in di vayse hemdlekh,
mit shlofndike oygelekh veynen mayne kinder.

This second poem is, artistically, a bad poem because those who don't know (and no one can possibly know) cannot understand the connection between her playing and his weeping, her playing and his children's weeping. It is also incomprehensible why Mani Leyb describes in such detail how he dressed his children in white shirts, put them to bed, closed the door, held the key in his hand for a long time, until he finally went down the stairs and came to the place where she was playing. And, after all, the reader doesn't know how his children suddenly came to the place where she was playing, after he had dressed them in white shirts, put them to bed, turned out the light, and closed the door behind himself. The reader doesn't know because he cannot know that in his fantasy, his children come to him crying when she is playing because her playing makes him uneasy, and his guilty feelings hound him because he sees them abandoned. This is one of those poems of Mani Leyb's that I call "stammering."

Nights with Mani Leyb II

In January 1915, our group undertook the fiction part of the journal *Literatur un lebn*, with the close collaboration of Yitzak Isaac Hurvitch, Jacob

Milkh, A. S. Zaks, and other Socialist and half-Socialist columnists. The group drew in Menakhem Boraisha, who several months previously had come from Warsaw to New York and was then, just as he was many years later, known simply as "Menakhem." I was chosen by the group to edit the fiction section. But I edited only the first of January issue and the fifth of May issue that came out after Peretz's death and was dedicated entirely to his memory. And since with that number the journal ceased to exist, Dr. Karl Fornberg—who was then, besides an editor of the journal, also a book publisher—printed a new cover and transformed that last number of *Literatur un lebn* into an anthology in memory of I. L. Peretz. I edited only the first and last numbers of the collaborative journal because after putting together the first one, it was decided that I should, in the interests of the journal, travel through the hinterland, mainly in the Midwestern states. I spent four months on the road, collected some 160 subscribers for the journal, sold quite a few books for Fornberg's publishing house, and came home before Passover with torn shoes and a torn hat; with a debt of 168 dollars to Fornberg, who in the meantime had been paying my wife an agreed-upon sum every week as an advance, according to a percentage of the sale of books and the recruitment of subscribers; and with a very pessimistic outlook concerning potential readers and the prospects for an audience for American Yiddish literature in America.

I came home around eleven in the morning. By evening, Mani Leyb and David Kazanski were already in my apartment. In a conversation about my trip, I told my friends, "Comrades, we are well off! We haven't a single reader and we can write however we want." Both burst out laughing, but Mani Leyb did not believe me. "No! Really, not a single reader?" I said that by "not a single reader," I was exaggerating, but my exaggeration was not far from the truth. From the books I had sold in the provinces, from the conversations I had had with the "best readers," from the response I had received to the lectures I gave on the road, and in general, from meeting all types of Jews and seeing who among them were potential buyers and readers of Yiddish books, I had come to the conclusion mentioned above. "Your *Yingl tsingl khvat*," I told Mani Leyb, "your *Der fremder* (The stranger), *Blimelekh krentselekh* (Flowers, wreaths), and other folktales and ballads will certainly have readers. But as for your lyrical poems and all of our lyrical poems and even stories and novels that describe Jewish American life, I am very unsure."

During my trip I came to realize why the first Yiddish writers and poets in America had found an audience and why we, who came later, would not (and perhaps never will). Having gone to various gatherings and having met all sorts of people, I saw that the writers who came before us in America had acquired an audience that they created for themselves. They had arrived with an audience that was mostly illiterate. That audience never read anything in the Old Country. Here, for the first time in their lives, they began going to the theater and to meetings where they heard speeches and where poetry was recited and songs were sung. Both the speeches and the poems that were read to them with great feeling spoke about their own suffering as immigrants and exploited workers, and that was enough to grab them. That the poetry and songs that were read and sung to them were beautiful, they didn't know and didn't care. For them, it was enough to know that they were being spoken to and sung to about themselves and their suffering. The speeches, songs, and poems became, as a matter of course, beloved and precious. And if many thousands reveled in the songs and the poems when they were sung and recited for them, hundreds—and in many cases, even thousands—bought all the songs and poems when they were collected in book form. The same was true of the stories and novels that were published earlier in the newspapers.

Those who bought and read books, then, were and remained proletarians. The audience that came to America the same time as us—the second, or rather the third generation of writers in America—was completely different. In the Old Country it consisted mainly of middle-class children, and a lot of them were yeshiva boys. And though most of them, in their first years of immigration, went to work in the shops, they could never get used to the idea that they would remain workers all their lives. In fact, a great number of them, especially in the hinterland, very quickly exchanged the shop for a business. That particular audience was no longer illiterate like those immigrants who had come to America with the first two generations of writers. The audience had, in the Old Country, already been reading not only newspapers but also books, and not only in Yiddish but also in other languages. It already had its own tastes and its favorites on that side of the ocean, and in order for what we wrote to appeal, it had to be in the spirit and taste of the writers that were liked on the other side of the ocean. The older Yiddish writers and poets could not provide this. For the new immigrants, the older writers were too primitive and too crude for them to read. In addition, the content of their work no longer made the impression it once had on the earlier immigrants, for the very reason that the new immigrants, though they went to work in the shops, could not, as I said, get used to the idea that they would remain workers forever. For them, we, the new generation of writers and especially the poets, were even more alien than the older writers. We didn't follow the spirit and taste of their favorites on the other side of the ocean, and we didn't concern ourselves in our poems with the themes that would be close to them, because they could only be themes that reminded them of the Old Country. They had fled from the Old Country because it was for them so confining and distasteful; yet once they arrived here, they missed it. The things they missed were *shabes-yontevdik*, and they wanted to find it in the things they read in Yiddish. In our lyrical poems, we couldn't and didn't want to give them that. We didn't want to be like the poor aunt who visits the rich uncle sometimes on a Friday night to eat a little gifilte fish. We wanted our things to be the daily bread of the reader, Zishe Landau said in one of his first articles, which had at the time "upset the geese" so much. However, *Yingle tsingl khvat, Blimlekh krentslekh, Der fremder,* and other folktales and ballads that Mani Leyb had already written, did have something of the *shabes-yontevdik* that the audience of that time longed for.

When I came back to New York, I found among my friends a broad-shouldered and heroic-looking man whose age at first glance was hard to determine. Both in his appearance and in the way he carried himself, there was something aristocratic but also theatrical. That was Yehoysh Gordon, a son of one of the wealthiest Jewish families in Kovne. With him was his wife, Flora, a small, very gentle, very elegant woman with a snub nose and amber eyes that seemed wise and naïve at the same time. She was the daughter of a German Jewish millionaire who had a large paper factory in Manheim and offices in London and New York. Yehoysh Gordon had a High European education, which he received in Germany, where he quickly became associated with Max Reinhardt.[3] From that time on, he had a great love for theater and dreamed of becoming a director. In his student days he became acquainted with the daughter of a Manheim German Jewish millionaire. She fell in love with him and they became man and wife. The Manheim millionaire did not, apparently, take his son-in-law's theatrical aspirations seriously, and like most industrialists, he wanted to take his daughter's husband into his business. As with most industrialists, his son-in-law would have to start at the bottom. So he sent Gordon away to work in his London office with a mutually agreed-upon salary.

When the world war broke out and the British government expropriated all German businesses in England and its possessions, Yehoysh Gordon was in danger of being interned. The fact that he was a Russian subject protected him. Still, he could no longer stay in London with his wife. So they came to New York, where he quickly became an employee in his father-in-law's New York office. Dr. Karl Fornberg, also from Kovne, was for a while in his younger days a bookkeeper in the manufacturing business of Gordon's mother. When Gordon came to New York, he immediately visited Fornberg at his publishing house in a half-basement on East Broadway where the editorial office of *Literatur un lebn* was also located. There he became acquainted with my friends and began to write about theater for the journal, under a pseudonym.

When I came back from the provinces, I found him among my friends, as if he were already one of our own. We very quickly became close. He lived not far from Columbia University, where he enrolled in some classes. There was not a week when my friends and I did not visit him and his wife two or three times. In the beginning, others came to his home as well. Among them were Menakhem, the painter Isaac Lichtenshtein, and Roza Lebensboym, who years later would write poetry under the pseudonym Anna Margolin. For reasons that I don't want to touch on here, and that created a tragic rupture in the lives of that beautiful and exceptional couple, Gordon never invited any of the others to his home again. But with

---

3. Pseudonym of Maximilian Goldmann (1873–1943); a well-known director, he worked at various theaters in Berlin from 1902 until the beginning of Nazi rule in 1933.

us, his intimate friendship remained just as whole as before. When, with the May number of 1915, the journal *Literatur un lebn* ceased to publish, Yehoysh Gordon confided in me that, though he had no money and lived merely from the salary he received as an employee in his father-in-law's New York office, he was ready to give our group five hundred dollars to renew the defunct journal, but only as a purely literary one. He asked me, though, to keep this a secret until he was ready to disclose it.

At the end of June, Gordon let us know that he wanted to visit us in Boro Park. I couldn't receive him in my apartment because it consisted of three small rooms in a private, two-family house that the owner had divided into four separate apartments. The biggest room was the kitchen, which also served as a dining room. That kitchen opened on two smaller rooms that were separated from it by curtains; one of them was supposed to serve as a bedroom and the other as a parlor, or "front room" as it was called. But for us, both rooms were used as bedrooms—for me, my wife, and my children. Neither of the two smaller rooms had a door that one could close—only openings; one of these was draped with a curtain of beads, the other with a heavy, wine-colored cloth. I was completely without work that summer, and there were weeks when there was no meat in the house and days when I had to walk all the way from Boro Park to East Broadway because I didn't have a nickel for the subway. So I couldn't receive any guests at my home. But Mani Leyb had an apartment with five rooms in a new apartment house that, at the time, was considered modern and even luxurious. So he invited the Gordons to spend a Sunday afternoon at his place. When Mani Leyb lived in Boro Park, his apartment became a literary center where young writers met every Sunday afternoon, though sometimes they met at Ignatoff's, so the Gordons met other young writers there whom until then they hadn't known.

The Gordons spent the whole afternoon and evening with us until midnight. When it was dark, we took them along the streets among the open, vacant spaces where, almost every night, Mani Leyb and I took our long walks. It was on these streets that Gordon revealed to Mani Leyb and Kazanski the secret he had confided in me a month earlier, that he was ready to finance the journal *Literatur un lebn* with five hundred dollars if we were willing to revive it. Of course, all three of us wanted to, because five hundred dollars seemed to us, in our poverty and provincialism, a tremendous sum with which we would be able to move worlds. (Landau was not in town then; he had already gone to stay in the country, in a basement somewhere in New Jersey.) Before going home, Gordon told us he would deposit the five hundred dollars in our name in a bank. He also told us he had rented a summer house for himself and his wife on the ocean in Belmar, New Jersey, and that he would like to have one of us as a guest every weekend.

Mani Leyb was the first to go to him. I was the second. But when I came home, I found my younger son, then three years old, seriously ill. We had no money to pay a doctor. Luckily, Dr. A. S. Schwartz, a Hebrew poet and a brother of I. J. Schwartz, lived nearby. Mani Leyb went running and brought him to my house. One look at the child and he told Mani Leyb he should leave the apartment because he had four children in his own home and he had to be careful not to bring something back that might be contagious. He didn't tell my wife and me what the child had. An hour later, he came back. This time he brought with him a serum, and after he had examined the child again, he told us that, unfortunately, he had to inoculate our other two children with the serum because the youngest one was suffering from diphtheria. Also, by law he had to put a notice on our door that the apartment was quarantined. That day, Dr. Schwartz came to us several more times and several times that night as well. At about midnight, when the child was wheezing and it seemed that we were losing him, Dr. Schwartz took him in his own car to the hospital. Two weeks the child lay in the hospital, and during that time I did not once go to East Broadway. At that time, Mani Leyb was not allowed to visit me. When we brought the child home and the notice of quarantine was taken off the door, Mani Leyb still did not come. I also did not rush to him, out of fear that I might bring something from my home. So it happended that our afternoon meetings on the empty streets in and around Boro Park stopped for a while. After my child became healthy again, I did go to East Broadway a few times to ask after Mani Leyb. But everyone I asked told me they had not seen him for a long time. Even our closest friend, Kazanski, had not seen him. I missed him terribly.

Then one night, very late, when my family was sleeping and I was sitting at the kitchen table reading a book, I heard a light knock at the door.
Not wanting to wake my wife and children, I tip-toed to the door. When I
opened it, Mani Leyb was standing before me with a strange smile on his
lips. "I'm glad you're not asleep yet!" he said quietly. "I need someone to
talk to terribly. Put something on and come with me!" His last sentence
sounded like an order. I was half undressed; throwing on a jacket and
looking to make sure everyone in the house was asleep, I quietly shut
the door behind me and went with him in the direction of the streets
that we had, until my child's illness, strolled so often. For a long time we
both were silent. Then Mani Leyb stopped suddenly and said: "If you find
these days that I am away from home you should not be at all surprised."
I didn't answer him, but looked at him as if he were speaking in a fever.

"Why are you looking at me as if I were crazy?" Mani Leyb asked
irritably.

"Because you're talking like a madman."

"Not like a madman, but like someone in love," he answered, and
burst out laughing.

But there was no joy in his laughter. Then he told me that for several
weeks he had wandered around as if in a dream. He had met a young girl
and she had captivated him so completely that now, for him, there existed
nothing in the world except her. He went to her at her home when she
allowed him to. He knew where she worked and he went there to wait for
her at the shop when he knew she would soon come out. Because of her, he
could not work. Because of her, he could not sleep. As he was speaking, he
interrupted himself several times with these words: "But you don't know,
Iceland!" When I finally asked him what it was that I didn't know, he
answered angrily—because he himself was frustrated with his stammering—that I knew nothing at all. I didn't know what kind of girl she was,
how beautiful she was, how smart she was, how wonderfully she dressed,
how beautifully she could speak, how beautifully she could be silent. In
short, I should see her, I *must* see her.

I had never before seen him in such ecstasy. Neither had I ever heard
such a speech from him. He stammered, he began to describer her, he had

fits of laughter and then began to stammer again. Sometimes you hear a drunk speak this way. And he was, then, completely drunk with love. When I looked at him and listened to him, I began to fear he might actually desert his wife and children and go off with the girl he was speaking about. But that didn't happen. That night we wandered till dawn. And after that I didn't see him again for perhaps a week.

One afternoon when I was sitting in Shapiro's restaurant, he came in and sat down near me in despair. But he did not stay for long. He had no time, he said, after he had sat with me for several minutes. He should and must leave now. Why he should and must leave, he didn't say and I didn't ask. Because when I saw how he kept looking at the round clock that was hanging over the buffet, I knew why he should and must leave now. It was getting close to the time when the workers leave the shops, and his girlfriend would be leaving the shop where she worked. But why was he so despondent today? After that, I again did not see him for several days. Kazanski told me he had indeed seen him, but had spoken very little with him because Mani Leyb was so terribly despondent.

One evening, before I was ready to eat dinner, he came to me. This time he was even more despondent than that afternoon when I saw him in the restaurant. He tried to joke with my wife, and he tried to play with my children. But all of that couldn't hide his despondency. When we left the apartment and started to go in the direction of our past walks, he suddenly stopped in the middle of his stride and asked me: "Tell the truth, Iceland. What is your Mini to you? I mean, besides a wife and the mother of your children?" I looked at him and shrugged. "What else can she be except a wife and the mother of my children?"

"And my Hasia is like a bride to me!" he said. "You understand? A bride! To this very day when I come close to her, she gives me such pure devotion, shy and trembling like a bride." Why he was telling me this, I didn't know and don't know today. But I suspected that somewhere it was linked to his relationship to the shop girl, whom I had, by then, seen once. I must confess: she truly was beautiful.

One week later there was such an angry scene between him and the girl while he was with her in her room that he grabbed his hat, slammed the door, and fled. And since then he had not seen her. Since then he also did not want to hear her name from anyone. What brought things to that head and ended that relationship is not entirely clear to me to this very day.

What did not happen that summer, did finally happen twenty months later. It was not, of course, because of the girl. He had come to hate her so much that he trembled when anyone mentioned her name. It was also not because of another girl, a young actress who was ready to sacrifice everything for him. It was because of a *third* girl, who was the true great love of his life. We have this love to thank for the poem "Ikh bin der vaynrib der vilder" (I am the wild vine), about which Itzik Manger wrote, and rightly so, that it is one of the most beautiful love poems in any language. I personally have that love to thank for his poem "Bloykeyt" (Blueness), with which Mani Leyb ended *Lider*, which was published in 1918 by Farlag Inzl together with a book of folktales and ballads and a book of Jewish and Slavic themes. In that poem he tells me, not calling me by name, what happened to him after an evening walk we had taken, not in the open spaces of Boro Park, but in the narrow, dirty streets of downtown Manhattan, until the blue dawn, when he appeared before me again. He describes, in a strongly idealized way, how in the middle of the night he was drawn to the woman he loved so much, how she welcomed him, and how he finally came back to see me. I must say here that the poem was built on a true story—or more accurately, not on one story but on ten or more, and that in "Bloykeyt" he "appeared" not at my window, as it says in the poem, but at my closed door on the first floor of an old tenement house on the corner of Ludlow and Houston streets, where at that time I lived alone.

In the autumn of 1915, after our group had published the first number of the revived journal *Literatur un lebn*, of which Mani Leyb and I were editors, poverty forced me to give up Boro Park and also to stop editing the journal; I had got a job working with my brother in a big delicatessen, where I was busy seven days a week from five or six in the morning to eight or nine at night. To be able to arrive at work on time and not have to drag myself around on my tired, overworked feet after my workday had ended, I took an apartment in the building that housed the store. After half a year working with my brother, I returned to the hat factory where I had once worked for seven or eight years, and I remained in the apartment. It was there, in that apartment, that my first wife, in the early winter of 1916–17 developed a strange, dry cough that ended with a sound like a rooster crowing. When she finally agreed to see a doctor, he sent her to a second one, and both of them told me that for my sake and that of our three children, it would be better to send them to my relatives and to send my wife away to the mountains. So I was living alone in the apartment just when Mani Leyb became drunk with love. And in front of the locked door of that apartment he shone in his "blueness," having spent the night with the woman he loved so much, because he could not, after such a night, go home.

Only those who saw Mani Leyb during those weeks can know how beautiful, how childish, how ancient, and how tragic a man in love can be. On the one hand, he could not under any circumstances refuse the woman he adored; on the other, he trembled when he realized that because of her he would have to desert his five children. Hasia was no longer a factor. In his great love for the other, Hasia ceased entirely to exist for him. Half a year earlier, she had been for him not only his wife and the mother of his children but also a "bride." All of that he had forgotten entirely or didn't want to remember. Finally the morning came when even his five children (he now had one more child than when we both lived in Boro Park) could not prevent him from leaving home. It was my fate to be nearby. For the rest of my life I have not been able to forget what played out in front of my eyes before and after he, catlike, sprang from his house.

I could not stay in my apartment for much longer. With each passing day it looked more abandoned. The dust and dirt were piling up, and the solitude was choking me. How long my wife would have to remain in the mountains and how soon I would be able to bring my household back together, no one could tell me. So I had no choice but to place in storage what little furniture I had and go live with someone as a roomer.

At Mani Leyb's there happened to be an empty room to rent, and at that time he wanted very much to have someone in the house with whom he was close. And since Mani Leyb wanted it, I didn't think about whether it was good for me, and I moved in with him. But soon it became clear that what he wanted for himself was not good for me. His Hasia had felt for months that something was going on with Mani Leyb. And that something was a lot different from the other somethings he had gone through.

Quiet by nature, she remained silent. But her face spoke. Everything in her spoke. The way in which she left the house spoke; the way the small child crawled on the floor leaving little puddles behind him that were not wiped up spoke; and more than anything, her eyes spoke with a lingering sadness that stuck to me and that silently demanded something of me. It happened that at that time I had to spend long hours in my room every day because I had begun to translate several volumes of Heinrich Heine's prose for M. Sheliubski's publishing house. So she had me constantly in her sight. And when her husband came home late at night, he entered very quietly so that she would not hear him. But she did hear him. She heard and in different ways let it be known that she heard. A few times, he slept in one bed with his eldest son. But the bed was too narrow and too short for him. So several times he slept in my bed. At first, Hasia swallowed this just as she had swallowed Mani Leyb's other goings on at that time. But one morning she could no longer stand it. As soon as the oldest children were off to school, she opened wide the door of my room and remained standing in the doorway.

Mani Leyb felt that something dramatic was about to happen. He sprang out of bed and quietly began to push her out of the room. But now that small woman who had always been silent suddenly found her tongue and cried out: "Enough!" She would no longer strangle herself. She would no longer suffer silently. Let him tell her, her dear husband, in front of me and to my face, let him tell her: Who does he drag himself around with the whole night long? "I will not keep quiet! Do you hear? I will no longer keep quiet! Tell me now who you drag yourself around with!" Mani Leyb was standing near her and wanted to shut her mouth, but she did not allow it. It came to a struggle in which she scratched his face with her nails. Then Mani Leyb quickly began to dress. After he got dressed she slammed the door of my room shut. The little child who was crawling on all fours on the other side of the door began to cry. She leaned her shoulder against the door and stretched out her hands like a cross and blocked the way out. But in the meantime, Mani Leyb had put on his coat. "You will not go!" Hasia screamed with a voice that was not hers. But by force, Mani Leyb tore her away from the door and with one leap was out in the corridor. Hasia must have felt that his leap out the door had ended her life with him. Because now she began a wailing that would have moved a stone. I don't know if she had ever taken a look at a *taytsh-khumesh* or read a *tkhine*. But her lamentation had all the grief and anguish that, during my childhood, Jewish women had poured from their hearts.

That same day, Mani Leyb got together with the woman he loved so much. As he had abandoned his wife, so had she abandoned her husband, but they remained together only one or two days. What ended that great love so quickly after they got together, that was for me—like the end of his first love—never entirely clear. Mani Leyb never gave me a clear explanation. I did hear an explanation from the woman, which partly made sense, but it was not consistent with what she told others. Nonetheless, the name of this woman—like the name of his first love—we were forbidden to mention for years. The great love had ended. But Mani Leyb did not go back to Hasia, just as that woman did not go back to her husband. With the end of this romance, an era in Mani Leyb's writing also came to an end.

My wife's illness, soon after this, took a turn for the worse, so I couldn't see Mani Leyb for several weeks. When, finally, I did meet him, Rashl Veprinsky, who became his wife for the last thirty-eight years of his life, was already with him.

Bright Joy of Summer

I am out in my summer,
roaring like a great river.
I have brought you the bright
joy of my summer.

I have wandered
from my appointed path—
open your doors to me
in my autumnal days.

Here before the doors a wild man
I lie like an outspread vine.
And like the wild vine,
I bear the beauty of death.

And from the paths and ways,
I bring you from my path

the sadness of autumnal rain,
the gold of autumnal days.

Likhtike freyd fun zumer

Ikh bin aroys in mayn zumer
royshik un groys vi a taykh.
Likhtike freyd fun mayn zumer
hob ikh getrogn tsu aykh.

Hob ikh gelozt zikh farfirn
fun mayn getseykhnte veg—
efnt mir ayere tirn
in mayne harbstike teg.

Do far di tirn a vilder
lig ikh vi vaynrib farshpreyt.
Un vi der vaynrib der vilder
trog ikh di sheynkeyt fun toyt.

Un fun di vegn un shtegn
breng ikh tsu aykh fun mayn veg
troyer fun harbstikn regn,
Gold fun di harbstike teg.

This is one of the "vine" poems with which Mani Leyb ended *Lider*. The poem was written in the beginning of 1917 when he was all of thirty-three years old and in the middle of the greatest love affair of his life. It has five stanzas, the first of which I have left out. The last three, in which he sees himself already in his autumnal days, were appropriate if not for his age then for his mood of powerful love, because both the young and those in love usually complain a lot about growing old and the approach of death. The poem's second stanza, which I have made the first, carries within itself, naturally, the same sadness as the other three. As soon as we hear the declaration that he is out in his summer, "noisy and great as a river," carrying with him "bright joy," we expect exactly what soon happens— the absolute opposite of joy. In that sense, the poem is entirely in the spirit of Mani Leyb's poetic period that ended with this series of poems. But as a motto, the second stanza—which for me is the first—would fit more appropriately in the second period, which began for Mani Leyb with the three poems, "Kum, pashtes . . ." (Come, simplicity . . .), "Mayne oygn in ayere shleyfn" (My eyes in your temples), and "Ikh hob lib di muberes vayber" (I love pregnant women), which he included in the second number of *Inzl* that our group published in 1925 and 1926.

In general, it is hard to tell exactly when a certain period ends for a poet and when a new one begins. That is not the case with Mani Leyb. Between the poems of one period and those of the next, there is such a great difference, especially between the first period of his writing and the second, that even a child would be able to distinguish between the two. In our youth, we kept repeating the argument that at the time served as a literary truism: what is important in a poem is not the "what" but the "how." I declared as much myself in my essay "Kunst un profanatsie" (Art and profanity), which had a paragraph that stated: "When one reads, in our circle, a foolish discussion about form and content, one might think that form is a kind of independent vessel that one can, if one wishes, fill with wine, and if one wishes, with water, and they don't know, the fools, that the juice determines the form of the grape." Of course the "how" is the most important thing in every work of art. But for a lot of writers, the "how" is determined in great measure by (and for a lot of artists, perhaps completely determines) the "what."

Mani Leyb's poetic periods are distinct not only in terms of technique but also in terms of themes. (Here I have in mind mainly his lyrical poems, though the same thing applies to his narrative poems.) His first poetic period began with the series of poems he published in 1910 in the second issue of *Literatur* (he did not, as I recall, include what he had written before that) up to the series of "vine" poems, which he wrote in 1917 and most of which were published in the anthology *Inzl*. His second period began with the three poems I mentioned earlier, published in *Inzl* in April 1925. How long it lasted is not easy to say, because everything he wrote after that, he published, with a few exceptions, in the *Forverts*, and for a long time he wrote only one original poem among untold translations he made from other languages. In the last seven or eight years of his life, when he wrote his sonnets, we see a third distinct period.

Throughout his first period, he is a romantic, and his themes are born of the dark temperament of an individual who cries out against a gray environment that he hates. Often he does nothing but complain about his fate. Another time, he struggles with himself or with his hated environment. Yet another time, he dreams of a fantasy world, one far brighter and more beautiful than the one in which he lives; and still another time, he sings of the joy and the sadness of a great and powerful personal experience that ought to have resulted in the happiness for which he yearned. With the tragic disappointment of that experience came a somberness that ended his first poetic period. Of course, in the first period, Mani Leyb also wrote poems of an entirely different kind, poems with national and even messianic themes, some of which succeeded extremely well. But it was the poems mentioned above that put their stamp on the first period. After that period there were some years that had echoes of his former theme, during which he repeated certain mannerisms. But like all echoes, they no longer had the strength to charge his lines as before. Of course, in between, there were some very important exceptions. But not enough for them to put a stamp on his works from that time and give them an authentic character.

The chief characteristic of Mani Leyb's first poetic period is haze. Everything in it is hazy; the mood is hazy, the experience that grows from it is hazy, and the expression he gives his mood and the experience is hazy—very often to the point of obscurity. The cause of that haziness, I think, was mainly that he again and again feared to ground himself in his emotions. The chief characteristic of his second period is sunshine and clarity. The poem that begins his second period is a kind program poem in which he demands of himself that he throw off the mist and reach for clarity.

> Come, clear simplicity with your gleaming knife,
> cut through the black muddle of my soul,
> let my world behind dark and blackened locks,
> shine for me like suns before my doorstep.
>
> And what in the deep darkness of my eyes
> is dazzled, blind, concealed and strange,

may it become clear like light from a rainbow
and like the white linen of my shirt.

And all living and nonliving things
that live far and turned away from me—
reveal as if through clear water,
like the precious ten fingers of my hands.

And on my ground of inexhaustible sadness,
the voice of everything that lies forged in sorrow,
like blood to blood may it ring in my ear
and in my word be purified through my song.

Kum pashtes klore, mit dayn blankn meser,
shnayd oyf dem shvartsn plonter fun mayn zel,
mayn velt fun unter tunkele un shvartse shleser,
zol oyfshtraln far mir vi zunen far mayn shvel.

Un vos in tifer fintsternish fun mayne oygn
iz blind, farblendt geven, farhoylt un fremd,
zol vern klor far mir vi likht fun regnboygn
un vi vayse layvnt fun mayn hemd.

Un ale lebedike un nit lebedike zakhn
vos lebn vayt fun mir un opgevendt—
dernen, dek oyf vi reyne vaser-flakhn,
vi mayne libe tsen finger fun di hent.

Un af mayn erd fun nit dersheptn troyer,
di shtim fun alts vos ligt in tsar geshmidt,
vi blut tsu blut zol klingen in mayn oyer
un in mayn vort gelaytert durkh mayn lid.

In the second poem of that beginning—which was, perhaps, in fact the first poem, because only the poet himself knows the chronological order of such things—there is openness, nakedness itself. So much so that another poet could very easily falter because what he is saying and wants to say may come out as cynical and even seem pornographic. Here we see before us, not the man who wraps himself in veils and who won't say clearly what he wants because he is afraid to come to a clear conclusion about it—no more the young, inexperienced man whose desires make him dream of romantic images—but rather the mature man who knows that all women excite him sexually and that he desires them all.

> Come with your rejoicing,
> As for God so for me you are all good.

He is even more naked in the third poem of that beginning, which I cite here in its entirety as an illustration:

> I love pregnant women
> with bellies bulging and swollen,
> when they drag their double flesh
> like cows in grassy valleys.
>
> What assurance they all have
> and their eyes like streaming sunbeams!
> But they smell from milk and kale
> like summer evening in the barns.
>
> You, with eyes like points of steel,
> you forget in the blaze of wounds,
> that the roses of their teats
> set fire to your lips.
>
> Ikh hob lib di muberese vayber,
> mit di beykher farshpitst un geshvoln,
> ven zey shlepn di toplte layber
> vi di ki af di grozike toln.
>
> Velekhe zikherkeyt trogn zey ale
> un di oygn vi shtraln vos kvaln!
> Nor zey shmekn mit milkh un mit kale,
> vi zumer farnakht in di shtaln.
>
> Du, mit shtolene oygn vi shpitsn,
> du fargest bay di sreyfe fun vundn,
> az di royzn fun zeyere tsitsn
> zaynen af di lipn getsundn.

Only the unsuccessful expression "blaze of wounds" recalls here the Mani Leyb of his first poetic period. Kolya Teper, in my apartment, once criticized Mani Leyb, saying that his poems were too soft and feminine. Mani Leyb, who was almost always ready to strike back, was offended by the accusation and answered with his characteristic drawn out, "ye-e-s," which always signaled that he disagreed. And indeed, he soon answered Kolya sharply that only insignificant, groveling men are afraid to reveal softness and gentleness, so that they will not be considered feminine. Signs

9. Group of writers and artists, ca. 1920. Top row: Reuben Iceland (in cap); second row: Moses Soyer (hands crossed); third row: Chaim Gross (far left), Mani Leyb (second from left); fourth row: Rebecca Iceland (far left).

of that femininity are still found, from time to time in his second-period poems, but very seldom. From then on, he is sunny and pure in almost everything he writes and manly in his purity, whether these are realistic poems or neoromantic, like "Ikh bin" (I am), "Du bist a hirsh gor a tsarter" (You are a gentle deer), and others of that sort; or descriptive, like "Der indisher foygl" (The indian bird); or social, like "A geveyn" (A cry), "Af shvere shleser" (Heavy locks), and tens of others; or poems such as "Baym kortntish" (At the card table), which Glatshteyn rightly described as Dostoevskyesque; or his grotesque poem "Hinter Chelm"[4] (The outskirts of Chelm); or his autobiographical poem (to my sorrow, I only got to read the beginning of that one). In everything there is the "Freyd fun zumer" (The joy of summer) of a poet who is mature, all-reaching, and colorful, like a beautiful apple tree covered with fruit, "rooted to the thigh in the ground."

The Last Years

In our youth, when we met we spoke only about writing, especially of poetry. At some point we realized that our children had become a large part of our conversations. Mani Leyb said that very quickly we would be talking about rheumatism, back pain, insomnia, and other sins of old age. But he was only half right. Because we quickly began to talk, not about getting old, but about being sick. The first to fall ill with a serious illness was, in fact, Mani Leyb himself.

That was in the early 1930s. He caught consumption—or "di katute," as he liked to joke about his illness, using the name that was used among Jewish shop workers. He had to go away to a sanatorium for a long time. After that, Landau became ill with heart disease. After Landau became ill, I had a serious heart attack. Finally, which at first no one realized, David Kazanski became ill. By the time we realized he had stomach cancer, he was already gone. So it happened that the youngest of our group—Landau and Kazanski—were the first to leave us.

From the criticisms that Kazanski made in his biting article in the anthology *Zishe Landau*, which we published on the first anniversary of

---

4. A town in eastern Poland presented in folklore as having a population of fools.

Landau's death, one could see that he, the only novelist in our group, accused Mani Leyb and me of betraying the principles of Di Yunge. In his words, we hadn't paid the IOUs we had signed. By this he was referring to the way we wrote and also to our behavior as writers. He was 100 percent correct in both his complaints about us. At that time, we had already thrown out a large part of our literary program—as much as we had one when we were a close-knit group—and also a large part of the unwritten codex concerning how a writer should conduct himself. Regarding the details of our program, he remained the only pure member of Di Yunge. That was, perhaps, his tragedy. Because writers usually outgrow the schools from which they come. And though Kazanski did outgrow the rules of our school no less than we, he did not want to admit it to himself. The result was a struggle between the new path that he had taken and the old restrictions that blocked his way to the new. One can see this best in *In yokh* (In the yoke), which was the third of five volumes of his novel *Arum un arum* (Around and around). The matter of Kazanski is too important— and too painfully intimate——for me to devote just a few lines to him. I had planned to write a longer work about him in this book. To my great sorrow, it has simply not been possible. I hope, though, that I will yet have the strength and time to do him justice, as befits that wonderful, unique writer and honorable man. Here I only want to add that we also could not keep to our program's hard and fast rules concerning how a writer should conduct himself. A lot of the unwritten rules were impractical from the very start, and we had to abandon them when they hindered our development as writers.

After Kazanski's death it became sad and desolate around us. Mani Leyb and I seldom met. There were times when I couldn't go anywhere because I was ill, and Mani Leyb couldn't come to me because between Anna Margolin and him, there were old grudges and old resentments that neither he nor she was ready to give up. And there were also times when he was ill, and he seldom went to East Broadway—the only place where we could meet. If it so happened that we both felt well and I went every day to the editorial office of *Der tog*, we met once or twice a week in the cafeteria. And when we met, we couldn't tear ourselves from each other for hours, just like the good old times of our youth. There came a time when Mani Leyb suddenly became very ill again, this time from bleeding ulcers. But to everyone's amazement, he quickly recovered, and the most remarkable thing is that after that illness he blossomed so beautifully that both his close friends and strangers could not take their eyes off him. Mani Leyb was very handsome his whole life, but now he was better looking than ever: healthier in appearance, sturdier in build, and straighter in his carriage. He, who was once the weakest and most delicate of all of us, now seemed the healthiest and strongest. His hair, which had been pitch-black, showed gray streaks for a long time. But now it was completely steel-gray, and this lent the dignity of age to his still young and flexible body. He was also filled with an energy that we had never seen in him.

I don't know exactly when he began to write his sonnets, which were the crown of his oeuvre and which introduced his third and last poetic period. If I'm not mistaken, this last period began with his recovery from that stomach hemorrhage. He had written sixty sonnets when he asked me to read them. I will never forgive myself for not honoring his request. With all my heart, I thank his widow, the poet Rashl Veprinsky, for sending me at least a part of that wonderful treasure that Mani Leyb left us. I had already read some by chance from time to time, when a summer issue of the *Forverts* fell into my hands. Already then, I was amazed at the tone in which they were written and the wisdom that flowed from them. But now, when I read and reread a greater number of the sonnets together, suddenly the amazement gives way to a different kind of deep joy—that Mani Leyb was worthy, no, that Mani Leyb himself brought about the privilege of creating something that made it seem as if everything that he had written previously, however beautiful and great it was, was nothing more than preparation for this last body of work.

All the sonnets that lie before me revolve around death. And perhaps it is the same with all of his other sonnets that I have not yet seen. It is self-evident that a melancholy mood flows from all of them. The poet feels he is coming closer and closer to death, and it fills him with indescribable sadness. The wonder is, though, that he is neither bitter nor rebellious. The wonder is also that he doesn't flirt with his readiness to resist death, as is the case with other poets. He doesn't want the end to come, and he cannot even imagine how the world will remain a world without him:

The sun without me will be ashamed to light
its fire by day and by night to set.

And the winds will no longer comb the grass
and will without a breath remain forever still.

Di zun on mir vet far di teg zikh shemen
ir fayer tsindn un in nekht fargeyn.

Un vintn veln mer dos groz nit kemen
un on an otem ebyik blaybn shteyn.

With these lines he ends one of his sonnets. Yet he welcomes his end with love and chastises himself because once, in his heart, he opposed his destiny.

One destiny awaits us all: to die.
And you shame and stubbornly deny
the silver flecks on your old head,
and on your forehead, furrowed notches.

For pride rampages in your narrow skull,
as the stallion gallops from the stable
in the time for sex when the ripe dill
fills autumn with the scent of its sheaves.

Forget that wise old age doesn't have
the strength that youth bestows. Therefore
it prepares for us the full measure of our reward
to know sorrow in sober thoughts
the joy of pure shining days—
the ornament of dignity on your last journey.

Eyn goyrl vart af alemen: tsu shtarbn.
Un du farshemst un layknst trotsik op
di flekn zilber af dayn altn kop,
un af dayn shtern dayne kneytshn-karbn.

Vayl gayves rayst zikh in dayn engn sharbn,
vi fun der shtal de oger in gallop

in tsayt fun biye ven der rayfer krop
farshmekt dem harbst mit reykhes fun di garbn.

Fargest, az vos di yunge koykhes shenkn—
dos hot di kluge elter nit. Derfar
fargreyt zi undz di fule mos fun skhar
tsu visn tsar in nikhtern gedenkn
di freyd fun reyne opgeshaynte teg—
di tsir fun verde af dayn letstn veg.

In our youth we spoke about resignation and demanded it of ourselves. Demanded it and sometimes achieved it, too. But who among us
and who besides us was uplifted through resignation to such a height as
Mani Leyb in his poem "Shtoyb tsu shtoyb" (Dust to dust)?

I have my long life walked through
all of God's ways. The broad way
of wisdom simpler than every day;
to offer the way of high illusion.

The other side—the side that holds fast
the eyes of the world on that shore
of things; also the tempting way
to the self that lies hanging in blindness.

Now I stand on the road, where all roads
end. The road is short and narrow.
It leads me to the depths of the valley.
Here an eternal one smiles at me
to rest. And all remnants of wisdom—
I shake off like dust to dust.

Ikh bin mayn langn lebn durkhgegangen
durkh ale vegn Got's. Dem breytn veg
fun khokhme posheter fun ale teg;
dem veg fun hoykhn anen tsu derlangen.

Di yene zayt—di zayt vos halt gefangen
di oygn fun der velt af yenem breg

fun zakhn; oykh dem shtroykhlendikn shteg
tsu zikh, vos ligt in blindenish farhangen.

Itst shtey ikh afn veg, vu ale vegn
farshlisn zikh. Der veg is kurts un shmol.
Er firt mikh tsu der nider funem tol.
Do shmeykhlt mir an eybike antkegn
di ru. Un ale khokhmes—drib un droyb,
ikh treysl op fun zikh vi shtoyb tsu shtoyb.

Mani Leyb, Mani Leyb

To his *shloshim*

Mani Leyb, Mani Leyb!
Marvelous man, wonderful friend, prince of poetry, the first of a generation, beautiful and beautifier of an era! Life is empty without you; in my heart it is dark without you.

Mani Leyb, Mani Leyb!
Only now will they see (if there is still anyone to see), only now will they understand (if there is still anyone to understand), what a light you were, what a song you were, what a gift you were!

How amazing is our gray, pitiful world.

With a mere nuance you could open gates, with a nuance build worlds, with a simple word you could untangle the thickest muddle, and with a puff of smoke lift yourself up to the highest heavens.

With your constant stress on worldliness—authentic Yiddish. With your apparent indifference to morality—deeply ethical. With your individuality—humane and universal. In your romantic exaltation—both feet on the ground. And on the ground—the passionate leap of a gentle deer, whose horns collide with a star.

Mani Leyb, Mani Leyb!
They hid your death from me. Days and weeks, they hid it. With cleverness and loyalty, they hid it.

But my heart had a premonition. And my tongue insisted. Constantly insisted. Demanded of friends and acquaintances: how is Mani Leyb? How is Mani Leyb feeling? What is Mani Leyb writing?

And constantly, I saw you in my dreams. In all different ways. And always remembered our last time together. Only the two of us, when all of our friends had left us. I at the edge of the bed and you near me. And our hands braided together and our glances magnetically joined.

And suddenly I bent down and kissed your hand, and you snatched your hand away and cried out. With anger, with tears in your eyes and suffocation in your throat.

You, who understood everything, did not understand what the kiss meant. With terrible sorrow, I felt that we were together for the last time, that we would not see each other ever again.

But did I really think that?

Mani Leyb, Mani Leyb!

On your lovely, bewitching head that now must lie in the ground, I weep.

On your sharp-gray eyes that could overflow with stars and now must be forever shut, I weep.

On your melodic voice with its vibrations and deep tones that is forever struck dumb, I weep.

On your slender hands that, with magical gestures, tried to charm from the air the most effective word in an argument and that from now on I will no longer see, I weep.

On letters and notes, written in tiny handwriting on narrow pieces of paper, in simple language like whole wheat bread and full of understanding and deep wisdom that will no longer exist, I weep.

Because, of an entire group, I now remain all alone without you, I weep.

"Not good, not good, not good. . . ."

Oh, how it is not good, Mani Leyb, Mani Leyb!

1953–54

✵ Moyshe Leyb Halpern

On His Tenth Yortsayt

Among Moyshe Leyb Halpern's colleagues, I was not the closest to him. At one time there had even been a quiet but bitter argument between our circle and him. We accused him of arrogance, bombast, melodrama, and burlesque. The last referred to his satirical poems. He, for his part, accused us of recycled lyricism and slovenliness because of our "resignation" and especially because of the "ordinary" that some of us then demanded in poetry, as a reaction to the clichés of which our poetry was then so full. This demand for the ordinary resulted in simplicity and clarity of expression, which was perhaps Di Yunge's most important contribution. But Halpern wasn't impressed and said so at every opportunity.

That was twenty-five years ago, when we were still relatively young and, like all young poets, were great zealots who thought that only *our* way was the right one and that all others were false. With time, not realizing it ourselves, we changed roles. We, Di Yunge, abandoned our "ordinary" theory when the method of opposing clichés itself became a cliché, at which time Halpern took it up. On his way to ordinariness, he went so far as to use vulgar language, but any vulgarity he used was only for effect, to be flirtatious. All of this I have already mentioned. I need to say that over time he and I grew closer. Indeed, I was the only one among all his colleagues to see Moyshe Leyb in the last moments of his life. That was a coincidence, but not entirely so. Members of his family knew that a short time earlier there had been something of a bond, a bit of closeness between us two, so when he collapsed and was taken to the hospital, they told me.

In the preceding months, I had been meeting with Halpern more often than before. I'm not sure whether he had actually changed much, or whether it simply seemed that way to me, but in those months the Halpern I encountered became entirely different from the one I had known for twenty-five years. Measured in his speech and his movements.

Still sure of himself, and still sure that his way was the true one, but also more tolerant of others' opinions and, more important, more inclined to listen to others. His face still expressed strength, though this was a distraction from the truth; as those closest to him tell it, he was then very ill. Those blue eyes no longer expressed brazen arrogance.

Fifteen days before his death, I spent perhaps ten straight hours with him. We had gone to a summer colony near Peekskill, where the I. L. Peretz Writers Union had arranged an evening for unemployed writers. With us were Avrahm Moyshe Dilon, Mark Shveyd, Beyle Belarina, Noah Nakhbush, and a musician whose name I have forgotten. Before and after that evening I saw Moyshe Leyb in a very different light than before. In his interactions with people, there flowed from him such a quiet goodness and lyrical gentleness that I sat there gaping. Was this the same Halpern whom I had known for twenty-five years? Was this the same man who, that evening, read poems that were exactly the opposite of all the others?

In the earliest years, Halpern was, for me, a poet whom I had to fight against. In the last years he was, for me, a mystery that I could not solve. The mystery became even greater that evening in Pine Lake Park near Peekskill. On Monday it will be ten years since Moyshe Halpern left us, and for me, the Halpern mystery is still not solved.

Moyshe Halpern was a very great poet, possibly the greatest after Morris Rosenfeld, against whom he fought so hard, perhaps because he was in more than one detail similar to him. But it was just as clear that his poetic powers were not always as well organized as they should have been and that he very often squandered them on nothing.

His admirers talk about the "strong" Halpern, and when they do, they mean mainly the satirical Halpern. But that is exactly where he is weakest as a poet. The argument I mentioned earlier ended many years before Halpern's death, and in one detail, also mentioned earlier, we had even changed roles. But what I and the poets of my circle found fault with concerning Halpern the satirist twenty-five years ago is pertinent to this day. True, in his satirical poems he used strong words, and in one period even vulgar speech, which he was proud of. But very seldom did he elevate his speech and himself to the level of poetry. With a few exceptions, he was, in his satirical poems, technically weak. He arrived at the secret of austerity only in his lyrical poems. Nowhere did he pour out such a flood of words as in his satirical poetry. It was the same with his rhymes. I don't know one poet among us who was so impoverished in rhymes as Halpern. And this poverty seems even stronger in his satirical poems. Very often it seems that Halpern did not possess more than five or six rhymes, which he kept repeating. But this is only a superficial impression; a closer look shows that it is not accurate. There are poems of his that are not only rich but also quite surprising in their rhymes. Not often, it is true, but those few instances show what he would have been able to achieve had he only made an attempt. Why he didn't, and instead took the easy way out, using facile rhymes that he recycled from his own work, should be researched. I would have said that it was partly simple laziness. Yet I also know that Halpern revised his poems a great deal. There was almost no poem that he did not write and rewrite many times. The reason why must be deeply hidden, and when it is discovered, the mystery of Halpern will perhaps be solved. His satirical poems also suffer from his joking around too much. It is the sign of a lack of true, lyric wisdom. By lyric wisdom, I mean that sum of those deeper experiences that accumulate from lyric-thoughtful experiences.

When they talk of the "strong" Halpern, they also have in mind Halpern the fantasist, and here they are closer to the truth. Though part of his fantasy writing was of the sort that Abe Kahan, in his pointedly Kahanic way, sometimes called "invented fantasy," still, Halpern often achieved true greatness in his fantasies. To that kind of invented fantasy I would attribute many of his grotesque images that don't live even as mush as marionettes in the hands of their manipulator. Yet Halpern wrote some fantastic poems that would have been jewels in the wealthiest poetic literature. The truly strong Halpern was to be found not in his satirical, social, or nationalist poems, some of which, such as "Di nakht" (The night), made such a strong impression in his time, nor in his fantasy poems, but rather in some of his lyrical poems. In that category I place "A banket reyd" (A banquet speech), which was found after his death among his papers, though it is too drawn out and has many redundancies and little refinement. In it he concerned himself with the eternal problem of life and death and the purpose of being, in that lyrical tone that never ceases to probe, though the tragic secret from which flows the sorrow of futility in all generations and all times was revealed to him long ago. The strong Halpern is revealed in all his greatness in the poem "Mayn umru fun a volf" (I am restless as a wolf), where he himself approaches the Halpern mystery. This is a great cosmic poem that in one burst, from the first to the last word, is profound in conception and classic in execution, with a tone and rhythm that captures, fascinates, and does not let go until the poem buries itself in your memory and becomes part of you, like all great poems.

To end, I will permit myself to quote an excerpt from an article I wrote about Halpern right after he passed away:

> Moyshe Leyb Halpern was one of an entire generation that caused an upheaval in Yiddish poetry, but of a different kind than the rest of his generation. Only the outcome was the same: the realization that we are all dealt a blind fate. Aside from that, they followed different paths. For most of the poets of the group, that realization led to quiet, lyrical resignation, but it provoked in him an everlasting protest.
>
> His whole life, Moyshe Leyb Halpern was a rebel. With his word he revolted against everything that stood in the way of man and his desired happiness. Like most rebels and protesters, he was not always careful with his word. The poet who seeks the truth for himself, searches, before anything else, for a word for his poem that is *convincing* to him alone. The poet who thinks that he has found the whole truth in his poem is like the orator and the propagandist, who seek with their word to *make an impression on others*. The effect becomes paramount. And in order to achieve effects, M. L. Halpern often chose such words that were intended to shock—and they did. At one time he was practically crowned the poet of "vulgar speech," and they thought with that they had reduced his poetry to its essence. But that is not my point. I only want to present Moyshe Leyb Halpern the rebel who, with his word, rose up against every sort of despotism, personal and communal, material and spiritual, traditional and that which is just beginning to create a new tradition;

but remarkably, he never opposed the most horrible despot of all, His Majesty Death. In his poems, he met death with the same resignation as the other poets of his generation.

Of all his poems, I remember best "Der zun vet aruntergeyn untern barg" (The sun will set behind the hill). A melody was composed for that poem that made it very popular. Most melodies weaken a poem. But in this case, the melody could not the least bit lessen the magic that Halpern had achieved with a minimum of means. Halpern touches on three of the most important moments in everyone's life: the moment of love, the moment of dream, and the moment of death. First, he experiences love. Later comes the dream in the image of the golden peacock that soothes him with singing, and at the end comes death and lulls him with the very same singing. Such beauty and such sorrow flow from that poem! And, as with most wonderful, lyrical poems, you don't know if the beauty comes from the sadness, or the sadness from the beauty.

I would like to give you the beginning of the same article in which I talk about the last moments of M. L. Halpern:

Of all his colleagues, it was my fate to see Moyshe Leyb Halpern in the last minutes of his life.

But did I really see him? Even now, I don't believe it. Because the man who was lying in the hospital bed with a wide-open mouth, as if he were using his last bit of strength to snatch a breath of air, definitely did not seem like the Moyshe Leyb Halpern whom I knew for so many years.

Twenty-four years he lived among us in New York. He was twenty-two years old when I met him for the first time. Already then, his hair was streaked with gray. But from his then not overly beautiful and sprinkled with freckles face, there spurted strength and health and that know-it-all impudence that one often sees in athletes. Only two weeks ago I spent ten hours in a row with him in a summer colony near Peekskill, where the I. L. Peretz Writers Union had an event. His hair was already entirely white. But through his glasses one could still see the same strength that gushed from his blue eyes.

And now a nurse leads me to a hospital bed that is curtained on three sides and I see before me an old man—a seventy-year-old man; a shrunken old Jew with hollow blue cheeks and a wide-open mouth from which there appears a single, orphaned tooth; and something is sawing in his throat and his chest moves quickly and his hands move quickly.

I step back because I want to see Moyshe Leyb Halpern. And this is not Moyshe Leyb Halpern.

1942

✿ David Ignatoff

DAVID IGNATOFF did not begin a new chapter of our literature. He was, though, central to a beginning. Historians will one day be very interested in the literary figure David Ignatoff because he was a uniquely expressive writer and mainly because he was an important literary activist. In the writer Ignatoff, historians will find a lot of pluses but also not a few minuses. Neither his pluses nor his minuses had any literary influence: one cannot find a writer among us from his generation and from the one that came later whose writing was visibly influenced by Ignatoff, as one can see the influence—for good or bad—of other prose writers and poets of his generation. However, with very few exceptions, there is not one important contemporary of Ignatoff's who did not directly or indirectly have something for which to thank the literary activist David Ignatoff.

Everyone who is the least bit acquainted with the course of American Yiddish Literature knows that with *Shriftn* there began a new literary era. And *Shriftn* would not have been possible without Ignatoff. Yet very few people know that Ignatoff's achievement in that respect began years earlier, before *Shriftn* was first published, when the literary activist Ignatoff came together with the writer Ignatoff. A struggle for the writer's right to be different began with his articles in the journal *Di yugend*, regarding which even his contemporary "revolutionary" beginners shrugged their shoulders—"Crazy!" The stubborn activist David Ignatoff assumed a very important position indeed at the meetings of the group Literatur, which published the two anthologies called *Literatur*. Meetings to which sixty or seventy young people used to come who had published poems and stories in the daily and weekly newspapers of that time, and others who were even worthy, sometimes, of having something published in a monthly journal.

Most of those young people had very little courage to stand on their own feet, and when it came to choosing an editorial board for the first issue of *Literatur*, the majority chose two people who were longtime colleagues at a newspaper, each of whom already had a name and a reputation: Yoyl Entin and the late Yoyl Slonim. The third whom they chose was Moyshe Yoyne Khaymovitch, who was also on the way to becoming established. He was not yet known by many people, but a lot of young writers looked up to him as one who knew and understood more than others and who already deserved respect. The result was that in the first issue of *Literatur*, it wasn't the young writers of that time who were published; on the contrary, it was the older, highly respected writers such as Leon Moyseyev, Moyshe Katz, Yoyl Entin. Thanks to the energetic stubbornness of some young writers, led by Ignatoff, that mistake was not repeated in the second issue of *Literatur*. The editors of the second were David Ignatoff, I. J. Schwartz, and Moyshe Leib Halpern, but the editorial board was guided mainly by Ignatoff.

That second anthology was an important moment in American Yiddish literature because it was the young writers who held all the levers, but even more because two things in that anthology made history, so to speak. One was Mani Leyb's series of poems, which the editors of the first anthology had rejected, but which, on being published, showed us literally a miracle— a poet full of sound, imagery, and nuance that had never before existed among us. His every turn was a wonder; his every word vibrated; his every line was dense and charged. The second thing was the story "Af yener zayt brik" (On the other side of the bridge), which almost overnight made a name for Joseph Opatoshu on both sides of the ocean. The third thing was a chapter excerpt from David Ignatoff's novel *In keslgrub* (In the whirlwind). The entire novel was published in the second *Shriftn*. That chapter was the most beautiful one of all in his first novel. However, it also had the short-comings that one finds in all his work. In the first *Shriftn*, David Ignatoff's "Der giber" (The hero), a biblical story based on the Yiftakh Legend,[1] was published, already demonstrating the two most important elements of his

1. Yiftakh vowed that if he was victorious in battle with the Ammonites, he would sacrifice to God whatever came out of the door of his house when he returned. It turned out to be his daughter. (Judges 11:31)

talent—his feel for language and his descriptive skills. But those were the very things that did not find appropriate acclaim. Only here and there could one hear a word of praise. Most of the critics ridiculed him. Derision is seldom a sign that the mockers are correct. Very often it is a sign that they themselves should be mocked because their spite comes from ignorance. The derisive outcry over Ignatoff's "Der giber" arose from just such ignorance. Most of those who ridiculed him chuckled over the fact that almost all the sentences in that story began with the word "and."

They didn't understand that the strength of that story lay in its biblical style, in which the word "and" is an important component. If the story deserved a little mockery, it was not because of the "ands," but rather for the prophetic pompousness behind them, for the way he rebuked the idol worshippers even while he relished the wonderful descriptions of orgies that were celebrated in the service of the gods he was thundering against. And why deny it? Aesthetic enjoyment, whether moral or immoral, influences the fine descriptions of the orgies more than the censure of prophets.

David Ignatoff was a uniquely talented man capable of wonderful, rhythmic language and great powers of description. But he was never satisfied with the gifts that were given to him, and he wanted to be exactly what he was not. He could certainly have been a true artist, and perhaps a very great one, but that was never enough for him—he needed also to be a prophet. His aesthetic accomplishments meant little to him—he yearned to have a moral impact. The result was pomposity instead of prophecy. That's how we saw him in his first important work, "Der giber"—he had great talent but he wanted to say too much. And that's what we would see in almost everything he wrote. Needless to say, his thematic ambitions caused his talent to be neglected and often even crushed that talent, for the tendency to be inauthentic does more than overshadow the authentic, it destroys it. The tragedy of Ignatoff was that he could not distinguish between the authentic and the inauthentic in himself. This is what led him to "improve" Nakhman Bratslaver's[2] stories, which resulted in

---

2. Nakhman Bratslaver (1772–1810), the great-grandson of the founder of Hasidism, the Bal Shem Tov; he was a charismatic rebbe whose many stories and parables were written down by his followers after his death.

monstrosities like "Dos likht fun der velt" (The light of the world), and to write "Di mayse fun der velt" (The story of the world), which is a kind of "Targum Shlishi" (Third Targum) of a not very crafty compiler. The finest thing that Ignatoff wrote in his whole life was *Fibi*, the only work of his that is, except for the introduction, free of redundancies.

The inability to distinguish between the authentic and the inauthentic is visible not only in his writing but also in his actions. As great as his achievements were as a writer, they were even greater as a literary activist. Without him the *Shriftn* anthologies, which were such an important land-mark in our literature, would never have existed, for no one else who took part in *Shriftn* had the energy or the perseverance to create the vehicle that would have such a strong influence on our group's literature. The main achievement of the *Shriftn* anthologies lay in the fact that in them, for the first time, those young poets and writers were fully represented who didn't want their works to be in the service of an idea, because they held that writing should not depend on the merit of anything other than itself. They wanted, more than anything else, for their organ to concern itself solely with writing; they also wanted it to publish only young writ-ers, who would earn their reputations through their own work and not by being published alongside older writers who would outshine them. Ignatoff, in that regard, wanted exactly the opposite: he wanted *Shriftn* to be the organ not only of Yiddish writers but also of painters, and he wanted it to publish things not only of young writers but also of older, established ones. There began to be quarrels about this between him and his colleagues, at first mild and then much sharper. He won the first quar-rel, his colleagues the second.

After the second issue of *Shriftn*, there was a split, though not because of the reasons I gave above; but this is not the place and I am not the man to speak about it. While the third *Shriftn* was being prepared, the group that split off made a stage for itself in the anthology *Di naye heym* (The new home). Before the third *Shriftn* was published, the group that had remained with Ignatoff agreed among themselves that it would be the last issue, which indeed it was. *Shriftn* would be revived, mainly under Ignatoff's editorship, at the end of the First World War, but it was no longer the same *Shriftn* as before. It was, perhaps, stronger in content and more beautiful in appearance. Certainly it was richer for the contributions of painters and graphic artists. But it was no longer the organ of a coherent group, partly because that original group had split into several others, but mainly because that era was already long past. No one needed an organ like *Shriftn*.

After the third *Shriftn*, there was a falling out between Ignatoff and the group that had stayed with him. At the beginning the rupture was minor. With time, though, it became much greater and they stopped meeting; some time later, they even stopped speaking to one another. It went so far that a few years ago, before Ignatoff collapsed, he published a series of articles aimed mainly at me. But though the rupture became greater, there remained, on my part, a very warm feeling toward Ignatoff. My heart remembered the "grace of youth" and the wonderful Sundays that, in the days of *Shriftn*, we spent in his bachelor room on Washington Avenue in the Bronx. My heart pounded when I saw him from afar or when I unexpectedly heard his voice on the telephone.

Several years ago, when I received the sad news that Ignatoff had collapsed while at work at HIAS (Hebrew Immigrant Aid Society), where he had been an official for forty years, I almost did the same. Only then did I realize how deeply Ignatoff was bound to me, even though we were estranged in terms of literature—and on his part, also personally. Later, when I heard that he had been brought home from the hospital and that he was well enough to see visitors, I persuaded Mani Leyb to do what I could not, and he promised me he would go and see Ignatoff, though those two were not on good terms either. And Mani Leyb, indeed, went to him. Not once, but in the beginning almost every week, and later almost every two weeks. And he went not only to visit his former dear friend at his sickbed, but also to help him in a way that Mani Leyb could—with preparing his last book, *Gidon* (Gideon), for publication. Until the last moments, Ignatoff remained the same as he had been in earlier years. The same man of great talent and the same man of great stubbornness. I know that from spoken and written accounts Mani Leyb gave me. In one of his last letters, when he himself was already a very sick man, Mani Leyb complained strenuously about the fate of the one who had meant so much to us in our youth.

David Ignatoff did not believe in death, and told us as much at various times, especially at the funerals of his close friends. For him, death was no more than a crossing from one life to another, higher one. I personally never believed this. I want, though, to comfort myself with the thought that he, until the last minute, believed it with perfect faith, and that because of that faith, the crossing was an easy one.

However long it is destined for me to be here, I will remember him with much sorrow but also with not a little joy, for the good and beautiful things that he brought to our literature, to our youth, and to our lives.

April 1954

✵ I. J. Schwartz

From My Diary

Yesterday, I. J. Schwartz and his wife Mary were our guests. Whenever Schwartz comes, it's like a holiday for us. But not yesterday. We were sitting outside in the long, narrow garden that stretches from my apartment to Washington Avenue, looking at the six banana trees that grow in two clumps not far from my windows. They extend their long, wide, wind-tossed leaves like outstretched hands, like a stylized upside-down *lamed*, from my apartment through the entire length of the garden. We spoke of various things yet felt at the same time that something was oppressing our hearts. Suddenly, Schwartz sighed: "Opatoshu is gone!"

By that time, Opatoshu's funeral had taken place in New York. But here, in the lovely, green garden, the corpse still lay before our eyes, so to speak. We tried to speak and dispel the quiet sorrow that oppressed us. But several times it leapt out—So suddenly snatched away! How did it happen?—and still other similar exclamations were sometimes torn from my mouth and sometimes from Schwartz's. We gazed at a row of papaya trees that grew in the long, narrow garden. We spoke about Schwartz's beautiful orchard behind his house and about the lawn with the beautiful trees in front of his house in South Miami, around eighteen miles from the place where I myself live. But Opatoshu's image remained before our eyes. And that night I could not close my eyes.

Now I sit at my desk, look out at my garden at the same banana trees, papaya trees, hibiscus bushes, and others, and my heart is just as distressed as yesterday when Schwartz was here and we were sitting outside. I ask myself: What was Opatoshu to you? And what were you to Opatoshu?

And I answer myself: Not very much. Both as a man and as a writer. From the very beginning when I was just getting to know him and the whole time that I knew him. He was not my kind of person and he was also not my kind of writer. Once we even came to blows, and afterward we did not speak to each other for years. So why is my heart so terribly stricken?

Apparently, however alien he may have been to me, both as a person and as a writer, he was also very close and even a little dear to me, like all writers and poets of that generation who came here between 1905 and 1915, and who were, at one time or another, counted among Di Yunge. How many of us remain of that generation? Oh, how few! In all, a small band that can be counted on the fingers of one hand even if one takes into account one who has been paralyzed for so many years in a home for the chronically ill. If he were not taken into account, we would be only four. All of them are dear and close to me, and I tremble for some of them as I tremble for myself. But especially close and precious to me is I. J. Schwartz.

How long have I known I. J. Schwartz? About forty-eight years, since he came to America in 1906. He was introduced to me on East Broadway near the library. And I liked him immediately for his appearance alone. Tall and thin with a finely formed face and a beautiful head with pitch-black curls, a thin smile on a fine, sensitive mouth. An impudent-happy flame shone from his brown eyes through a pair of glasses. And just as handsome and just as straight is he today after celebrating his sixty-ninth birthday and beginning to come closer to the age of the "sweet singer" in Israel.[1] One can often still see the fine smile on his lips, though not as often the impudent-happy smile. Of course his head is completely silver. But that lends dignity to him.

When I saw him for the first time, I already had read his poem "Afn Nieman" (On the Nieman), the first thing that he had published here in America in *Tsukunft* and perhaps also the first thing he had ever published. And I have to say that the poem made me like him even before I had met him personally, even though it was quite rough and had, in

---

1. Probably a reference to King David, who is said to have died in his seventies (Professor Ruth Wisse).

general, more faults than virtues. And if my memory isn't tricking me, in that first poem of his that I read, I could already find signs of the virtues and the shortcomings that we find in everything that he has written until now, especially in his two great works, *Kentoki* (Kentuky) and *Yunge yorn* (Young years).

Kentoki became a classic for us that was worthy of three editions. For quite a while, it was taught in our high schools. Now Schwartz has translated *Kentoki* into Hebrew, and I am almost certain that in Hebrew this work will have exactly the same success and perhaps even a greater one than in Yiddish. The success is certainly well deserved, because with all its faults, it has no equal in our poetry. But since I wrote about it in *Inzl* right after it came out in 1925, I will rewrite that article here, in a condensed form, because I think that what was effective then is still effective today:

> Schwartz's greatest virtue is his intense and sensual sensibility. Wherever Schwartz trusts his instincts, they accomplish their mission completely. They pry, snort, stick their nose into everything, touch and taste, aren't satisfied until they discover everything. What Schwartz achieved through his instincts is authentic, direct, and complete. And wherever we come across a passage that is dictated by his instincts, it is masterful.
>
> This is true of his early, smaller poems and also of the poems and idylls that he wrote in his last few years and that are now published in a separate book with the name *Kentoki*. And if only Schwartz had always trusted his instincts. As with every artist, they would have led him further to psychological insights and revealed to him that deeper core that lies beneath the outer gloss of things and events. But it is also necessary to make intensive efforts on the one hand, and discard superfluous methods on the other hand. And one does not always find those qualities in Schwartz's work.
>
> The lack of intensity that one feels in Schwarz's work is in the poverty and often watery quality of his language, and in his weakness for images, jokes, and allegories as old as the beginning of time, and mainly in the Jewish outlook that he often had on things and events—that Jewish outlook that is so well known to us from our long, boring *Haskole* language and Jewish nationalistic articles that have a ready, intelligent explanation for everything, and that is like poison for artistic creativity.

Where Schwartz is free from that Jewish outlook—as, for example, in his early landscapes and his current, smaller idylls—we don't see his other shortcomings as strongly, and very often they disappear altogether. Because as soon as Schwartz is freed from that curse, he has to, willingly or not, bring together all his intellectual strengths, and that helps him to create something worthwhile and, sometimes, even something that is truly great, as, for example, the two best things in his current book, "George Washington" and "Der sof fun Tomasn" (Thomas's end).

In "George Washington," Schwarz succeeded in creating not only an entire, complete work but also—what is much, much more important—an entire tragic-comedic gestalt that breathes with vibrant life from beginning to end. As with every lively, fictional character, we come to love the heedless, foolish, slow-witted Negro, although we would, perhaps, not eat with him using one spoon and we can often hardly keep ourselves from smiling when we see the humor in that black person who is so purely primitive and so frighteningly helpless in his every move.

Like every primitive creature, George is not, for even one minute, the lord over his instincts. At the same time, he doesn't have the strength to comply with the demands of those instincts. By nature lazy like a cat, yet he must work like a mule; clever as a fox, but dense as a klutz when the least bit of sensible exertion is needed; always on the watch and always irritated at his wife, Meggie, whom he suspects of infidelity, and yet blind while, right before his eyes, she deceives him with his worst enemy, the libertine Thomas, and so on, forever.

This poem is rich in unique passages that prove what a fine observer and masterful portrayer Schwartz can be. It's enough to cite the scene in the little Negro church at a weekday service. Or the Thanksgiving dinner that George unexpectedly finds when he arrives home, exhausted and frozen after a hard day of work.

> The beautiful turkey perfumed the air
> and shone golden brown
> with clear drops of fat like pearls;
> and rabbits, as if alive in every limb,
> as if they were frozen leaping,
> remained stuck among brown potatoes
> and all kinds of fresh vegetables.

The sweet and sour cranberry sauce
made his mouth water
and from a wicker basket shone
red, gray apples and oranges,
and cool aromas spread out in the heat.
And on the ground, from a deep washtub,
with necks stretched out in a line
like soldiers, bottles of beer
peeked out from shards of ice.

Der sheyner indik hot aroysgeshtekt
un hot aroysgeloykhtn goldik broyn,
mit klore tropns fets azoy vi perl;
un hozn punkt vi lebedik, mit ale glider,
zey zaynen vi farglivert shpringevdik
geblibn shtekn tsvishn broyne bulbes
un kolaminim lebedike grinsn.
Der zoyer-ziser zaft fun zhuravines
hot im gemakht zayn moyl tsu vasern,
un s'hobn fun geflokhtn korb geloykhtn
di royte, groye epl un oranzshn,
un kile reyekhes in der hits farshpreyt.
Un af der erd fun tifn kubel funem gret,
mit heldzer oysgreshtrekt sherengevayz
azoy vi zelner, hobn flesher bir
aroysgekukt fun ongebrokten ayz.

Such masterful descriptions can be found also in the other smaller poems, especially in "Dos zaydene hemd" (The silk shirt) and "Der sof fun Tomasn," where the chief figure in both poems is Thomas the libertine.

Thomas's characterization, as a whole, is not Schwartz's most successful, although he puts more into him than into George. But how wonderful the fragments are in which the arrival of Thomas's end is described. Here Schwarz proves masterful not only in descriptions of outer appearances, but also of inner experiences. And as with every true artist, they are both so intertwined that one grows out of the other. When Thomas lies hidden in the woods and hunger finally forces him to stick

his head out from his hiding place, and he wants to entice a squirrel that
is playing not far from him to come closer, we sense how everything in
him is concentrated on the little creature that could still his gnawing
hunger, and we see "the head / with its dull bloodshot eyes." Or later,
when Thomas was captured and brought to the courtroom wounded,
exhausted, and dirty,

> His face was grayish-blue:
> around one eye a lump like a big fist
> gleamed and howled. His other eye
> like a hounded, red mouse,
> darted over walls and heads. . . .
>
> Dos ponim iz geven groylekh bloy:
> arum eyn oyg hot shrayendik geglit
> a beyl vi a kulak groys. Dos tsveyte oyg
> iz vi a royte un geyogte moyz
> arumgelofn iber vent un kep. . . .

Together with him, we experience the fear of the unknown fate that
awaits him and that will soon be revealed.

And finally, when Thomas suddenly feels that the unavoidable and
evil end is approaching and a terrible horror falls upon him, and his
young, hot blood wants to cry out, wants to burst out in an animal's roar,
his glance meets another's and it becomes uncannily clear: "that it cannot and will not be otherwise." We remain frozen as if we ourselves were
face to face with the unavoidable.

In these two works, Schwartz allowed his instincts, and only his
instincts, to lead him. And it resulted in two, true masterworks in which
most of his shortcomings are absolutely wiped out. In "Dzho" (Joe),
they show themselves here and there. And there are entire sections that
indicate that the poet was afraid to trust his instincts and went to his
ideological intelligence for help. But his shortcomings are clearest and
strongest in the longest poem at the beginning of the book. Nowhere is
Schwartz's language so poor and so watery as in this, the chief work of
the book. Even in the best places, you suddenly come up against words
and expressions that are in no way suitable there. You feel that Schwartz
used one or another expression only because he was too lazy to search

for the exact word. Here, we collide with proverbs and even whole sentences that are not Yiddish but badly translated English, and sometimes with entire verses that one comes across only in bad newspaper language. Here are some examples:

> Di daytshe brider velkhe zaynen shoyn
> bay yener tsayt geshtanen af di fis.
> The German Brothers who were already
> at that time standing on their feet.

or:

> Un als azelkhe hobn zey gevirkt
> And as such, they had an effect.

or:

> Dos lebn is dervayl gegangen forverts vi
> s'geyt der zeyger af der vant.
> Life meanwhile went forward like
> the clock on the wall.

And many other examples of that sort.

Of course the chief work of the book is also not lacking in wonderful descriptions of true mastery. But they often become drowned in banal, watery language, flat jokes, sweet smiles, and exaggerated, solemn sorrow that come from the same two places—poetic laziness and Jewish conceptions. The same defects that one finds in the details also cry out from the general conception of the work.

That ends the shortened article about *Kentoki*. The same strengths and shortcomings that we find in Schwartz's *Kentoki*, we find also in his second work, *Yunge yorn* (Youth), which is, perhaps, superior in quality to the first. Also, here we find—and in greater measure than in Kentoki—supple descriptions of great mastery. And also, here we see entire pages of skimpy, bad Hebrew that one has to trudge through as if through sand. As in *Kentoki*, the defects of *Yunge yorn* are, to a great extent, a result both of poetic laziness and of Schwartz's Jewish view of things and events.

But why do the defects in *Yunge yorn* bother me much less than in *Kentoki*? Perhaps because between one work of Schwartz's and the second,

I became a mere thirty years older and the shortcomings of a thing cannot irritate me as much as before. And perhaps because I, personally, am now more envious of a poet who wrote great work, even with a lot of defects, than I am of one who wrote perfect things, but small and few. And perhaps the cataclysm that befell our people in the horrible Hitler years made even me look at everything with Jewish eyes, so that the great sorrow that cries out from even the prosaic phrases in Schwartz's *Yunge yorn* over our savagely murdered world that once existed but now is gone, grabs me more now than any beauty that meant so much to me in past years.

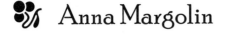 Anna Margolin

The Most Important Details of Anna Margolin's Life

The complete picture of Anna Margolin will be revealed only when someone is found who will read, sort, and put into order the hundreds of letters she left behind, which fill quite a large valise. The letters are in Russian, Yiddish, and Hebrew, and some also in English. Most of the letters were written to her. A great number, though, are from her to others. The letters to her are mostly from people who knew her from when she was a girl of fourteen until her early thirties. No one who wrote to her during those decades was entirely indifferent to her. Most of these people, for a longer or shorter time, were in love with her, some of them passionately. And in the case of one, that love lasted several years. The more one loved her, the more one suffered. This was especially the case in her youth, because she liked to play with those who loved her until she had hurt them. This is not to say, though, that she herself emerged whole from the game. In most such games, she was the greatest victim. Every true love that she experienced was for her a tragic love. A love affair for her was a conflagration. And she always came out singed from it.

Also in the valise is a mass of letters from her family. Most of them from her mother, a few from her father, some from an aunt. There are also twenty or more from her son Na'aman Stavi, who after the founding of the State of Israel was that nation's first military governor. Soon after Anna Margolin died, I sent him all the letters and most of her photographs of him, together with a huge crate of books in several languages. Of the last thirty years of her life, almost 90 percent of the letters are from her to me and from me to her. These letters themselves are wonderful material for a future biography of Anna Margolin; they will provide the key to many of her poems, and to the tragedy and confusion of her last years, and perhaps also to the mystery of why she stopped writing poetry as suddenly as she began.

Family

Anna Margolin was too close to me and our lives were too intimate and too tragically intertwined for me to write about her properly. But I feel that I should point out the most important details of her life, as much as they are known to me. Because if I don't do it, there won't be anyone else. If, however, people are found who know something more about her or her family, and if they want to correct me or complete this endeavor, I will, of course, be happy, because every new detail will help portray her more fully. Here are the details of Anna Margolin's life as they are known to me.

Anna Margolin (Roza Lebensboym) was the only child of Menakhem and Dvoyre Leye Lebnsboym, both raised in Brisk-Dlito. This "onlyness" is surely one of the chief conditions that determined the direction of her life. Of her father's family, Roza knew very little. Her father's father she remembered as if from a dream. In her eyes, he was very, very old, the few times that she saw him as a child. In reality, he was not nearly as old as he seemed to her in her childhood years. She also remembered that her father held her grandfather in high esteem and told her he was brilliant. The name "Lebnsboym" tells us that her father came from a learned family. Perhaps the forebear of the family was the author of the *seyfer Eyts Khaym*.[1]

From her childhood she remembered that she was once taken to a wedding, to which the Grodner Rabbi had also come with his daughter, who embraced and kissed her as if she was one of them. Her father told her then that the Grodner Rabbi was his cousin. Her father, Menakhem

---

1. "Lebensboym" can be translated as "tree of life." Here, Iceland is comparing the name to *Eyts Khaym*, which has the same meaning in Hebrew and is the name of a well-known and revered Kabalistic book by Rabbi Khaym Vital (1543–1620), who was called The Eyts Khaym. (Ben Sadock)

Lebensboym, had the reputation in his childhood of being a genius. At that time he was also a Hasid—a Kotsker Hasid.[2]

Later he became a Maskil and a Zionist. From his former days as a Hasid, there remained only one friend, who was a Kotsker his whole life. That friend used to come to him from time to time to play chess. At the chessboard they both used to hum a Hasidic melody that Roza liked very much and that she never forgot. It was the only Hasidic melody she liked. She remembered that her father had a short Van Dyke, dressed in European fashion, and spoke *daytshmerish*. That was because he lived many years in Konigsberg as a commissioner of wheat and flour. He used to return home only a few times a year. There were also times when he came home only twice a year, for Passover and for the high holidays. When he came for Passover, he sometimes stayed until after Shvues. And when he came for the high holidays, he stayed all through the days of Sukes. The fact that her father was seldom home during her childhood was certainly one factor that strongly shaped her life. She used to say that her father was a very handsome and elegant man and that women loved to be in his company. He had an open mind, was very learned, read a lot of Hebrew, German, and Russian, and was much beloved in Zionist circles, first in Brisk, later in Odessa, and finally also in Warsaw. Among his friends during her childhood years were the then famous Zionist activist *matef khazn*,[3] the Finkelsteins, Avrahm Goldberg, the brother of Menakhem Boraisha, Sh. Yatskan, and others. She described her father in her poem "Mayn shtam redt" (My ancestors speak):

> Merchants from Leipzig and Danzig,
> Bright cuffs, fine cigar smoke,
> Gemore wit, German civility.
> The glance is shrewd and opaque,
> shrewd and sated.
> Don Juans, merchants and seekers of God.

2. A follower of the renowned Kotsker Rebbe, Menakhem Mendl (1827–1859), based in Kotsk, Poland.

3. Literally, orator singer; it is not clear who Iceland is referring to here.

Soykhrim fun Leipsk un Dansk
blanke manketn, eydele sigar-roykh,
Gemore vitsn, Daytshe heflekhkeytn.
Der blik is klug un mat,
klug un iberzat,
Don-Zhwanen, handler un zukher fun Got.

Her father had two sisters: one older than he, Fradl, and a younger one, Leye. The older one, apparently, became widowed early and ran a whole-sale wheat business by herself, from which she grew wealthy. Khuker was her family name. She had several sons and daughters and ruled over them all. One of her grandchildren, Dora Barkai, who is in Israel and has a post in the Haifa technical college, wrote to me that she was the "Mirele Efros" type.[4] She is, by the way, the only one of the Khuker family who was left after the Hitler annihilation, thanks only to the fact that she left for the Land of Israel not long before the Germans arrived in Poland. When Anna Margolin speaks in her poem about "grand dames in calico and linen," she means her aunt. From childhood on, she had great respect for Aunt Fradl, who always went around with a large ring of keys stuck in her wide apron, behind which there always hung a large linen bag with money she had earned in her big flour store. This aunt of hers was the old-fashioned Jewish type.

A completely different type was Anna Margolin's second aunt, Leye. Apparently, she was already a bit of a Maskil, read German, and knew whole pages of Schiller by heart. She realized very early that there was no future for her in Russia and was among the very first middle-class Jewish girls in Brisk to go to America. Here, in America, Leye became "Lena." She was beautiful. She soon found an admirer.

She was no less practical than her sister, it seems, and from the very beginning thought about business. She had as much business ability as her sister Fradl. Several years after her marriage, she was already very well-to-do, so that when Roza was still very young, her Aunt Lena could allow her-self the enjoyment of going home to Brisk on a pleasure trip with her two

4. The eponymous character in the play by Jacob Gordon; a strong and willful woman.

children and showing the others in the family how successful she had been in America. She arrived all dressed up city style with the attitude and bearing of a wealthy, big-city young woman whose old-fashioned title "Mume" no longer fit. So Anna Margolin from her childhood on used to call her not "Mume" but "Aunt Lena." She, her father, and her aunt had in common one trait, which apparently they had all inherited from someone in the family: they could never forget a wrong that someone had done them. And of course, they could also never forgive a wrong. Aunt Lena loved her husband very much, but the first time he sinned against her, she never forgave him; she divorced him and remained a divorcee the rest of her life.

Anna Margolin's mother came from a humble family. I cannot, unfortunately, remember her mother's father's first name. His family name was Rosenblum. Anna Margolin described him to me as a plain but very observant and pious Jew. In his youth, he ran a village inn. In his middle age, he moved to Brisk. It seems that he was very wealthy when he moved to Brisk, because there he could buy for himself a big house across from the "Czar's Orchard." In one part of the house he had a bar and an inn. In the other part he had several apartments to rent. He came from the village with a wife and several daughters and sons for whom he had to provide. He also brought with him an old mother, whom everyone in the house considered learned and a saint. In Brisk he married off all his children well. And though he gave his daughters large dowries, almost all of them did poorly and they with their children had to return to him.

Anna Margolin's mother, Dvoyre Leye, was his eldest daughter. For her, he searched for a really good match. And when they proposed a match with the very good-looking, very successful and well-bred Menakhem Lebensboym, he promised a dowry of two thousand rubles—a tremendous sum for that time—and the match was made. Several years after her marriage, Dvoyre Leye still had no children. Finally she became pregnant, and on the 21st of January, 1887, she gave birth to a daughter, the only child she would ever have. They named the daughter Roza.

Childhood and Youth

Of Anna Margolin's childhood and youth, I know, of course, only what she herself told me. And she, naturally, did not sit down and tell me everything in order and with dates. It was only after returning, on count-less occasions, to those years that we all remember as the happiest in our lives that I gained a general understanding of her childhood and youth. My understanding, though, is clear enough that I can lay out the early course of the life of that complicated person and remarkable poet, Anna Margolin.

Anna Margolin remembered her very early childhood as if from a dream. It seems that after their marriage, her mother and father lived in a small apartment looking out on a courtyard. The courtyard seemed huge to a child's eyes, and in her imagination the world ended at the edge of it. So she once became confused when she went through the gate of the courtyard and saw before her a new world. In her confusion she let her-self go farther and farther. How her walk ended, she did not remember. But as her mother used to tell her often, she became lost and because of that her mother almost went mad. She also didn't remember whether her father was home at the time. Years later, though, when her mother and father no longer lived in that little apartment, but in a large, comfortable apartment with three rooms in her grandfather's house, her father was already seldom at home. At that time he spent most of the year abroad, working as a grain and flour commissioner, mostly in Konigsberg. He came home, as I mentioned, only a few times a year. Her mother loved him very much. When her father came home, it was, understandably, a joyous time for both mother and daughter. But the holiday lasted only for the child. Her mother soon became dejected after the first days of radiant joy. She felt insignificant compared to her handsome, successful, and in her eyes worldly husband. And even more important, she was afraid of him. As soon as the first joy of being together was over, she felt the critical glances of her husband, and they made her very unhappy. And this had a bad effect on the child from her earliest years. She noticed, very early on, the quiet estrangement between her father and mother, the almost slavish servility of her mother and her father's harsh contemptuousness. She also, very early on, took the side of the stronger one—her father. As a child, she worshipped him. Very early on, she began looking down on her mother.

In the few weeks that her father was home, her mother could not properly show him the great love that she had for him, because she was afraid of him and felt inferior. She quickly found herself sacrificed to the caprices of her one and only daughter. The result was fatal for both. The child ruled over her mother every day of the year no less than her husband ruled over her in the short periods when he was home, and her feelings of inferiority grew even stronger. The child, from her earliest years, became used to her every desire being a command. Thanks to her beauty, intelligence, and womanly charm, her requests were almost always commands for all the men with whom she came into contact when she was young. She knew it, and she used it left and right with all her strength. It brought her countless victories, but also defeats, even in her most charming, blossoming years. And later, when she was still in her youth and she suddenly realized that her word had ceased to be a command, it was such a blow that she never recovered. That was, perhaps, one of the main things that led to her distancing herself more and more from people and, finally, separating and cutting herself off entirely from the world.

When Anna Margolin was six years old, her father sent for his wife and child to join him in Konigsberg. Anna Margolin told me many times that her father must have missed her mother sexually, because her mother had, perhaps, the most beautiful body that she had ever seen. The trouble was that her mother did not know how to maintain her body, take good care of it, and use it. She also didn't know how to dress and how to conduct herself among people. The result was that her father was ashamed of her. When he sent for her to come to Konigsberg, he was sure that there, in the new environment of a European city, his wife would become different, dress differently and conduct herself differently. But what happened was just the opposite. There, her mother felt so foreign and lost that she was afraid to leave the house. And if it happened that her husband almost forced her to go for a walk, or even took her to the theater, she came home in pain and unhappy. Almost always something happened during the excursion that made her feel hopeless; she could never become sophisticated, as her husband would have liked. Anna Margolin and her mother were in Konigsberg only three or four months. In that short time, she learned to speak German and even to read a little.

When she was seven, her father hired a teacher to come for an hour to teach her the Bible, Hebrew grammar, and Modern Hebrew books. Her father said that she should absorb Jewish culture and learn Hebrew before she began to learn Russian and other European languages. And since he would not be home, he told his wife she should watch her and see that she never missed a Hebrew lesson. The several times a year that he came home, he tested her severely to see how far she had progressed in Hebrew. And since she, in those years, literally worshipped her father, she studied very hard in order to please him.

A year later, they also hired a Russian teacher. She took to Russian with eagerness and enthusiasm; she would have neglected Hebrew entirely if she had not remembered that she could, through such neglect, lose her father's love. When she was nine, her everyday language was already Russian. All of her friends spoke Russian, and the boys she knew also spoke Russian. The only ones she had to speak Yiddish to, because they didn't understand any other language, were her mother, her grandmother, and her aunts. And it seems that the women's side of her mother's family spoke a rich, idiomatic Yiddish that returned to her when she, years later, became a Yiddish writer. This was especially evident in the translations she wrote for *Der tog*, which, with only one exception, were always anonymous. She was, incidentally, one of the finest translators that we had.

All her life Anna Margolin spoke with great nostalgia about the several years that she lived in Odessa with her mother and father, where she went to the gymnasium. How old she was when her parents moved to Odessa is not clear. Both from what she told me and from certain poems of hers, one can deduce that it was the years when the young girl in her had awakened and everything in her and around her became a romantic wonder. That wonder she carried with her all her life, and the most beautiful expressions of it are found in two of her poems, "A shtot baym yam" (A city on the sea) and "Odes" (Odessa). At the heart of both poems is a yearning to remember, a desire to return to a net of memories, the delicate, girlish expectations that were themselves deep experiences. At the end of "Odes" she captured the most beautiful impression of the city that she loved so much:

And can you remember
everything that has no name
and is merely a fragrance and a secret?
In the breath from the steppe,
and from the sun and from the tar?

And to the singing sea, the city,
as if with a silken train
descended a thousand marble steps.

Un kont ir zikh dermonen,
alts dos, vos hot nisht keyn nomen
un iz bloyz a duft un a sod?
In dem otem fun step
un fun zun un fun smole?
Un tsum zingendikn yam hot di shtot,
vi mit a zaydene shlep,
genidert fun toyznt mirmelne trep.

From Odessa, Anna Margolin returned to Brisk a complete young lady. From conversations with her, I have the impression that she was around fifteen years old. Menakhem Boraisha, who was a year younger than she and who knew her from childhood on, told me that she was then magically beautiful, smart, well read, and completely grown up. She had big blue eyes and a forest of ash-blond hair that reached to her knees. She could bewitch both with her eyes and with her hair, which, when she let it, fell in long, thick waves over her shoulders and down over her hips. She knew her good points and the strength she possessed. And she used them in full measure. She was quickly surrounded by boys her age who fell for her. There was flirting and playing that hurt both her and the boys she captivated. She was always so sure of her strength that when a boy fell in love with her, she pointed out one of her friends and convinced him that her friend was prettier and more interesting than she. But if she succeeded in persuading one of her admirers, and he indeed fell in love with her friend, she used to suffer terribly. As Anna Margolin told me, she had this trait not only in her years as a just-awakened young woman, but also later, in the full ripeness of experience. And she always suffered when an admirer, because of her own persuasiveness, actually fell in love with another woman. Yet the boys who loved her suffered more from her caprices than she did. As a young girl she liked to test her strength, and when she saw that a boy was caught in her net, she pushed him away.

A boy named Abrasha suffered terribly. As Anna Margolin remembered, he was very handsome and very talented, had a phenomenal memory, and wrote Russian poems. But Abrasha suffered from epilepsy. The first seizure she witnessed came on after she had teased him. As she did with the other boys, she told him to go away because she couldn't stand the sight of him. Of course she became quite shaken when she saw the result of her teasing. But when Abrasha came to himself again, he began to speak to her so beautifully that she was bewitched. Later, several times, she teased him in the same way so that he would have an attack and afterward again speak to her so beautifully. In her last years, when Anna Margolin herself suffered physically and spiritually from all sorts of illnesses, real and imagined, she often became melancholy from a superstitious conviction that she was being punished for the sins she had committed against others in her youth. More than anything, she felt that she was being punished because, in her younger years, she had played so cruelly with Abrasha.

Her Father Abandons Her Mother

At the same time that she was so busy with herself and her flirting, her mother experienced the saddest time of her life. Menakhem Lebensboym, her husband, left Konigsberg for Odessa, mainly because of business. His business in Konigsberg had never quite prospered. In the years he spent in Konigsberg, he often had to go to his father-in-law for loans he could never pay back. When he felt that the water was reaching his neck, he gave up Konigsberg to try his luck in Odessa. At the same time, he made a decision that was, for him, not much less important. The longer he stayed in Kongsberg while his wife remained in Brisk, the greater grew the distance between them. With each year, he became in his own eyes more of an urban man and she more backward. His one attempt to bring her to Konigsberg had failed. In great measure, he blamed this on the fact that his uneducated, small-town wife could not adjust to Konigsberg's foreign, German, and thoroughly Gentile environment. He thought it would be entirely different in Odessa. However foreign she might feel in southern Russia's greatest city, she wouldn't feel entirely an outsider because she would encounter plenty of other Jews. And a great many of them would be Jews from foreign places—not from Odessa, but from different cities and towns, many of them even from Brisk and its surroundings. With them she could speak, with them she could spend time, and from them she could learn how to conduct herself. But his reckonings turned out to be incorrect: he was no more successful in business in Odessa, and his wife did not become more sophisticated. Indeed, his wife felt even more out of place in Odessa than years earlier in Konigsberg, and this was precisely because in Odessa she met other Jewish women who just a few years earlier had been as simple and as provincial as she and who in a short time had become city women—a thing that she was always convinced she could never become. The result was that the whole time she was with her husband and child in Odessa, she was afraid to be among people, and if she went somewhere with her husband because she had to, the outing was always a failure. After each such outing, she felt that her husband was becoming more distant, and when they finally returned to Brisk, he was entirely alienated from her.

Her husband could not remain in Brisk for long. To go back to Konigsberg was also not an option. So he began to travel here and there, from Brisk to Warsaw and from Warsaw to Brisk, and after every trip he returned more distant from his wife. He was then in his best and healthiest, most masculine years—more handsome than ever, more elegant than ever. In his daughter's eyes, he was the most handsome and most elegant man in the world. And when her father sometimes took her for a stroll, she felt proud and happy that she could go with him, arm in arm through the street, so that her friends would be jealous of her.

Once, when her father had taken her for a walk, he confided in her a secret—that very soon he would be leaving Brisk and never coming back. Her mother, he told her, was not refined and he did not love her and could not waste his whole life with her. His daughter, of course, was distraught and burst into tears. But at the same time, she thought her father was right. In her eyes, her mother really was backward compared to her father and therefore she was not worthy of him. And she knew from all the novels she had read that a man and woman should not live together without love. So by the end of the stroll she had taken upon herself the mission of telling her mother the sad news and convincing her that she should divorce her father. How cruel it was for her father to give her such a task, and how foolish it was for her to take it upon herself! Anna Margolin realized this only in her later years. But in those early years, when she was considered not only a beautiful and well-educated girl, but also a wise one, it seemed natural to her that, since her father didn't love her mother, she must free him, and that the responsibility lay with her, the daughter, to persuade her mother to let her husband go.

But her mother, who had never stood up to her husband or her daughter, considering herself inferior to both of them, when it came to precisely this matter demonstrated an independence and stubborn determination. She had felt for a long time that her husband was becoming more remote, and she expected that one fine day he would leave her. All the same, when the unhappy hour arrived and her daughter brought her the sad news, it was such a blow that in one day she seemed to have aged several years. There were no heated scenes between her and her husband because her husband was not home at the time; and later of course there were none because it was not her nature to make scenes. But there were hysterical outbreaks, and after each outbreak, her determination not to divorce her husband grew stronger.

There began a very sad time for her and her daughter. When Mena-khem Lebensboym saw how determined his wife was not to free him, he decided to break her stubbornness by withholding the money she needed to live. Mother and daughter actually went hungry. In her penury, her mother had no choice but to return to her father. What that meant to her, a good twenty years after her marriage and with a grown, capricious daughter on her hands, one cannot even imagine. As if that wasn't enough, a huge fire broke out in Brisk during which almost the whole town was burned to the ground. Anna Margolin's grandfather's large house was destroyed, and since it was not insured, the fire made him a pauper. On the site of the large, spacious house where her grandfather had lived until then, he now, in his old age, had to move into a tiny apartment. And in that crowded apartment he also had to take in his eldest daughter, Dvoyre Leye, with her daughter Roza, as well as a second daughter and her children who had lived with him earlier because her husband died young and left the widow and orphans naked and barefoot.

It is not entirely clear to me what happened first—the fire in Brisk or Anna's father's decision to rid himself of her mother. Their loneliness was a hundred times worse for the mother than for the daughter, who was a beautiful and charming young girl. It made no difference to the boys who hung around her that she lived worse in her grandfather's house than she had before. She was the flame to which they were drawn, and this gave her pleasure. She enjoyed seeing how they were singed by coming close to her. In addition, a new world quickly opened for her that made her forget not only her mother but also her entire circle of friends. Her father left Brisk altogether and settled in Warsaw. For her, it was natural that she should leave her mother in her solitude at her grandfather's in Brisk and go to her father in Warsaw. Natural, first, because she still worshipped her father and looked down on her mother, and second, because she was young and pretty and thirsty for life and knew that life would be better with her father in Warsaw than with her mother in Brisk.

And indeed, life for her in Warsaw was broader and richer. It was as if in one night, from a half-grown girl she had become a ripe woman among adults. For the first time, she met Hebrew and Yiddish writers, teachers, and activists face to face. Like most young people in Brisk at that time, she had been inspired by the revolution and had joined the Social-ist-Territorialist (ST) movement. Now in Warsaw, she met several leaders of that movement, who lived in Kiev but who visited Warsaw from time to time. It was also in Warsaw that she stopped flirting with love and began great and boundless loves. And when she was in love, she forgot everything and everyone. More than anything else, she forgot about her mother. For every ten letters she received from her mother, she answered one, and sometimes not even that. What that must have meant for her mother, who had now lost everything, including her only child who had been the apple of her eye, she should have remembered, no matter how greatly her new life in Warsaw distracted her. But Anna Margolin did not let herself remember. So it came as a terrible shock when one day she left the lodgings where she lived with her father and saw her mother sitting, bent over tearfully, on the steps. In her great longing for her only child, her mother, after long and sleepless nights, had decided to travel to Warsaw and see her. But when she came to Warsaw and went to the house where she knew her husband and daughter were living, she went only as far as the building where they lived. To go to the door, to knock and enter—for that, she did not have the courage. And since she wanted so badly to see her daughter, she had sat down on the steps to wait. Perhaps there would be a miracle and her daughter would come out and she would see her.

The miracle happened, but only for her. Her daughter felt as if a hammer had struck her on the head when she saw her mother sitting there. Anna Margolin in her later years always became hysterical whenever she remembered that moment. And as she told me several times, she then, for the first time in her life, felt profoundly guilty. Seeing her mother so debased and dejected, almost on the threshold of her and her father's door, she remembered all the suffering and grief she had caused her through the years. All the pain, great and deep it was. That day, she did not turn away. And from then on, she knew that she could no longer remain with her father in Warsaw all the time, however good it might be there, but must divide her time between Warsaw and Brisk and be with her mother as much as with her father. Indeed, she did return soon to Brisk, but she was not happy living with her mother. This was partly because she was always restless there, but mainly because her first true love had just then stormed into her life. And as I have already said, she knew no limits when it came to love. I don't remember where she met the boy, who is today a prominent journalist and community activist in New York. I only know that he came from a small Ukrainian town and that he spent his bachelor years in Vilna and Warsaw. Apparently he had also been in Brisk for a short time.

Like Anna Margolin, he was a follower of the ST, in which he held a key position on a local committee. That was, perhaps, how she met him, but it did not take long for that to be forgotten. Tens of letters from him that I have found from that time show that this was one of those great loves for which both sides are ready to sacrifice everything. He literally would have walked through fire for her. And indeed, she became a ball of fire who brought everyone around her to grief. In her love, she forgot her father and mother, her friends and acquaintances, all her customary manners and social graces. When he was in Vilna and she wanted to be with him, even though her father would be very upset when he learned of it and her mother wouldn't be able to sleep at night and people would talk, she suddenly flew to him. And when he had to go away for a little while to his hometown, she followed him there. That resulted in her going so hungry that the landlady from whom she rented a room in that town once caught her red-handed, in the middle of the night, standing barefoot in front of a shelf about to steal a piece of bread.

How long can such a love endure? Sometimes for an eternity and sometimes only briefly. Anna Margolin burned with love for a year or a little more, the boy very much longer. Her mother slowly got used to her daughter's circumstances, and as she knew and liked the boy, she began to look on him as a future son-in-law. Her father, though, became very upset by the whole affair. He had never until then seen his child consumed by such an unbridled passion, and like all fathers he feared the consequences. Besides that, he didn't like the boy. He had expected his daughter to choose for herself someone wealthier, more successful, and better educated. He also expected a lot more from his daughter. He thought her a talented girl with the mind of a genius. He dreamed of a great career for her. He tried to stop his daughter's love by every means possible, and of course none of his ploys worked. Meanwhile, he wrote about the whole situation to his sister Lena in America, pouring out his bitter heart and asking her to help, if possible, even if only with some advice. From their letters, a plan was born. Her brother would send his daughter to her in America. She was, after all, rich enough to own her own house. There was enough room and there would be no lack of food, even clothing would not be lacking. Her brother need only send his daughter fifty rubles a month for her education. First, a private teacher would be hired who would come to the house and give her English lessons; later, when she had mastered English, they would prepare her for college. Her father pounced on the idea, and to his amazement, his daughter did not reject it. But she would have to discuss it beforehand with her fiancé. That did not please him at all. After all, he had jumped at the plan mainly because it would separate her from the one she called her fiancé. But he knew that when she said she would have to discuss it with him, she would do it whether he liked it or not, so he agreed.

Anna Margolin had a frank talk with her lover. She could not and would not continue as they had. She had to consider the future. And for her the future meant being an educated woman. Until now she had squandered her time on foolishness. But now an opportunity had appeared for her, and she must begin her education and not treat the opportunity cavalierly. She would go to America, where she would immediately prepare for university, and if he didn't want their bonds to be severed, he would have to do the same in Europe. He must give up all the business connections he had by then made in Vilna and go study in Switzerland. However difficult that would be for him, he nonetheless agreed to it. A month later she was on a ship to America. Not long after, the boy severed his business ties and went off to Switzerland.

In America for the First Time

Anna Margolin was eighteen and a half when she went to America for the first time, in 1906. Her Aunt Lena welcomed her as her own child. She got her own room in the spacious house on Rodney Street, in Williamsburg, and was dressed and cared for as a daughter. A tutor was soon hired who came to the house every evening to teach her English. In the house were her aunt's own two children, one of whom later became a prominent doctor. They were both, it seems, younger than she and very respectful of her. For several weeks, Anna Margolin felt that her aunt's house was a paradise. Her aunt and uncle would leave the house soon after breakfast to go to their business. The children were away at school, and she was left in the house by herself. She had nothing to say to the maid, and besides, the maid was busy with her work. The few books that Anna Margolin found in her aunt's house she quickly read. She began to grow bored.

A former friend from Brisk looked her up, and one evening the friend took her to East Broadway, where she met other friends whom she knew from Brisk, Warsaw, Vilna, and Kiev. They all spoke Russian, and so did other people she met on East Broadway, and she felt warm and at home among them. She came home late at night, and when in the morning she was left alone again, her aunt's large and spacious house seemed empty and cold. And when her aunt and uncle came home in the evening, they

10. Anna Margolin, ca. 1910. Courtesy of the YIVO
Institute for Jewish Research.

did not find her there. They waited hours for her for dinner, which was
the main meal in their house. The teacher wasted an hour waiting for
her. And everyone in the house was worried because of her. Her aunt
became angry with her, and it came to an argument. She admitted that
it was her fault and promised she wouldn't do it anymore. And for several days she actually kept her word. But then one day she was again
drawn to East Broadway and forgot about her promise. She did, however,
remember to come home on time, and she was also careful to be on time
for her English lesson. But soon after, she got dressed and went back to
East Broadway.

A little later, visitors began coming to her from East Broadway. Her
aunt didn't like them. In her eyes, they were all too "green" and not the
sort she wanted to have in her house. The boys pleased her least of all.
And least of all could she stand one who, it seemed to her, was fifteen

years older than her niece. He appeared no better to her even after her niece said that he was an editor and was prominent among the intellectuals on the East Side. In her eyes, he was an idler, and besides, what did a man of his age want with a girl her niece's age?

Aunt Lena was not a person who can keep something that doesn't please her to herself. And since it didn't please her that Roza was running around constantly on East Broadway, she said so. And not only said it, but also asked that she do it less. Of course Roza did not, in such a matter, allow herself to be dictated to. From her childhood on, she had been used to people obeying her, not the other way around. And so they began to have conflicts with each other. The conflicts became more frequent when the niece began to neglect her English lessons to the point that the teacher finally stopped coming. Even greater conflicts arose when her aunt noticed that letters were arriving from Switzerland two or three times a week and that her niece wasn't even opening them. Driven by feminine curiosity, she allowed herself to open one of the letters and read it. Soon she began to read all the others.

She had a hard and domineering nature, but she could also be deeply sentimental. And what she discovered in the letters made her more than sentimental. Her niece found her in tears when she came home that night from the East Side. From the letters she had read, she was so full of sorrow that for a long while she looked despondent and remained silent. Then suddenly she began to berate her niece. How could she have in herself so much cruelty? A person loves her so much that he sacrifices everything, leaves his home, a business, and goes off to study abroad where he goes hungry, suffers want, and all for her sake, and it doesn't begin to bother her, as if he were a stranger, as if he were a dog. She hardly stops seeing him than she no longer knows him, as if he never existed. He almost dies from sorrow because he hears nothing from her, doesn't know what to think, tears himself apart writing to her, and she doesn't even open his letters. How can she act that way? How can she be so inhuman? To all the accusations, her niece answered with the same question: What right did her aunt have to open her letters? This drove her aunt wild. Letters that lie around weeks at a time unopened are "her" letters? And she is not ashamed? Of course her niece was ashamed, and of course she knew she was at fault concerning her lover in Switzerland and her behavior was cruel. But pride wouldn't let her admit it. And besides, what was she to do when she no longer loved him and he no longer meant anything to her? Should she not let him know it? Yet she did feel guilty, and the guiltier she felt the more she insisted that she didn't want her letters opened. She would not allow her letters to be opened and she did not want to be told where she could go, whom she could meet, to whom she should write and to whom she should not write. The first break between her and her aunt had arisen. Neither of them had to wait long for a second.

Her aunt informed her father. Letters upbraiding her began to arrive from him. I found three of them among Anna Margolin's papers after her death and sent them, together with other things, to her son in Israel. The conflicts between the two happened more and more often until one fine day when her aunt was not home, the niece gathered her things, left the house, and never came back.

Her Relationship with Dr. Khaym Zhitlovski

I have dwelled longer on certain details of Anna Margolin's life than on others because through them I wanted to describe her background, which certainly contributed a great deal to the person she became. All the other important details of her life—with a few exceptions, perhaps—I will merely mention. One of the most important periods of her life was certainly her relationship with Dr. Khaym Zhitlovski. Because that relationship, to a great degree, determined her future.

When she left her aunt's house, Anna Margolin went to live with three other girls in a small, half-dark room on the East Side. They were, as was she, middle-class girls from the Old Country, where they had studied in secular schools, taken part in the revolutionary movement, and dreamed beautiful dreams about their own personal futures. Here, however, hard reality forced them to work in shops. As long as Anna Margolin was with her aunt, she had avoided that fate. But now she, like the others, was also forced to work in a shop. But she could not stand it for long. She worked for a total of eight or nine weeks, in two trades and in three shops. She earned between four and five dollars a week. Enough for bread with herring and a warm meal with meat every other day, sometimes only twice a week. She could have gone back to her aunt at any time, but she did not want to. Among her papers, I found a letter from her father to her aunt in which he complained that his daughter had become a mere shop girl. He consoled himself with the thought that this was, perhaps, no more than one of her wild caprices, which surly would soon pass. His prophecy did indeed come about, but not the way he thought it would.

Winter arrived quickly, and with it all the lectures, concerts, and dances of which there were so many in New York. Once a week, young intellectuals came in droves to hear a series of philosophy lectures that Dr. Khaym Zhitlovski gave in Clinton Street Hall. His lectures in that hall, which held eight or nine hundred people, were always packed. Very often the audience was so large that all the aisles were blocked and people stood pressed together against the walls. And the hall was packed for good reason—his lectures were spiritually enthralling and intensely enjoyable. He structured them masterfully, and he had a gift whereby, while he was speaking, the audience could see clearly how he was preparing the foundations on which to build a marvelously logical edifice. He was, besides, unusually handsome, and had a beautiful voice and gestures that helped emphasize his thoughts.

Among those who went to hear Zhitlovski that winter were Anna Margolin and her roommates. She became intoxicated with the lectures but even more with the lecturer. She left the hall completely in love with him. And so sure was she that he would also fall in love with her that on the way home she was ready to place a bet with the other girls. And she might well have bet them. It didn't take long for Zhitlovski to notice her. It took even less time for him to want to know her better. Before you knew it, he had asked her to become his secretary, and within a few weeks she had become his lover and there was not once place that he went without her. In New York at that time, a lot of women were in love with Zhitlovski, and he had, to put it mildly, allowed them to love him. But with her arrival in his life, all others were erased. Everyone came to look on her as the future Mrs. Zhitlovski, and they respected her as if she already was. And he wanted her to become his wife. And her intelligence said, "of course," because it was no small thing to be the wife of the most famous man on the "Yiddish Street." But her young blood argued against it. She was hardly nineteen years old. He was in his forties, as old as her own father and perhaps even older.

The relationship lasted a year, and during that time she became, spiritually, more mature. Since she was gifted with an alert, analytical mind, a good memory, and a piercing perceptiveness, she naturally must have benefited greatly from being in the company of one of our finest minds, a man for whom thinking was as necessary as breathing. But for Zhitlovski, to live near a person like her was also a spiritual prize. Zhitlovski considered *Historishe ideyen-farbindungen* (Historical idea-connections) to be his most important and original work. And right in front of me, he said to Anna Margolin that he had her to thank for it, because she had inspired him. And I can attest to the fact that she could inspire someone intensely. She had inspired me to write two-thirds of the poems in my book *Fun mayn zumer* (From my summer). Hardly had I, in conversation with her, blurted out a well-expressed phrase than she would say: there you have a poem, why don't you write it down? And she wouldn't budge until I had written it down. As Zhitlovski's secretary, she had found among his papers some examples of historical idea-connections. Based on those, she had suggested that an entire work be written about them. Zhitlovski's beautiful green eyes lit up at her suggestion, and he soon got down to work.

Zhitlovski told her this right in front of me some twenty years after their relationship. It was at a table in Sholom's Café. He met us both one evening and asked if he might sit with us. That evening he also mentioned to Anna Margolin that she was always her own worst enemy. And if it weren't for that, who knows whether both their lives might have taken an entirely different course? What exactly he meant by that, I don't know. But Anna Margolin herself told me many times that their relationship ended because Zhitlovski, in a moment of jealousy, accused her of betraying him. That was just before an excursion on a boat up the Hudson. He felt so wounded by the "betrayal" that throughout the excursion, he didn't "see" her. He also didn't "see" her when they got off the ship, and the next day, and the day after; he didn't appear. This upset her so much that she lay in bed several days and wept, and Dr. Pavel Kaplan, one of Zhitlovski's closest friends, sat near her and protected her, for fear that she would commit suicide. But when she finally got out of bed, she cut Zhitlovski out of her life completely. Zhitlovski by then knew the truth, that his suspicion had been senseless. But she felt so wounded by how he had treated her, by his suspicions, that she could not forgive him for the rest of her life.

The most interesting part of the story is that just after, she did indeed fall in love with the man whom Zhitlovski had suspected. And the man was none other than the above-mentioned Dr. Kaplan, who was ten years older than Zhitlovski. How the wonderfully beautiful Anna Margolin, at the age of nineteen, could fall in love with such a man as Kaplan, who could have been her grandfather and who was, with his short, thick appearance, far from attractive, is one of those mysteries that only a good psychologist could solve. One factor was certainly his tremendous goodness and readiness to come and help.

Paris, Warsaw, Marriage, and Divorce

Around that time, Anna Margolin wrote some stories and sent one of them to the *Fraye arbeter shtime* under the pseudonym "Khava Gross." Sh. Yanovski, the editor of the *FAS*, liked the story. However, because he had had some experiences with beginners who sent him things under women's names, he invited Khava Gross, through his famous mailbox, to come see him at the editorial office. And when she came to him and he saw who it was that was hiding behind the name "Khava Gross," he asked her to join the editorial staff as secretary. She gladly accepted, though he paid very little, because she had no other prospects of earning money. She held the job about six months. But she didn't like the work and also didn't like the environment in which she found herself in New York; without Zhitlovski's brilliance, all of New York seemed banal and gray. She grew restless and began to dream of returning to Europe.

Soon after leaving her aunt, her mother had let her know that she had finally agreed to divorce her father. Now she received news that her father had remarried, this time to a very beautiful and wealthy woman. This news both weakened and strengthened her desire to return to Europe. Finally, she made the decision to go. Friends helped her with money for a ship ticket and with letters of introduction. Sh. Yanovski gave her a letter to Prince Piotr Kropotkin, the great theorist of anarchism, who lived in a villa outside London. He also gave her a letter to Vladimir Burzev, the Socialist revolutionary who had in his time caused a tremendous sensation with the revelation that (Yevno) Azev, who had posed as the leader of the terrorist organization of the Socialist revolutionaries, was in fact an agent provocateur for the Czarist secret police. Burzev at that time lived in Paris, where he often exposed the double life of many such people who in various parties posed as revolutionaries but were actually spies and provocateurs. Both letters were of use to Anna Margolin, both spiritually and materially: thanks to the Kropotkin letter, she met one of the most noble, spiritual, and cultured people of that time; and thanks to the Burzev letter, she was able to spend several months in Paris and to acquaint herself with the great masterpieces in the Louvre and other museums in the French capital, which was, for artists and writers of that time, the center of the world.

She spent four weeks in London. And during those four weeks, at Kropotkin's request, she went to him every day. The old anarchist-theoretician had chosen a young Russian, a devoted follower of his, to bring her to him every day. And he came every day at exactly the same time and took her to Kropotkin. In letters to various people, Kropotkin mentioned her name several times, praising her highly; in one letter, he even wrote that she was the only person who had made him think about the Jewish Question. From Paris, Burzev gave her enough material about the secrets of the Russian Revolution that she could send frequent correspondence to the *Forverts* in New York. This was her source of income the whole time she was in Paris.

As Anna Margolin told me many times, Paris was one of the two cities where she truly felt at home, even though at that time she did not speak one word of French. It seemed to her that in Paris, everyone must feel at home wherever he comes from and to whatever people he belongs. The second city where she felt absolutely at home was Tel Aviv, which was just then being founded. But however comfortable she may have felt in Paris, she was dissatisfied. She felt herself drawn back to Warsaw. And after several months in Paris, she departed for Warsaw. And even though she had not been away for more than two years or so, still, she did not recognize the city. During those two years, a new generation of writers had arisen—the third generation after Peretz. Everyone was talking about A. M. Weisenberg, Moyshe Stavski, Efraim Kaganovski, and many others. One who had a very special place among that group was the poet Mena-khem, who was from her hometown of Brisk and who at one time had been a very close friend—Menakhem Goldberg [Boraisha].

She was soon drawn into that circle. And very quickly she also became a visitor at Peretz's. She fell in love with Moyshe Stavski. They married and soon after they both went to Israel, where they lived first in Jaffa and then in Tel Aviv. There, their son Na'aman was born; after the founding of the State of Israel, he was chosen as the military governor of Galilee. But life with Stavski was not good. She warned him that as soon as her child was weaned, she would leave him. And in fact she did. Hardly had the child stopped nursing than Stavski had to give her a divorce. She left the child with him and returned to Warsaw. I have a picture of Anna Margolin with her child in her lap. And this picture shows the saddest woman that I have ever seen in my life. Anna Margolin always kept that picture hidden away so that she could not easily come upon it. Because when she did see the picture, she became so hysterical that she beat her head with her fists. And afterward she would lie sick in bed for days. The picture reminded her of the day she left Tel Aviv. So that the child would get used to being without his mother, several days before her departure, they took him and kept him in a friend's house. On the day of her departure, they brought him to her for a few minutes. But as soon as the child spied his mother, he threw his little arms around her neck and squeezed so hard that they could not tear him away. Whenever she looked at the picture she always felt the nails of her child, how they had dug into her neck, so she hid the picture away so that she wouldn't be able to find it.

Warsaw, Krementshug, and Again New York

As sad as Anna Margolin was when she left Tel Aviv, she became even sadder when she arrived back in Warsaw. During the two years she spent in Tel Aviv, she heard that her father was doing very well in business and living lavishly. When she returned to Warsaw, naturally she went to him. Even before her marriage, her father had been living very nicely with his second wife and her three young daughters. When she returned to Warsaw, he was in a spacious apartment, beautifully and richly furnished. But the welcome she received in the apartment was very cold. Not only her stepmother but also her father immediately made her feel that she was not a welcome guest. For her wedding, her father had given her a dowry and had a very rich wardrobe made for her. Besides that, she had received wedding gifts, and with that her father felt that he had rid himself of all responsibilities toward her. He would have had no desire to have her back on his shoulders even if she had been a good daughter. But in his eyes, she was far from being a good daughter. She certainly had given him no pleasure with her behavior up until her marriage. While she was his only child, he had tolerated her, but now she was no longer his only child. His new wife had given him a son, and on his son who was then still an infant in a cradle, he placed all the hopes that he had earlier placed on his daughter. In addition, the new authority was not he but his new wife. She had brought him wealth when he married her. Thanks to her, he was now doing very well, and of course her word in the house was law. Her stepmother simply could not stand to have Anna Margolin in her home; her husband and her three daughters from her first husband were enough for her. She did, though, see to it that Anna Margolin would have the kind of financial support that would make her flee as soon as possible.

Indeed, Anna Margolin wanted to escape from the very first day. But to her sorrow, she couldn't, because she had returned from Israel almost naked and barefoot. The dowry had been spent on expenses for her and her husband's trip to Israel and to live on for the first several weeks. The wedding clothes had become torn in the two years she was there, and the wedding gifts had been slowly pawned and sold to provide a meager subsistence. In Warsaw she didn't have anyone to whom she could go for help. And even if she had had some acquaintances, she could seldom have visited them because of the sorry state of her clothing. There were several months in Warsaw when she simply couldn't leave the house because her shoes were torn and her father didn't want to give her any money to have them fixed. And this was during the winter months, when it was impossible to go around in torn shoes.

Her father and stepmother were cruel to her. Only her older two stepsisters were good to her. One of them was not far from her in age.

Her two stepsisters even became her friends, and thanks to them she was able to remain in her father's house as long as she did. For his cruel behavior toward her that winter, Anna Margolin came to hate the same father whom she had once idolized. So strong did her hatred become that when, years later, she received a letter from him, she ripped it up without opening it. And when years later Sh. Yatskan came to New York on an extended visit and brought greetings from her father, who was his good friend, she said that for her, her father was dead. However, when the same Yatskan, several months later, brought her the message that her father had died after a short illness, she became so hysterical that she had to take to her bed. By then, she remembered not only her father, whom she had once loved so much, but even more why she later came to hate him. And for the rest of her life she could not speak of him without hatred. Even when she remembered his virtues and the qualities that he had inculcated in her. She thought that his greatest virtue was his wonderful mind. She was sure that if he had had a secular education, he would certainly have succeeded in anything he put his hand to. The most important quality that he instilled in her was a love for truth—a quality that she herself carried to a much higher level and that would make a lot of trouble for her. Her love of truth was so strong that she could not keep herself from telling the truth to many of the people with whom she came in contact. And people hate it when they are told the truth. Almost all of my closest friends did not like her, and all because she told them her true opinion of them.

How long she was in her father's house after her return from Tel Aviv is not clear to me. My impression is that it was around three-quarters of a year. It was her mother, who at that time was married to a bookkeeper in Krementshug, who rescued her. Her mother sent her money for clothes; she also sent her money for expenses and brought her to Krementshug. She stayed with her mother for several months, where everyone showed her love and respect. But one could not even speak about her remaining there. However little her mother had for herself, she nonetheless saw to it that her daughter did not go without. And when her daughter could no longer stand the constricted life in Krementshug, she managed to get the money for a ship's ticket and train expenses, and on the 13th of May, 1914, she came to America for the second time. She would remain there for the rest of her life.

The first few months after she came to America for the second time, she very often went hungry. She was not close with her former circle that had gathered around Zhitlovski. The only one of that generation who remained close to her was Dr. Pavel Kaplan. But he had aged greatly in the few years that she was away from New York. Now, in addition, he was suffering greatly from asthma. He still kept up his practice, but patients seldom came to him. He could not, therefore, help her much financially. The younger generation of poets and writers that had come into their own in the years she was away were, most of them, just as poor as she. To the young poets, she was a beautiful lady with a great deal of worldly knowledge and an original, rare, musical voice that bewitched many of them, though others considered it unnatural and affected. There were those who fell in love with her, and those who were afraid of her, but almost everyone had great respect for her.

In the beginning of November of the same year, *Der tog* was founded in New York, and it revolutionized the Yiddish daily press, as had *Der fraynd* (The friend) in its day, when it was published in Petersburg. With Kaplan's help, she became a contributor to that newspaper. Her weekly column, *In der froyen velt* (In the woman's world), was read with great pleasure by her fellow writers and by discerning readers; in it she showed herself to be a journalist with a brilliant and original style that captivated even such a *faynshmeker* as Kolia Teper and such a stylist as Moshe Nadir.

Very soon she became a full member of *Der tog's* editorial board, a post she kept until the fall of 1920. She left the job for various reasons. Later, she again became a contributor to *Der tog* with a regular salary, but not as a full member of the editorial board, only as a contributor of one or two articles a week. Until the fall of 1920, she was known only by her own name, Roza Lenensboym. But two years later, she began to write poems under the pseudonym "Anna Margolin." In later years, she was known only as Anna Margolin. Only those who knew her from the past knew her as Roza Lebensboym.

Once, a very good-looking boy came into the editorial office. He was blond with blue eyes and appeared so young and in the flowering of his youth that compared to him all the staff at the newspaper seemed old and faded, though several of them were not much older than him. He was Hirsh Leyb Gordon, who is today a well-known psychiatrist. One look at him was enough for Anna Margolin to fall in love. They soon had a relationship, and though Hirsh Leyb Gordon was five years younger than she, they became man and wife. When America entered the First World War, Gordon joined the Jewish Legion and went with it to Israel. When the war ended, she began to hear various rumors about her husband. She did and did not take them seriously, but nonetheless she felt that something between them had been spoiled. The difference in their ages determined from the beginning that they would not be together more than a few years. Now there came signs of the beginning of the end.

In the fall of 1919, I came into her life. In the first few years there was great intensity and struggle between us. Many of the poems in my book *Fun mayn zumer*, which came out in Vienna in 1922, and a very great part of her book of poems, which came out in New York in 1929, describe in different ways that intensity and that struggle.

July, 1954

The Poet Anna Margolin

Anna Margolin: Lider (Poems) (New York, 1929)

Anna Margolin—like all true and mature poets—constantly judges herself. Sometimes she determines that she is correct, sometimes not. But there is always that deeper recognition that, one way or another, there is a higher court with its own last judgment that we cannot fathom, yet we imagine it with our entire being. From the interminable grief and joy that radiate from Anna Margolin's poetry, as from all true and mature poetry, there is the grief of consciousness and the joy of having arrived at that consciousness.

The immature poet distinguishes himself from average people only in that his instincts are more alert and his impressions sharper. The mature poet distinguishes himself from the immature by adding objectivity to his instincts—that is, that blessing or curse of being able to detach from oneself and examine oneself as a separate being. The expression of the immature poet is a scream; the expression of the mature poet is form. This constant shaping and reshaping of one's own emotions enables one to judge oneself.

In order to judge oneself and to be honest with oneself, one must weigh and measure one's sensibilities as well as one's deeds; one must cast away ready-made, conventional concepts, but always return to one's original feelings. And only he who weighs and measures his sensibility also achieves weight and measure when he expresses it: The exact word, the exact nuance, the concealment of things that must be concealed and the revealing of things that must be revealed, sometimes through one particular word and sometimes through that magical arrangement of word groups, line, and verses, that at times soothe us like music and at other times grab us with a different kind of magic and do not let go, and ring in our ears for days, weeks, and sometimes years.

Only a few other Yiddish writers can find the exact word and magical arrangement of word groups to the extent that Anna Margolin can. Her word, whether a simple statement or a description, or when it says one thing and wants to suggest something else, is in most cases so apt that one can in no way change it for another. I know very few poets whose poems and individual lines and stanzas resonate for me for as long as Anna Margolin's poems:

> The glance and the gesture, the whisper of love and dying things
> Der blik un der zhest un geflister fun libe un shtarbende zakhn
>
> Blossomed and ripened and practiced playing with life and death.
> Geblit un gerayft un ge-ibt zikh in shpil fun lebn un toyt.
>
> But their flesh is a weeping willow,
> Their fingers, like dried leaves, in their laps
>
> Ober dos layb iz a veynendike verbe,
> ober vi trukene bleter, di finger in shoys
>
> The night opened its golden eyes,
> I became the fiddle and you the bow.
>
> Di Nakht hot ge-efnt di goldene oygn
> bin ikh fidl gevorn un du der boygn.

Sad as rushes,
gentle as the names of flowers.

Troyerik vi tsheret
tsart vi di nemen fun blumen.

Or "Dos lid fun a meydl" (The song of a girl), which begins with these wonderful lines:

That hour, that rapture I will always remember,
like a song without words, like a poem by Verlaine.
I am so afraid, what if I stop yearning.

Yene sho, yene reyts, vel ikh eybik gedenkn,
vi on verter a lid, vi a lid fun Verlaine.
Ikh hob azoy moyre, tomer her ikh oyf benkn.

Only the purest poetic intuition and the finest artistic weight and measure can create such an unexpected yet natural, psychologically authentic, and uniquely magical passage as in the last example.

The Poet Anna Margolin, 2

We often speak of form and content, and most of those who speak of form cite examples that indicate that they are hardly authorities on the matter. Because the thing they call form is really no more than clichéd, irrelevant technical *form methods*, certainly not *form elements*. All of these things can be learned. And of course every poet has to master them, but as a wise Gentile once said, only in order to be able to throw them away. True form develops from content and is organically joined to content like a shell is organically joined to the kernel. The true artist can play with clichés and show that even with them one can still create something that is formally unique. But this is certainly not a requirement. In the end, the artist only wants unity in his work, and the unity is achieved in a work of art only when all the details have been abandoned for the sake of the artistic goal.

Anna Margolin achieved this unity in many of her poems, for example, in "Ikh bin amol geven a yingling" (I once was a boy), "Muter erd" (Mother earth), "Mayn shtam" (My ancestors), "Ful mit nakht un geveyn"

(Full of night and weeping), "Azoy vi mayn blik der fartroyerter" (Like my mournful glance), "Iz di goldene pave gefloygn" (The golden peacock has flown away), "In gasn" (In the streets), "Harbst" (Autumn), and such from the cycle *Mary* that were, with a spare means of expression, brought to such perfection that they are among the finest in Yiddish poetry.

We will cite as an example the poem "Muter erd," which is built on the well-known and, if you will, even banal idea that a woman does not live her own life, but rather lives through the life of the man she loves, and that the man is what he is thanks only to her. In the hands of Anna Margolin, this abstraction becomes flesh and blood and is transformed into a wonderful poem:

> Mother earth, well-trod, sun-washed
> dark slave and mistress
> am I, beloved.
> From me lowly and sad,
> you grow—a mighty trunk.
> And like the eternal stars, and like the flaming sun,
> I circle in long, blind silence
> your roots and your branches,
> and half awake and half drowsing,
> I search through you, the sky.

> Muter erd, fil getrotene, zun gevashene
> tunkele shklafn un harn
> bin ikh, gelibter.
> Fun mir der nideriker un batribter
> vakstu aroys—a mekhtiker shtam.
> Un vi di eybike shtern, un vi fun der zun der flam,
> krayz ikh in langn un blindn shvaygn,
> in dayne vortslen un dayne tsvaygn,
> un halb in vakh un halb in driml,
> zukh ikh durkh dir dem himl.

Tone, rhythm, and image, everything here is harmonious, as if one grew out of another, and all three together express in ten lines, so beautifully and profoundly, what woman in every generation has felt in her blood for man.

Or take this poem, "Ful mit nakht un geveyn" (Full of night and weeping):

A silence sudden and deep
between us,
like a bewildering letter
with a message of parting
like a sinking ship.

A silence without a glance, without a touch,
full of night and weeping
between us,
as if we, ourselves
had closed the door
to paradise.

A shvaygn plutsem un tif
tsvishn unz beydn,
vi a tsetumlter briv
mitn onzog fun sheydn,
vi a zinkende shif.

A shvaygn on a blik, on a rir,
ful mit nakht un geveyn
tsvishn unz beydn,
vi mir voltn aleyn tsu a ganeydn
farshlosn di tir.

What a wonderful and original simile, "like a bewildering letter," and how frighteningly cut short is the rhythm up to the finale, which is completed with an echo of resignation.

Resignation lends sublime simplicity to "Mary's tfile" (Mary's prayer):

Lord, meek and silent are the ways.
Through the fire of sin and tears
all paths lead to You.
I have built a nest of love for You
and of silence a temple.
I am Your guardian, servant and lover,
and Your face I have never seen.

And I lie at the edge of the world,
and You go darkly through me like the hour of death,
like a broad, flashing sword You go.

Got, hakhnoedik un shtum zaynen di vegn.
Durkh fayer fun zind un fun trern
firn tsu dir ale vegn.
Ikh hob fun libe geboyt Dir a nest
un fun shtilkeyt a templ.
Ikh bin Dayn hitern, dinst un gelibte,
un Dayn ponim hob ikh keynmol nit gezen.
Un ikh lig afn rand fun der velt,
un Du geyst finster durkh mir vi di sho fun toyt,
geyst vi a breyte blitsndike shverd.

And only a form artist could utilize the dancing meter, anapest, in a clean, elegiac poem like "Mary un der toyt" (Mary and death) and still have the poem benefit from it:

Mary went out of the bright house,
bowed before the walls, bowed and went out,
and went away in the night, like a stroll in the woods,
where God's breath is near and every shape frightens.
. . .
And behind her, happy and gaudy, went
beggar, drunk and vagabond.
Like sad, sick birds in love,
cripples limped behind her.
And lepers shyly approached,
and hid their wounds with their hands,
and at the front, yearning, went
Death, the boy with the dark flute.

S'hot Mary zikh gezegnt mitn likhtikn hoyz,
far di vent zikh geneygt, geneygt un aroys,
un avek in der nakht, vi men geyt in a vald,
vu Got's otem iz noent un s'shrekt yede geshtalt
. . .
Un gegangen nokh ir zaynen freylekh un bunt

betler un shiker un vagabond,
vi troyerike feygl kranke farlibt
hobn kalikes nokhgehipt,
un kretsike hobn farshemte genent,
un zikh di vunden farshtelt mit di hent,
un foroys iz gegangen farbenkterheyt
der yingele toyt mit der tunkeler fleyt.

But it's not only in entire poems that one can recognize the full-blooded poet and artist. One can touch the genuine poet even in single lines, turns of speech, metaphors, adjectives, and similes. And Anna Margolin amazes us with her similes, though she doesn't have a single one that is forced or facile, as is often the case with our poets. Similes for Anna Margolin bring the far near and with a leap carry away the nearest to infinity. And how different and original her similes are: "sad as rushes, gentle as the names of flowers"; "you go darkly through me like the hour of death"; "trample through me as if through a dark house"; "materialize from the silent, gray night like a mist from mist, like a night from the night"; "all this is far away . . . like an enchanted shore in a sunny mist"; "like the aroma of fresh bread in all the streets and houses, your good-morning"; "to the singing sea, the city / as if with a silken train, / descended a thousand marble steps."

The Poet Anna Margolin, 3

A woman emerges from Anna Margolin's poetry as someone for whom every experience is keen and profound. She is never indifferent. Everything becomes an elemental, shocking experience. And from it there issues a gamut of feelings: refined love and barbaric hate, deep humility and stubborn pride, admiration and scorn, explosive drama and serene resignation, heroic daring and almost childish fear. Fear has big eyes, as the saying goes. I don't know even one Yiddish poet who sees as many huge, weird things as Anna Margolin. The air, for her, is literally inhabited by nightmares, with "good" devils and "romantic" monsters. Utensils, walls, houses, streets, trees, clouds—everything for her is alive and everything takes on a strange, grotesque image to frighten her.

An immature poet with such keen experiences would be full of wild cries. The artist in Anna Margolin, though, does not tolerate the cry, but tones it down, hides it and uncovers it at the same time by means of an image. Sometimes she stumbles and indeed cries out, which is so unfitting. Like all poets, she often stumbles. Sometimes she lacks the appropriate rhythm and sometimes the rhyme is clumsy. Here and there, adjectives turn up with the *daytshmerish* ending "de" instead of "dike" (libnde, veynende, shtarbnde, and so on, instead of libndike, veynendike, etc.), and sometimes she wants to force everything into a poem, even things it doesn't want and can't accept.

But these are trifles, like withered twigs on a live tree. They are visible but insignificant. And in truth, what kind of significance does any flaw have for a poet that carries,

> . . . carefully
> your voices, smiles and grimaces,
> as one carries a song on one's lips,
> like a costly ring on a finger!

The Last Years of Anna Margolin

Der tog, July 27, 1952

In the last eight years of her life, Anna Margolin left her home only twelve or thirteen times. Five times the heat drove her out and, against her will, she had to spend the hot months in a summer colony in the company of other people. Three times she was taken from her home on a stretcher and an ambulance took her to the hospital. The third time she did not come back. I lost the dearest and most precious part of my life, and our literature, the greatest poet we had in either of our languages.

The tendency to cut herself off and separate herself from other people first began to appear not long after her book of poems was published. There were many different factors. One of them was certainly that her book, here in America, did not receive the notice she had expected and that she knew it should have had. Poets are by nature sensitive people. Anna Margolin was hypersensitive. Like a fine instrument, her intellectual and creative apparatus received a terrible shock from the least unfavorable vibration. Anna Margolin had a wonderfully clear and logical mind that could fathom the deepest thoughts and disentangle the most confused feelings, even her own. Her mind was admired by such intellectuals as Piotr Kropotkin, Dr. Khaym Zhitlovski, Dr. Nakhman Sirkin, I. L. Peretz, and C. N. Bialik. Zhitlovski insisted that she take philosophy courses. Kropotkin mentioned her several times in letters to Burtsev and Sh. Yanovski. All of the above mentioned, except Zhitlovski and Sirkin, knew her only by her maiden name, Roza Lebensboym. Only later did the poet Anna Margolin come into being. But however wonderful her mind was, it had no influence over her emotions. Like a lot of poets, she was very impulsive and could love deeply and hate even more deeply. Both her love and her hate wounded her terribly, and the slightest insult hurt her deeply and left eternal marks on her soul.

Outside New York her book caused a sensation. In Warsaw, Aaron Zeitlin and Melech Ravitsh wrote about her with the greatest astonishment, and Ber Horovitz gave a lecture about her and read from her book in the Literary Club. That, of course, made her very happy. No less happiness did she have from the reactions to her book that she received in letters from other poets. She received some tens of them. The greatest joy was given her by a short letter from Bialik that read:

Dear Anna Margolin,

Thank you for your book of poems. Who are you? It seems that until now I have not come across your name. Your poems are genuine. You are a true poet. I wolfed down your book as soon as it fell into my hands. Thank you very much.

Respectfully,

C. N. Bialik

If Anna Margolin, in her attached letter, had given her true name, Bialik wouldn't have had to ask, who are you? He knew her very well. When she and her first husband, Moyshe Stavski, stopped for a short time in Odessa on the way to Israel, Bialik was a frequent guest of theirs, showed great friendship, and respected her for her mind and for her great knowledge. But she did not want to give the name by which Bialik knew her for fear that their friendship would influence his opinion of her as a poet. That was, by the way, a fundamental feature of her character: she never wanted to pass for something she was not, just as strongly as she did want the fullest acknowledgment for what she was. Among her papers there were poems from other poets that she liked very much. For fear that someone would by mistake think they were *her* poems, she wrote on some of them the name of the author in large letters. She was, in general, a woman of truth. In that trait, she went to extremes. Because of that I used to jokingly (and quite often not jokingly) call her "Brand in a skirt"; like Ibsen's hero of that name, she often had deeply tragic experiences. And for her lack of acknowledgment here in New York especially among the local poets, she had in part to thank God for her great love of truth.

But as I said, this was only one of the various factors that led first to estrangement and then to complete withdrawal from people. Here it should be said that it was far from being the most important. In her last twenty years, she had several very strong experiences, most of which I had caused, directly and indirectly. The direct ones I am not strong enough to talk about. Indirectly, I broke her with my becoming sick and with a string of circumstances that my illness brought with it. The last blow she received eight years ago, when I had one heart attack after another—three in one summer—and had to be brought to the hospital. When I was taken the third time, she could no longer visit me. As soon as she went home, she herself would have to lie down in bed, and by then she could no longer recover. Because of the shocks she had from me that summer, and because of her own personal tragic experiences, she had a blood pressure of 250.

Always impulsive and always very temperamental, she was, with her terribly high blood pressure, constantly irritated and ready to flare up. She knew her condition and knew that her constant irritation must be hard on others. And consequently, she developed the tendency to cut herself off. In the end she arrived at the point where, physically, she simply could no longer have a stranger near her.

In the very last years of her life, when she had locked herself away so completely that even the building superintendent could not enter our apartment to fix something except when I was home, and only then after she had locked herself in her room, precisely in those years, many people literally knocked on the door wanting to meet her. Some of them loved her. A few of them she respected, and she herself was dying to meet them. But the thought that she would have to meet them face to face frightened her so much that she suppressed her own desire. She very much loved the poet Itzik Manger. Among her papers I found two of his poems that she, still in her thirties, had cut out of the *Literarishe bleter* (Literary pages). She did not begin to know that Manger also thought highly of her. When over a year ago she heard that Manger was coming here, she was very happy, but when Manger, directly on his arrival, came and rang our bell and said he wanted to meet Anna Margolin personally, she was overcome with fear. In a letter to him she wrote that she wanted to see him more than he wanted to see her, but that would never happen. And indeed, it unfortunately never did happen. I say "unfortunately" because Manger bought her much joy, and if they had met she would certainly have given him a lot of joy also, and God knows how much poets, who are orphans among us, need joy.

In the last years of her life, Anna Margolin literally did not have one good day. She had stopped writing poetry in 1932. Now it was even hard for her to write her weekly article for *Der tog* under the pseudonym "Clara Levine." She used to become enraged when someone praised her articles. But as if out of spite, her work was highly praised, and not for nothing. There was style in everything she wrote. Once she edited a fashion section for *Der tog*, and the section read like poetry. Despite the suffering she went through in her last years, her mind remained clear and sharp until the last minute, when she suddenly fell into a coma from which she never came out.

In her younger years, she did not have any interest in political matters. That changed with Hitler's coming to power. After that, her mind was alert to every political event, and she became so wonderfully astute politically that from one event she could predict all possible results. Tremendous joy and, perhaps, just as much suffering were created for her by the rise of the State of Israel. But above all, there was always her interest in poetry. She followed every new trend in poetry in Yiddish, English, Russian, and also French. She did not get a lot of enjoyment from the new poetry. In her opinion, poetry was going through a period of decline. Yet this did not stop her from swallowing every new book of poetry that I brought home and every individual poem that she came across in the better American magazines.

She had learned a little French in high school, which, afterward, she completely forgot. But at forty years of age, she began to study French again and learned enough to be able to read such favorites of hers as Baudelaire, Verlaine, and Rimbaud in the original. Some poems by the Spanish poet Garcia Lorca made such a great impression on her that she began studying Spanish when she was over fifty. But she did not get very far with Spanish. The less she liked the current poetry, the more she returned to the poetry of the past. And mainly to her French favorites. Twenty years earlier, through Lupus Bumenfeld, she had ordered all of Verlaine's work, and of course she immediately read everything that was worth reading. Just a few months before her death, she took two of Verlaine's volumes from the bookshelf, and they were among the last ones she kept on her bed table. The others were a book of poetry by Dylan Thomas, three books by Itzik Manger, and A. Sutskever's latest book of poetry, *In fayervogn*. Manger was her favorite for a long time. The true Sutskever she recognized only in his last book. In the cycle of poems from *Negev* and poems from *Sodom*, she found some that she considered great achievements in our poetry.

Her love for poetry was so great that a good poem was for her a personal experience, regardless of who had written it. She had never liked Zishe Landau's work, and she had enough reasons to hate him personally, to hate him tremendously. But about ten of his poems she liked very much. And her great hatred for him did not stop her from saying that they were some of the best poems in our literature. The woman in her, naturally, was interested in all our woman poets, and when she found something good among them, she became intensely enthusiastic. Several months before her death, she found in Leyeles's *Velt un vort* (World and word) a poem by Sophie Guberman in which she saw something truly new. That was the first time that she had come across the name, and she did not rest and did not let me rest until I found out who Sophie Guberman was. And when I found out that she was the wife of Wolf Yuni, she immediately called him at *Der tog* editorial office and asked him to tell his wife what a strong impression the poem had made on her. And just as a good poem could inspire her, a bad poem could make her sick. God knows how many bad poems have been written among us in recent years. For her personally, our post-Holocaust Yiddish poetry was one of the signs of the destruction of Yiddish.

> a simple woman from Lithuania
> a child of merchants and Talmudists,
> with a quick intelligence sharpened
> to understand by a hair
> the chess game of life
> and a heart ground and torn
> by heartless reality.

> a poshete froy fun Lite,
> a kind fun soykhrim un lerner,
> mit a seykhl sharf un farshnitst
> tsu banemen biz af a hor
> dos shakhshpil fun lebn,
> un a harts tsekritst un tserisn
> fun der harter vor.

I found these lines among Anna Margolin's papers on a page marked number two. Where the first page went, I don't know. Probably she tore it up. The paper and the handwriting show that the lines were from the time when she had just begun to write poetry. The contents show further that they were a crude first draft for the poem "Mayn shtam redt," which had in its time made a great impression, and rightly so. In these few lines there is also a painful path to self-awareness that she followed for the rest of her life. From that self-awareness there blossomed poems of great beauty and unusual depth that were a treasure in our poetry. The path to self-awareness, though, was also overgrown with thorns that scratched and wounded her body and her soul. It was my good fortune to be the person who helped her endure the suffering. It was not easy. Anna Margolin was, among all her virtues, blessed with a wonderful, musical voice. And it was painful, indeed, to hear how that wonderful voice changed as a result of her constant suffering, which often led to fits of weeping. For the fine, sensitive poet's nerves, even in her healthy years, were so tense and keen that even a landscape could wound her with its beauty.

> The hour plays now on silent flutes.
> Even tenderness can wound . . .
> Di sho shpilt itst af shtilste fleytn.
> Afile tsertlekhkeyt kon vey ton . . .

she wrote in one of her last poems. Even more strained and keen did her whole existence become under the physical suffering in her last years. That, too, was not easy. But how much would I not give to hear her voice, even her groans and wailing. Without her, life has become empty. Without her, I keep whispering to myself the last lines of the same poem:

> Oh, softly, softly
> Every touch can wound.
> O, shtiler, shtiler,
> yeder rir kon vey ton.

July, 1952

Addendum

Among Anna Margolin's papers I found some twenty complete poems and about twenty fragments of poems. Both the complete poems and the fragments were written between 1929 and 1934. Of the complete poems, she published five or six in the weekly *Yidish*, and another two appeared in other publications. Among the published ones were some true pearls. The unpublished ones should in fact not have been published. Anna Margolin was too self-critical to allow it. And what she did not want to appear while she was alive, naturally must not be published now that she is gone. A great number of the unpublished poems and almost all of the fragments revolve around one theme, which provides, perhaps, the key to the mystery of why, in the last years of her life, she withdrew from the world and locked herself within the walls of her home.

Early in our relationship, Anna Margolin had a kind of waking dream. One afternoon she was sitting by herself in a room with half-closed eyes, when she sensed that a woman was standing behind her, bending down behind her head, and that she whispered to her: "You will be ashamed!" Anna Margolin could never forget this waking dream, and she tried to embody it in most of the finished unpublished poems and in almost all the fragments. Tried by every means possible, but not one attempt succeeded. This shows that Anna Margolin, in the last years of her life, was possessed by a feeling of shame, and such a feeling is capable of isolating a person. How much I was at fault for that feeling of shame—that I do not have the moral strength to say.

Among the published poems that I found, there was an epitaph for herself that she wrote in 1932. The epitaph, which soon after her death was published in *Der tog*, reads:

> She with the cold marble breasts
> and with her thin bright hands,
> she squandered her life
> on garbage, on nothing.
>
> Perhaps she wanted it, perhaps coveted it
> to her misfortune, to seven knives of pain
> and spilled her life's holy wine
> on garbage, on nothing.
>
> Now she lies with a shattered face.
> Her ravaged spirit has abandoned its cage.
> Passer-by, have pity and be silent—
> say nothing.

> Zi mit di harte marmorne brist
> un mit di shmole likhtike hent,
> zi hot ir lebn farshvendt
> af mist, af gornisht.
>
> Zi hot es efsher gevolt, efsher geglust
> tsum umglik, tsu zibn mesers fun payn
> un fargosn dem lebn's heylike vayn
> af mist, af gornisht.
>
> Itst ligt zi mit a tsebrokhn gezikht.
> Der geshendter gayst hot farlost di shtayg.
> Farbaygeyer, hob rakhmones un shvayg—
> zog gornisht.

In the last two or three years of her life, she asked me to promise that if she died before me, I would have the epigraph engraved on her gravestone, but without the first two lines. Her will was done. A gravestone with the epitaph marks her grave in the New Carmel Cemetery of the Workman's Circle.

October 1954

 I. Kisin

IT DOES NOT SEEM SO LONG AGO that we started complaining that our ranks were thinning. And already half a generation is gone. The last to leave us was I. Kisin, poet, translator, and reviewer. As a journalist, he was associated with a newspaper for twenty-five years, yet he was unknown to the general public. And only among writers and a few readers is it known that, with his passing, a modest but honored place in our literature has become empty.

He never collected his works in book form. And this is clearly a shame. Because in the current, sad state of the Yiddish book market, and the costs of typesetting, printing, and binding, it is very doubtful that people will be found who will take upon themselves the task of looking through his writings and trouble themselves to ensure that his worthwhile things are collected. The expenses would not have been great. A small book of his collected poems, a large book of translations, and a book of essays would make his literary achievements available. He wouldn't, perhaps, stand out as a towering figure, but he would be remembered as a very original and interesting one.

He appeared in our literature before or around the First World War. From the beginning, he was close to Di Yunge, though he was too social a person to be able to set out on Di Yunge's asocial path, especially in the early years. For us, the others in the group, he was too much of a "Litvak" and too much of a *takhles mentsh*—in the spiritual sense, of course—for us to accept him as one of us. He worked with us on our journals and anthologies. He joined in our quarrels. He suffered, perhaps more than any of us, from the attacks that were made on us. But he could never join with us completely.

The most interesting thing about this Litvak and *takhles mentsh*, however, was that he was the most romantic among us and, with regard to Yiddish literature, a fantasist who went around hatching all sorts of quixotic plans. One of his greatest dreams, one that persisted year after year, was the project of a world poetry library in Yiddish. He often called me on the phone and told me we *must* meet because he had something very important to discuss with me. He needed to see me about various matters. But until the very last years before his wife became ill, there was seldom an occasion that he didn't also speak about his beloved plan. From the beginning, he worked it out in detail. He knew exactly which poets would have to be translated into Yiddish. But he never wanted to deal with the fact that we didn't have people who could translate the great poetic works of all languages into Yiddish. And second, even if we had the translators, we would never have had the means to publish the translated work, and in any case, very few people would be interested in reading it. If I'm not mistaken, he once tried to interest someone in the plan who had money and who also liked Yiddish literature. But it seems that the love this person had was not big enough for her to open her purse for him.

I. Kisin was one of the few people for whom reading a poem was a wonderful, personal experience. In exactly the same way, he could feel personally offended when he saw a bad poem published. He couldn't keep his feelings to himself, but had to share them with others. Of course, opinions, sooner or later, reach those about whom they are spoken. Good comments warm one a little and are forgotten. But bad comments wound forever and one cannot forget them, they hurt. Moreover, the one who is offended becomes, naturally, an enemy. But Kisin used to become so personally offended by a bad poem that it was not the writer of the bad poem that became his enemy, but rather Kisin who became the enemy of the offending poet. He could, generally speaking, love deeply and hate deeply. But to his credit, it should be said that he loved more than he hated and always looked for the more beautiful and finer side of a person. Once he liked someone, he could no longer see anything but the good in him.

There was a time when Kisin completely isolated himself from people. None of his friends saw him. Probably during that time he experienced something deep that will always remain hidden from us. Not long ago, in my desk drawer, I came across some tens or more of letters from him, written to me at different times. But none is from that time, when he had distanced himself from everyone. In the last years of his life, I rarely saw him. His wife's illness and death broke his heart, and as always when he was heartbroken, he was seldom seen with people except those he worked with. In the middle of February I met him by chance and we were both very glad. We agreed to meet the following Saturday evening in the cafeteria on East Broadway and chat a little. But apparently he forgot about it, or perhaps he felt too ill. Because only a few weeks after, I heard the sad news that he had been operated on and that the doctors had given up on him.

After that, I could only receive greetings from him, and the greetings were not good. The report of his death, therefore, was not a surprise to me. Nonetheless, it cut me like a wound in my heart. Kisin, too, is now gone!

"Here and there, it is already evening, my soul!"

July, 1950

❧ Herman Gold

I JUST, but really just, only four days ago, sat at my desk and read in a letter concerning a remark that was made about me: "Herman Gold smiled into his beard and drank another glass—'L'khaim! L'khaim tovim, arukhim v'l'sholem!' (To life! To a good, long life and to peace!) and we enjoyed ourselves immensely."

The letter was from my friend and colleague, Sh. Erdberg, with whom Herman Gold was often a guest and through whom he almost always sent cordial greetings to me.

When the letter arrived, Herman Gold was 1,500 miles from me in the north. I, almost at the farthest southern corner of the United States. Still, I felt he was literally like a living presence near me.

He stood so lifelike before me, in his threadbare but always clean jacket, and I could see that one of his eyes was squinting and the other laughing and that his red lips smiled and that his thick, heavy beard embraced his full, healthy, red face, tilted a little to one side, as if mocking me.

And I could even hear how he said, accompanied by his characteristic laughter, "Say, boyele, good, it's good for you there. As it is written: 'kapoys-tmrim' (date palms) and 'al sfas hayam' (on the seashore). Say peasant, are they real palms, all those brooms you see through your window?"

And here I sit, still at my desk, reading the newspaper the mailman just brought me, and before my eye can see correctly, I spring up—"Oy gevald! It can't be! Herman Gold? Brought to his eternal rest? That hunk that hung around with us? When? And how did this happen?"

Great surprise and deep wounds always arise from such an unexpected message. Even though we already know so well what we can

168

expect and even though we are, to our sorrow, so rich in this kind of sad experience.

With his writing, his attire, his way with people, his speech, his gestures, his actions, the sharp contrasts and contradictions of his character, Herman Gold was the opposite of the whole generation of writers with whom he had arrived. Yet he was also an integral part of it and, in a certain sense perhaps, the most visible expression of the generation, at least in the eyes of his milieu.

That generation of writers, with whom Herman Gold arrived, could blossom and grow only in the Jewish American soil and climate and the local surroundings. The local surroundings gave that generation so much, yet it felt foreign here. Perhaps because its roots, physical and spiritual, were somewhere else, and perhaps because the environment, for which this generation had so much to thank, was essentially foreign to it—to its ideas and aspirations, artistic, aesthetic, and ethical.

Such alienation must give rise to mutual hatred and contempt. Herman Gold was with his whole being the clearest expression of the contempt that the writers of his generation had for their surroundings. Often to such an extent that he became repugnant even to his colleagues. Indeed, perhaps because they saw themselves in him. Because Herman Gold was the crooked mirror in which his generation saw itself. Not the way it wanted to see itself, but the way it was seen in the eyes of its milieu: strange in its ways, impractical in its deeds, unintelligible and even senseless in its speech.

Consequently, there was both a closeness and a great distance between Herman Gold and his generation. And also, consequently, so many contradictory opinions among his generation about the person and the writer Herman Gold.

I personally don't know what kind of niche Herman Gold carved out for himself in the edifice of our literature. I do know, though, that with his departure the Yiddish literary landscape here has been robbed of the most visible, most colorful, most interesting character that came out of it.

Already on his first appearance—different from everyone else. Different face, attire, gestures, speech, and deeds. Sometimes a face like a caricature of a young moon. His pointed chin jutting out. His forehead jutting out. His mouth fallen and sunken in. Later on a thick, wild beard made his face fuller and rounder and the contours gentler. But his eyes were the same. Always half squinting and always laughing. The "funny man," my children used to call him when he showed up and gave out strange Chinese nuts that he had, like a juggler, pulled out of a deep pocket of his Charlie Chaplin pants.

Herman Gold always remained the "funny man." The funny man in him was by nature and culture, so to speak. Born and created. Consciously elaborated and cultivated. So his sudden appearance could awaken great joy in children, alarm among the philistines, and mixed feelings among his own friends.

Herman Gold was a complicated nature, full of contradictions and therefore a mystery to everyone. Wanton bohemian and practical businessman. Stingy with pennies and generous with fifties and even hundreds. Dressed in shabby clothes but punctiliously clean. He looked like a tramp and could, like a beggar with dirty fingers, eat off someone's plate, yet he was very careful with his body, which he diligently cared for with physical exercise and cold showers.

And as he was personally, so he was in his writing: a deranged, senseless phrasemonger. And one of the most original sentence builders. Here he drags out a long story without a beginning, without an end, without a middle, pointless and without reason. And here there falls from him a story of ten or twenty lines that is so good, so organically whole, so full of flavor, that you want to hold it, chew it, and remember it countless times like the taste of a wonderful fruit. And here, the rubbish of word heaps in which you drown as if in mud, and there, the clearest simplicity in which everything is delightfully transparent and pure.

I knew Herman Gold from the years 1907 to 1908, when he peddled radical booklets and brochures at meetings. I remember his beginning as a writer with a melodramatic story, "In hoyz vu men veynt un men lakht" (In the house where there is crying and laughter). I remember how he amazed me with an introduction that he read aloud to me of a messiah novel. A novel that he never wrote but that began with a beautiful description of a New York square where tables have been set up and preparations made to welcome the Messiah with a great banquet under the open sky. I remember the beautiful short stories that he once wrote that had the style and the flavor of the specifically Jewish story as we know it in all its transformations, from the Bible through Talmudic legends, from the medieval morality books to Hasidic stories. And I remember, also, how he began to occupy himself with twisted ways and only he knew where they would lead.

From the first years until his last days, Herman Gold was always the funny man, the oddball, the ridiculous one with the beard, the teller-offer and the told-off, the weaver of the weirdest, wildest word plays, and one never knew if he wanted to reveal something with them or hide something.

The impression was that all this was, in great measure, a mask, a disguise, a defensive means to keep one from coming too close to him and getting to know him. Few knew that Gold could also, at certain moments, be intimate and have heart-to-heart talks. The same few people also knew that Gold, the ridiculer of everything and everyone, had essentially great respect and love for those whom he had ostensibly derided. They also knew that Gold had a grandiose dream for Yiddish writers and literature in America.

In that dream was a plan for a writers' and artists' house, without the guardianship of party and community busybodies, a subsidized publishing house and a brotherhood among Yiddish and American writers that would lead to a partnership in a bilingual journal for the best things that were written in Yiddish and English.

Someone was even found who was so interested in the plan that he was ready to finance that dream, if a small group of Yiddish writers was formed that would take upon themselves the task of realizing it. To what extent that man actually existed and how much he was a fiction, a part of Gold's dream, is hard to say. Because however hard Gold tried, he never succeeded in putting together such a group. Almost everyone he turned to wanted before anything else to see the man who was ready to take upon himself such a heavy financial burden on behalf of Yiddish writers and Yiddish literature.

Now the funny man is no more, the writer is no more, the clown is no more, the comedian is no more, the dreamer is no more, and it has become much emptier and sadder in my soul.

May, 1953

🏵 A Home for Yiddish Writers

WHEN SOMEONE, at some future time, writes the history of Yiddish literature in America, he will again and again have to mention the name of Dr. Yekhiel Kling. And that is because he often appears in the memoirs of Yiddish writers. His apartment was always a gathering place for writers. And most of the poets, novelists, and essayists who made a name for themselves in the past forty years repeatedly found themselves there.

A group of writers felt so much at home in his apartment, warm and intimate, as if they were in their own homes. I, too, belonged to that group. And to this day, there rises in me a loving warmth when I remember those Saturday and Sunday evenings and the wonderful hours that I spent alone or with friends in his apartment. At other homes you decided beforehand to go there; at Dr. Kling's, you simply dropped in and were always welcome. Such a home pulls you in. And I don't know any other home that pulled one in like Dr. Kling's. It's no wonder it was, for so long, a home and a center for so many Yiddish writers, musicians, and painters.

It is close to forty years since I crossed the threshold of his apartment for the first time. It was around this time of year: before Sukes or on one of the intermediate days. The leaves on the trees were already changing color, but the days were still hot. I also spent such a hot afternoon with David Ignatoff in his room on Washington Avenue, which was the cradle, so to speak, of Di Yunge. There, the second *Literatur* anthology came to an end. There, the *Shriftn* anthologies were born. And there, for a long time every Sunday afternoon, almost everyone who was involved with that anthology came together. I have already, on other occasions, written about those Sunday afternoons and what they meant for everyone who came of age in that wonderful springtime of our Yiddish literature. The future historian will also have to speak of them, but the afternoon that I am going to talk about was not a Sunday at all, but a humble weekday.

Most of those who are today well-established writers were then beginners who lived from labor such as shop work. One wrote only in the hours that one was free from work, or that one stole from work. Only those who were still free could steal a lot. I was then already married and the father of two children. How I could have escaped from the shop in the middle of work that day, I don't remember. I also don't remember how Ignatoff and I spent that whole afternoon in his room. I can, however, not forget the half hour in the evening that we later spent on the hill in Claremont Park, which was not far from Ignatoff's room, and where, when we left the park at the exit, there loomed before us two purple ash trees with their fat gray trunks like the feet of elephants and their shiny, damp, thick leaves that changed their colors three times in one season and were then quite red. And more than anything, I cannot forget how Ignatoff led me out of the park onto Bathgate Avenue and 164 Street and practically dragged me to the home of Dr. Kling.

In my youth I was shy. In a strange apartment I don't feel entirely comfortable even now, when I am old. Then, I struggled when someone wanted me to meet strangers or to take me to a home where I had not been before. So Ignatoff practically had to drag me to Dr. Kling's that evening. But I felt so much at home when I got there, as if I was an old member of the household, even though Dr. Kling and his dear Bertha did not try to make me feel at home. And perhaps it was just because of that, because they didn't try. Because it was natural for them to welcome new people as if they were old acquaintances. I had then certainly not published more than twenty poems and some stories. And I don't know if Dr. Kling or his dear wife had heard of me. But the way they invited me to sit down, the way the doctor immediately began to chat with me as if he had known me for who knows how long, and the way I was invited to the table, not like a stranger who happened by chance to stop by, but like one who was expected—all this made me love these two people at my very first visit, and for years after I was a constant guest in their home.

It didn't take me long to discover that I was not the only one. All the writers of my generation whom I had met at meetings of the Literatur group in Goodman and Levine's restaurant, which was in a cellar where *Der tog's* mailroom is now, I found, from then on, at the Kling's. In the middle of the week—one or two. Saturday and Sunday evenings—in large groups. This was especially the case after the Klings had moved from the apartment house, in which the doctor had his office, to the private house across the way, where there were more rooms in which we could spread out.

It was an old, wooden private house, with several rooms below, two or three above, and one more in the attic with sloping walls, high under the roof. At one time, Zishe Landau and Moyshe Warshaw lived in that attic room. They were good friends and Bundists from the Old Country, and here one of them—Moyshe Warshaw—became a seeker of God. At that time, both were going hungry, both wrote, and both—partly under the influence of Kolye Teper—nourished themselves with Christian mysticism. For Landau it was only temporary and no more than play. But Warshaw, it seems, was searching for some kind of support that he could lean on. Searching, but not finding, and in the end, some time later, when he was living somewhere else, he took his own life.

I have already written about that. I mention it here, in passing, because for me it is impossible to imagine that home of the Klings and not see, floating before my eyes, the image of the physically weak and deeply ethical man, who was often to be found there and who at the age of twenty-something looked like a monk with one foot in the next world. Incidentally, Warshaw was a tremendous contrast to all the other people who were at that time habitués at the Klings.

Saturday or Sunday evenings, one could almost always find David Ignatoff, Joseph Opatoshu, Avrahm Moyshe Dilon, Moyshe Yoyne Khaimovitsh, Dr. Sh. Faks, and I. J. Schwartz, in addition to Peretz Hirshbein, who after his arrival in America lived not far away and spent no less time at the Klings' then he did in his own lodgings. Moyshe Leib Halpern, Alexander Zeldin, Yoyl Slonim, Joseph Rolnik, and B. Rivkin used to drop in from time to time, and Mani Leyb stopped by when he happened to be in the Bronx. Later, H. Leivick and others. And at one time, every Sunday, a young Christian American journalist, whose name I have forgotten, used to come.

With few exceptions, we were all young men in our twenties. And like all young men, hopeful and sure of ourselves, contemptuous, insolent, and provocative, which, though these traits are not always signs of self-assurance, clearly emphasized Warshaw's lack of self-assurance. That was, perhaps, one of the reasons why, precisely at a time when the room was full of guests, he would hide himself in his garret, and one seldom, on such an evening, could get him to come downstairs.

When writers get together, there is always a danger of conflict. But when writers get together, there can also be a mood of happiness and celebration. At the Klings', it was almost always happy and almost always celebratory. I am speaking about regular Saturday evenings and Sundays. Several times a year, though, there were special holidays when people came from all over the city. Every room was full and every face beamed. Those holidays were distinguished by the fact that they were never literary. No one ever read there for an audience. But there were little groups sitting in different corners and they read quietly for one another, or they had literary discussions that irritated and sometimes infuriated and led to quarrels with insults and sharp, cutting words. Berta Kling in those years had not written any of her own poetry, and since she always had a fine voice and liked singing, on those occasions she sang all kinds of songs for her guests and always ended with the wonderfully beautiful, spiritual, folk-style *Shir haMayles,*[1] and God only knows where she got it from.

From Bathgate Avenue, the Klings, years later, moved to East 180 Street, and only then did their home become a true gathering place. Others joined the group, and besides writers, one began also to see musicians and painters. But there in the apartment, where the Klings live to this very day, I was not such a frequent guest and neither were most members of the group. Partly because, in the meantime, Di Yunge had split into two warring camps, and partly because we no longer lived nearby in the Bronx but had scattered to different parts of the city. But several times a year, we still came together at the Klings'. And the apartment was still full of *yontev.* One saw a lot of new faces of older and younger colleagues, and in time

---

1. Songs of Ascents—Psalm 1.

even newer and younger ones. It was the same holiday, however, perhaps bigger, because the crowd had become bigger.

I don't know how it's been in recent years now that I don't go anywhere. But it wouldn't surprise me if I heard that at the Klings' there is still the same center and the same home for Yiddish writers and artists, and that everyone who comes now feels just as much at home, and warm and intimate there, as my friends and I did in former years. I know that at one time Dr. Kling was very interested in Yiddish schools and that he gave a lot of time to the school movement. That expanded even more the circle of his acquaintances, who were, perhaps, just like us in our time, much more than mere acquaintances. Dr. Kling, in my time, preferred to listen rather than speak. Nonetheless, it often happened that he used to sit with me in a corner and have a long discussion about various matters. The matters were mostly ordinary, but the conversations were always intimate. I always had the feeling that Dr. Kling spoke so intimately only with me, but perhaps I was not the only one who felt that way.

This, I think, is the key to why Dr. Kling was loved by so many people. He could always make the person with whom he was speaking feel that he was very close to him. He could sometimes make you feel this way with a mere glance or with a smile from a distance. Today, they still warm me, those glances and smiles.

Goodman and Levine's Restaurant

TODAY, IN THE BASEMENT OF *DER TOG*, you'll find the mailroom and the presses. And where today it smells of ink, lead, paper dust, and postal sacks, years earlier, before *Der tog* was born, it smelled of cooked fish and roast herring, sour borscht and fried pancakes, bad coffee and scorched milk, and still other odors that were so thoroughly mixed up, it was hard to distinguish one from another. The few steps that led to the cellar on East Broadway were in those years always alive from very early until late at night; today, they are used only during the hours when the newspaper is being distributed. There, in that cellar, was the dairy restaurant of Goodman and Levine, and there, all the young writers then in New York used to pour in. Not because they were in love with the food, God forbid, but because this was the center of Di Yunge. There, you could read or listen to a poem. There, you could always hear and learn something about poetry and stories, because discussions about literature never ceased. There, you could meet the few young writers whom talent or luck had lifted above all the others and who were already famous, while others were unknown. And there, one could also expect to hear—with a pounding heart—how things were going with one's own status as a poet or writer.

To the general public, our literary center was almost unknown. The general public—so far as it had shown any interest in Yiddish writers—knew that on Division Street there was a *kibitzarnia* previously known as Herrick's Café and after that as Sholem's, and that there, the older Yiddish writers whose names appeared in the newspapers would gather. The general public did not know that, besides them, there were other Yiddish writers, and even if it had known, it wouldn't have much cared. The existence of the *kibitzarnia* of the older writers was also known in the "provinces," and almost all of the habitués at Sholem's were considered very important people. When I, at the end of 1914, in Cleveland, mentioned the name of a certain writer and how I happened to have had a little debate with him about modern literature, they winked at each other behind my back: "The boy is bluffing." And if those people are still living and remember it still—perhaps to this very day—I remain an empty bluffer.

There were two reasons why Di Yunge went to a different café. One was purely financial. The *kibitzarnia* on Division Street was simply too expensive for the young writers, most of whom were then poor factory workers or had no work at all. To spend a few hours in Sholem's Café you had to have at least a quarter in your pocket, and a quarter, for the young writers, was quite a bit of change. In Goodman and Levine's restaurant, you could sit and talk for several hours for only ten or fifteen cents, and if you didn't have even ten cents—which was not at all unusual at that time—you could order a glass of coffee or tea with a roll or a cookie and sit for the same long hours for only five cents. The second reason was a snobbish one, if you will. The spokesman of Di Yunge simply considered it beneath him to spend time in the same café with the older writers.

There was quite a bit of childishness in that snobbish separatism. It was dictated, however, by a healthy instinct. Di Yunge had arrived with something new and original, and they felt that in order for the new to endure, they had to separate themselves from the old and entrenched. One must not have anything to do with the newspapers and magazines where the older writers pulled the strings, because there, one would have to make compromises and submit to the taste and will of the older writers. One mustn't have anything to do with the newspapers and newspapermen when one had in mind pure literature, and if one truly wanted to protect oneself, one must shun the café where the older writers set the tone. Writers must have a place where they can meet. Writers must also have a place where they can publish. To avoid having to go to the newspapers, we began to publish our own journals and anthologies. So as not to be under one roof with the older writers, we went to a separate café.

The separation was good for our writing. But it also led to comical situations and—not seldom—tragicomic ones. One incident, I remember especially clearly. It was in the first months of 1915, a short time before *Der tog* had moved from Pearl Street to the building on East Broadway, where it is to this day. The days of the *kibitzarnia* of Di Yunge were numbered. A few weeks later, Goodman and Levine's restaurant closed and we, Di Yunge, had to give up our own place and mix with the older writers, who had by then switched from Sholem's Café to Lamed Shapiro's restaurant, also on East Broadway, not far from Rutgers Street. In Shapiro's restaurant we immediately realized that the change was not a bad one. The food was better, the coffee was, of course, better, and at the new tables, we didn't feel out of place any more than we had at the old ones in Goodman and Levine's cellar. Here we also convinced ourselves that we no longer had to fear the harmful influence of the older writers because by then we had matured enough to be bad influences ourselves. We were also prominent enough that the older writers would no longer be able to dominate. Now it was we who dominated every place we entered. And in any case, we didn't leave the cellar before we had played the following trick:

One night, when about ten of us were sitting in Goodman's cellar, a disciple of one of our most famous poets barged in and announced: "Friends, come! At Shapiro's there's a banquet and you're invited to come. Everyone is invited."

No one had to tell us for whom the banquet was being held. Because the famous poet, in those years, had a habit of throwing himself frequent banquets. Publish a book—a banquet. Two books—of course a banquet. No books and no anniversary—he found another excuse. Today I understand that all the banquets were nothing more than an excuse for a little carousing, to drive away melancholy, or just because he wanted a drink with some friends. At the time, however, we were quarreling with him, and as always in a quarrel, one sees in one's opponent only bad intentions. We saw in these banquets the pursuit of honor and fame, so that night we decided, "Enough! We won't help him with his farce." And no matter how much his disciple insisted, no one from our table got up, and he left as he had arrived—alone. The famous poet was mortified. What? There is a banquet for him and they are sent for and they don't want to come?

In short, one delegation after another came to us in the cellar. And *everyone* was in the delegations—the greatest big shots of the time. But none of us got up from our table, and the delegations returned as they had come, without us. We were secretly a little ashamed of the whole thing. Our stubbornness began to seem to us foolish and haughty, but the more delegations that arrived, the more stubborn we became. Only one single person got up from the table. The rest of us did not move from our place, and for a long time afterward, we considered this simply heroic.

Only four or five tables in the cellar were "reserved" for writers. They stood in a corner, to the left of the entrance, between the buffet and the kitchen. Nothing good came to us from either side. From the buffet, we were often pierced by the hostile stares of one of the partners, especially when the restaurant was full and it didn't even occur to the freeloaders that sometimes it would be decent of them to vacate the tables for more genteel customers. And always from the kitchen there wafted fumes, bad odors of fried things, the clanging of utensils and the clatter of dishes being washed. Very often our eyes smarted from the smoke that drifted from the kitchen door and coiled under the low ceiling where it joined the smoke from countless cigarettes. In the summer it was terribly hot, and in winter your feet froze from the cold that came up from under the floor and from outside whenever anyone opened the door. The food was, as in most of the East Side restaurants at that time, barely edible and the coffee was simply terrible. The things you often heard about yourself as a writer could have curdled your mother's milk, yet the cellar pulled us in like a magnet.

I have already mentioned that most of the young writers were then shop workers. To miss a day of work often meant not having a pair of shoes for a child or lacking three dollars for rent. Yet when you entered the cellar, you found friends whom you knew should have been at work in the shop. Several of Di Yunge were house painters and paperhangers. It was not unusual for them, in the middle of work, to climb down from their ladders and come to the café in splattered work clothes that once were white, and with paint smeared on their face and hands. For a long time I ate lunch in the shop for fear that if I were to go and eat in a restaurant, I would not go back to work that day, because the café would pull me in and I wouldn't be able to resist the temptation. Once, I had the following experience:

One Saturday in summer, when I worked only half a day, I came home, ate lunch, and went to a barber for a shave. In the evening I was supposed to take my young wife and our six-month-old daughter to visit a relative somewhere. I lived on Fourth Street near Avenue B. The barbershop was somewhere on Houston Street. In the barber's chair I suddenly "smelled" the café, and I could hardly wait for the barber to finish shaving me. It even occurred to me that it would be better to go home first and say where I was going. But my feet were already pointed in the direction of East Broadway, and it would have been a shame to turn back. It was a hot day, and I was sure that in the café I would find few colleagues and, for that reason alone, I would perhaps stay no more than an hour or two.

It turned out, though, that the cellar was full. From the sea of faces in the clouds of smoke, there emerged the image of Mani Leyb with a finger wagging and pointing in front of his nose, and with tipsy green eyes squinting at the homely, strewn-with-freckles, but strong and impudent, perspiring face of Moyshe Leyb Halpern; Joseph Rolnik, with a thick mustache that cast a shadow of an intelligent smile on his usually wary and constantly sad face; Zishe Landau, as always (judiciously) bohemian, with an impudent look, saucy blond locks tousled over his handsome white forehead; I. J. Schwartz, with the most handsome head and graceful face in the whole gang; the eternally disheveled and eternally morose, stuffed-with-plans and almost exploding with energy David Ignatoff; the dark, bony, and bearded-up-to-the-eyes A. Raboy, with the eternal pipe in his hand and with a sparkling smile in his large, black eyes; Moyshe Yoyne Khaimovitch, who was in the middle of testifying, here with this one and there with that one, did he not say this and did he not say that, this many and that many years ago; Zuni Maud, always with some kind of trifle in his hands and a saying on his lips that made everyone laugh even though it was not at all funny; the small A. M. Fuks (or "Fuksl," as we used to call him endearingly), with the eyes of a decadent and the sharp nose of a bird that shudders like a young girl in love; and on and on, ten or twenty others.

I no longer remember what everyone was so excited about when I came in. I only know that I, too, was soon in the middle of it. And it boiled for an hour and then two and then three. From one theme, they leaped to a second, from a second to a third; soon they went back to the first and tried to affirm their opinions with citations from poetry and from what this or that authority said about the matter. And in the same way, others tried to affirm just the opposite, and for that also, they found convincing evidence from other authorities. Some of the writers left. Others came in. Still others left and again still others came in. We drank coffee and tea and ate pancakes, blintzes, cookies, and rolls, but mainly smoked cigarettes. Hour after hour flew by. Night fell and we didn't notice. Of the big crowd, half had already slipped away. But we who remained still sat there talking. Sweat was pouring down. Still we sat and talked. From the buffet, Goodman kept throwing contemptuous glances at us. But we didn't see him or his angry looks and we dragged out the discussion longer. Finally Goodman said, "Even in hell there is time to rest. Go in good health, already!" But it sounded like—"Go to the devil!"

It was then around two o'clock in the morning, and however many of us were left strolled out through little Seward Park to Delancey Street, and from there to Essex Street, to Avenue A, over to Thompson Square to Avenue B; from there on Tenth Street to the river, where someone knew about a wonderful place near a lumberyard where it was nice and cool. From there, back to Thompson Square Park and then to the numbered streets. The whole time, our mouths did not shut. We always found something to discuss.

Finally, however, the group became smaller and smaller, until there remained only two—Mani Leyb and me. I wasn't far from home. Mani Leyb, though, lived in Brooklyn, and he suddenly became very sad to be going home and asked me to accompany him at least until Delancey Street, where he would catch the streetcar that would take him home. But at Delancey Street, he decided to accompany *me* home, and then right in the middle we turned again on Delancey Street. All the literary discussions had by now run their course. Now we felt the haunting sadness of *Minkhe* time though it was almost dawn. And we spoke about the difficulties of daily life, about the sadness of our hard lives, and about the gnawing and longing that creep from the houses through the nights, and how everything, all the long and boring talk, was, in essence, just an escape, a desire to stifle that yearning and that longing. And at that, he told me in passing that whenever he came home very late at night, he didn't enter his apartment by the front door, but climbed up to the roof and from there, by the fire escape, descended to a window of his room and crawled in like a thief, so that his wife wouldn't hear. Once, in his confusion, he had opened his neighbor's window, and an Italian, who thought he was a thief, lunged at him with a stiletto.

By the time Mani Leyb finally boarded his streetcar, the sun had already risen on the Brooklyn side of the East River. Only now did it occur to me that this was the first time that I had been away from home the whole night and that I had not said before leaving the house that I might be late and that I was supposed to go with my wife to visit a relative. And my heart was aching when I approached Fourth Street. As I arrived at the house, the grocery store on the ground floor was already open, and the grocer, who was standing at the door, looked at me with great contempt and asked: "Young man, was that your wife who ran to the police to search for you?"

❧ Sixty Days with Abraham Liessin

IT WAS IN THE MIDDLE OF WINTER, soon after New Year's, 1938, when B. I. Bialostotski told me that the couple Malke Lee and Aaron Rappaport, both poets, had built a summer colony at the foot of a mountain in a beautiful area of Ulster County. They had built five cottages, and almost all of them were already rented. The biggest one, which was intended for two families and had a large porch in front, was rented by A. Liessin. The second, in the same row, was rented by Miriam Kahan, widow of the well-known folklorist I. L. Kahan. The third, by Bialistotski himself. The fourth, by a teacher in a New York public school. There remained only the last, or rather, the first, which Malke Lee and Aaron Rappaport had built for themselves. Later, though, they figured that until the colony started to pay they could stay in the big house that belonged to Rappaport's father, and the cottage they had built for themselves they could rent to someone else. If I wanted him to, he, Bialistotski, would speak with Malke—or "Archie," as he called Rappaport endearingly—and they would hold the cottage for me.

In my youth I was always wandering. But I married early and soon became the father of three children, and could not allow myself any long trips. So I stilled my wanderlust with Saturdays and Sundays that I snatched from time to time to go to Westchester County, northern New Jersey, and many places on Long Island. I made these short trips on the trolleys that used to circulate among the different cities and towns, on buses when they replaced the trolleys, and on local trains. Later, when friends and acquaintances began to own their own cars, some of them allowed me to coax them to take me with them to upstate New York. And in that way, over time, I got to know large parts of New York State

11. Abraham Liessin. Courtesy of the YIVO Institute for Jewish Research.

and to know almost all of its choice spots. But that particular spot, where the new summer colony was built, I happened not to know. Bialistotski, however, described the beauty of the area, which he had seen during the winter, so enthusiastically, that when I came home, I immediately discussed it with Anna Margolin, and within half an hour that evening I had rented the cottage.

That summer, the Bialistotskis and the Liessins went to the colony in mid-June, two weeks before the schools in New York closed and the crowds set out across the land. One day I received from Bialistotski a letter in which he told me they had had heavy rain lasting over three days and that the whole colony was so flooded that you couldn't leave the cottages. But when they woke on the fourth day, the rain had stopped. True, the sky was still overcast, with frightening, black, low-flying clouds. Liessin stood on the porch, and from his large cottage, with a hand shading his eyes, he looked and looked on all sides to see if the flood had really stopped. That image of Liessin standing in a sweater and a pair of broad white slacks, his eyes shaded like Noah of old on the deck of his ark, I could not forget that whole summer, though I never actually saw Liessin in such a pose.

Anna Margolin and I came out to the colony on the fifth or sixth of July. It was about five o'clock in the evening when the car that brought us turned off the main road onto a side road that farmers' wagons, over the years, had cut with their wheels. The car went through a small orchard of old apple trees, turned again to the left, and stopped in a long, broad, grassy clearing that was glistening with gold from the setting sun, in front of a small white cottage with green windows, a pointed roof, and a small, open porch in front of the door. Before Anna Margolin and I had placed our feet on the ground, I spied on the other side of the grassy place two cottages, similar to mine except that one of them was almost twice as big. A man was coming toward us, middle-sized, in broad, white slacks and a white shirt with short sleeves and an open throat. "Noah of the Ark!" I said quietly to myself in my heart, and walked toward the man. We met in the middle of the road and remained standing opposite each other. Liessin stood before me with a big, good-natured, and very friendly face. When he smiled, his nose became full of thin wrinkles. He stretched out to me his large, broad hand: "Sholem aleykhem!"

Liessin and Anna Margolin Quarrel

That same evening, Liessin, Anna Margolin, and I went strolling on the road that passed by the gate to the colony, and as usual among writers, we talked shop. About poetry, poets, the state of our literature, and again—as is usual among writers when they come together—also a little gossip. The second evening we again went out together the same way, and so it was on the third evening too. But the third evening, we didn't return to the colony all three together, because Liessin stormed off by himself, leaving Anna Margolin and me in the middle of the road. The reason was an argument between Liessin and Anna Margolin about the Russian poet Valery Bryusov. I don't remember what led to the argument. Though

I do remember how Liessin disparaged Bryusov and how Anna Margolin defended him. Both stubbornly maintained their opinions, and every minute the debate became sharper. Both were very subjective people, and not for long could the discussion stay on an appropriately objective level. Soon, spiteful words were said on both sides. They ended with a very angry remark from Liessin at the expense of Anna Margolin and with an angry remark from Anna Margolin at the expense of Liessin. From him: he had never considered her a poet, and he had published her in *Tsukunft* only out of pity. From her: that's what he said about every poet he ever published in *Tsukunft*, and she had a letter, from him, in which he praised her to the skies. And she gave his praise as much weight as his criticism because only the opinion of poets mattered to her and he had never been a poet. The poet Liessin meant nothing to her. I didn't interfere in the discussion because I didn't know any Russian and Bryusov was for me only a name I had heard from Anna Margolin and my closest friends, Mani Leyb and Zishe Landau. Perhaps one of them had tried once to translate one of his poems for me. Since I didn't interfere, my heart trembled as I watched the storm grow, feeling that any second there could be an explosion. That Anna Margolin could go so far as to say that the poet Liessin meant nothing to her—*that* I never expected. And it seems that Liessin was deeply offended by that remark, because he wheeled around as if he had been shot and strode quickly back to the colony.

That night, neither of them could sleep. Anna Margolin could not forgive herself because, in the heat of the argument, she had forgotten herself so far as to say that as a poet Liessin didn't exist for her. Especially since it wasn't true: she thought very highly of him even though he was not her kind of poet—in her estimate, he was old-fashioned in method and very often dated, as well as neither precise nor unique in expression. She had been punishing him for hurting her unjustly. Liessin for his part could not sleep because that night he had heard from Anna Margolin something that he had, until then, never heard from anyone. He had already become famous in his early years on the other side of the ocean, and here in America, from the very start, he had been pampered like a gifted only child, so that even Abe Kahan could not have any power over him. Later, as the editor of *Tsukunft*, he became a central figure and his house became a meeting place for writers and artists. Most of those who visited him in his house praised him to the skies. Others were servile and flattered him. Of course, there were many who, just like Anna Margolin, did not consider him their kind of poet and who behind his back even disparaged him as a poet. But no one dared say so to his face. Anna Margolin was the only one who had such nerve. In the morning, as soon as he got up, he telephoned several friends in New York and told them about her *khutspe*, and two or three days later it was being talked about in the literary *kibitzarnia*.

In the morning, when Anna Margolin got up, she said to me, "Reuben, right after breakfast I want you to go over to Liessin. With me, he will never speak again. Don't say he will. I know him better. You were never with him in his house. I was a frequent guest and I know that the slightest insult, he never forgets. And yesterday evening, I insulted him deeply. I'm sorry, very sorry. I would go and tell him myself. But I don't want there to be any ill feeling between the two of you. Because first, you have to be with him here for two whole months and it will be awkward for everyone if you are angry at each other. Second, I feel guilty because you know very well that I think highly of him as a poet even though he isn't *my* poet. And also, Liessin is the greatest scholar, the greatest erudite, the sharpest journalist, and simply the man with the greatest accomplishments, and I shouldn't have forgotten myself."

So right after breakfast, I went over to Liessin's. He was sitting outside on the porch when he saw that I was coming in his direction. His daughter, Rokhl, was sitting near him. Both looked at me severely when I drew near them. I was afraid that Liessin would get up when he saw me and go inside. But he didn't. I came to say good morning, and he answered "good morning," and we had a long talk about a lot of things, which could not have happened the evening before, with Anna Margolin. But he looked at me coldly and, from time to time, cast a suspicious glance at me. Nonetheless, we spoke for a long time. The whole two months we were at the colony, Liessin never again looked at the place where he had seen Anna Margolin and never came closer than a hundred feet of our cottage. However, this often caused him inconvenience and quite often he had to take the long way around in order to avoid our cottage. But I went to him almost every morning and, very often, even several times a day, spending hours with him on the porch. Often we met near a row of ash trees where Liessin liked to hang his hammock in the afternoon, and often one of us waited for the other in a hayfield behind the colony or on the road to the colony. Between the two of us, there wasn't even a moment of anger. On the contrary, that summer—which was, unfortunately, the last summer of his life—I became very close to him and he to me. Though I had known Liessin since 1905 or even earlier, I only truly knew him that summer of 1938. I never went to his house as a poet goes to his editor. I was in his house only once in my life, and at that, when he happened not to be home. I had gone there fortuitously, accompanying a woman who had to see Liessin's sister-in-law, Beyle. I really only got to know him in that summer colony. Met him and got to know him, and had for him great respect.

Liessin's Porch

As we sat on Liessin's porch, the luminous panorama of the Catskills lay before our eyes as they formed a half-circle, three chains, each behind the other and each higher than the other, in a northwest direction. Like all mountains and cloud formations, they took on different images at different times. Parts of the mountains always kept the same image. One, the bend from north to northeast, looked like a huge head with a nose, chin, eyes, and forehead turned toward heaven: Mussolini as if he were posing at a parade, but many times greater and more powerful, Bialistotski once remarked. And Mussolini remained the name of that mountain the whole summer. From afar, all the mountains were blue and the highest one was very often mistaken for clouds. Like everything that towers high, the awesome mountains dominated the landscape. Between the mountains and the colony ran a semicircular valley through which, in various directions, there twisted and snaked the Rondout Creek, one of the longest and most beautiful of the narrow streams between the Hudson and the Delaware. The valley met the mountains through small, round hills at the foot of the Catskills. On clear days, the play of light and shadow revealed and hid clusters of houses and entire villages on the backs and plateaus of those mountains as they shone white and red and various shades of green.

Liessin's cottage porch was almost always crowded with people. Those who were sitting there did not come to see the luminous landscape, but rather to see Liessin. There were, that summer, several writer and art-ist families in and around the colony. But the center of the colony was Liessin, and everyone was drawn to the center. And when we came and sat on the porch, we mainly sat with our backs to the surrounding beauty and with our faces to Liessin. We came to visit him from early morning on, but mostly the porch was occupied in the late afternoon and evening. His daughter Rokhl was almost always with him, and also his sister-in-law, Beyle. One could see that Liessin was very happy that he was the cen-ter and that everyone was drawn to him. He also felt good, it seemed, that he was sitting with those who were closest to him. And just as everyone's eyes were fastened on him, his eyes were fastened with great love on his daughter, and very often, in various clever ways, he tried to bring her into the conversation.

Rokhl was born with hydrocephaly, and the older she grew, the big-ger her head seemed and the more crippled and shrunken her body. She was a strange, helpless freak who had to be led by the hand because she couldn't walk by herself; she even needed help to sit down and get up. I was not even sure if she didn't also have to be fed like a child, because I never saw her when she was eating. That crippled little body suffered all kinds of pain. When she was in pain, her eyes clouded over. But hardly did she become free from the pain than her eyes became large and bright and showed more than average intelligence. Liessin saw that however much his guests tried not to look at this only daughter, they couldn't help it. The deformed and helpless repels even when it evokes pity, and attracts glances, like everything that is outside the norm. And so we saw that Lies-sin, with his wanting to bring his daughter into the conversations, wanted to show his visitors that they shouldn't look at the outside of the pitcher, but at what was inside of it. He knew that his crippled daughter had many intellectual virtues, such as a clear head and a wonderful memory, and that she was well versed in Yiddish and English literature.

A. Liessin, the most Jewish among all the writers and poets of his gen-eration and circle, had, of all people, a non-Jewish face, almost a Russian face. In any case, at first glance he appeared more like a Slav than a Jew: wide face and high cheekbones, peasant's nose and straight, unruly hair that fell over his forehead. The resemblance was even sharper in his broad

chin and his homely, slightly crooked mouth—its fleshy lower lip, in contrast to the upper, was thin and sharp and became even thinner when he
was angry or being ironic. This homely face, however, possessed a unique
charm and even a loveliness that drew you to it, though it often seemed
that this was the face of a man from whom you must protect yourself. His
face was especially attractive when a smile played on it and it became
softened by countless tiny wrinkles. One saw him often that summer with
such a smile, sitting on his porch. Especially when he noticed that the visitors who came to him were amazed when his daughter let fall a remark
that showed that though physically she was almost a child, intellectually
she was grown up. One could also see such a smile when he contemptuously destroyed an argument with which he didn't agree.

But not always. Because with him, contempt often led to irony. And
then his expression was very different. Contempt for someone's opinion
always comes from confidence in one's own opinion. This, however, is not
always the case with irony. Very often, irony is no more than a diversion, a
blockade. One is ironic about the opinion of others exactly when one is not
entirely sure of oneself. Irony, as a diversion, is a psychological assault. It
irritates and provokes, becoming sharper at another's expense. The smile
that appeared then on his face was no longer the good-humored smile that
one sees on a man who is amused by someone's weak thinking. On the
contrary—it is angry and bitter. And Liessin could be angry and bitter.
But to his credit, it should be said that after the conflict with Anna Margolin, during the whole sixty days that I spent with him that summer in the
colony, I seldom saw him that way. I often saw him sad and often in deep
sorrow. But angry and bitter—very seldom. I saw him become sad very
often over a trifle about which someone else would have paid no attention.
All poets are sensitive and therefore moody, but Liessin was hypersensitive. If it seemed to him that someone thought his latest poem was not one
of the best he had ever written, that could upset him for several days.

And very often, a lot less than that could sadden him. I once saw Liessin walking in the hayfield behind my cottage in the direction of the apple
orchard where I was sitting in the shade of a tree reading a book. Suddenly he changed directions as if he had changed his mind and made a
long arc over the same field and approached the row of ash trees behind

Bialistotski's cottage, where his hammock was hanging. But before he got there, he changed direction again and again came toward me, again changed his mind and again made the same arc in the direction of his hammock. I surmised that Liessin wanted to speak to me about something. Therefore, he came toward me. But he was afraid that perhaps he might also meet Anna Margolin, so he cut short his route in the middle and turned back. So I got up from my place and walked over to him. I met him sitting in his hammock with a gloomy face.

"What's the matter, Liessin?" I asked.

"Nothing," he answered. But his face showed that something was troubling him. For a while we both stood quietly. But soon he said to me with a sad voice: "Malke came to see me not long ago and made me very depressed." Malke Lee was called by everyone in the colony by her first name.

"How could Malke make you depressed?" I asked.

"She told me," he said, "that the Order (meaning the International Workers Order[1]) is publishing a book of her poetry in four thousand copies and they will all sell. My set gets published in no more than fifteen hundred copies and I am sure they will all remain lying in the cellar." By his "set" he meant his collected poems in three volumes, which at that time had already been printed and a lot of them were already sewn and had only to be bound in covers. That his set was published in only fifteen hundred copies, while Malke Lee's book would have four thousand, was enough for a deep melancholy to fall upon him, never mind that Malke Lee was certain that the entire edition of her book would sell out to the very last copy, while he was certain (a certainty that, unfortunately, turned out to be almost entirely true) that his three books would remain lying in the cellar. But since I never get excited when I hear that a book of poetry is selling well, because I know that no matter how many copies are sold, it will be read by very few people, I asked him: "What is the difference between one cellar and four thousand cellars?" Liessin looked at

---

1. The IWO, founded in 1930, a fraternal organization affiliated with the Communist Party.

me a while as if he did not understand what I was asking him. Suddenly, though, his eyes sparkled and his face lit up with a smile.

Liessin the Talmudist

When you see a person day in and day out for a long time, it's hard to have respect for him. You see him in his everyday activities and so you see his weaknesses. Someone's weaknesses obscure the virtues that make you respect him. I saw Liessin sixty days in a row, and most days more than once and in different situations in which his weaknesses were quite apparent. Yet it did not diminish my respect for him. On the contrary— with every day it became greater. And as with me, so with all his visitors who came that summer to sit on his porch. That is, according to Carlyle, one of the clearest signs of a great man. I don't know how great Liessin was as a poet. I personally cannot know because he was not *my* poet, as he was not the poet of my entire generation of poets. Liessin the poet had weaknesses that were considered by us to be fatal sins, so to speak. Exactly as we had our own weaknesses that were later considered by the Introspectivist poets to be even greater sins.

Artistic weaknesses are the first things that a group of artists notice in another group, so they are not able to see the good and positive sides of the other. In my eyes, the weakest side of Liessin was his not being selective enough in his choice of words, the lack of feeling for austerity and suggestiveness, the overblown rhythms that were too driving, his great attention to the theme of the entire poem at the expense of the workmanship of the individual lines, but mainly, the outmoded poetic idiom. These weaknesses never allowed me to see the overall poetic image of Liessin.

Nonetheless, I always knew that Liessin was an authentic and seminal poet. Just as authentic and seminal, and perhaps even more so, than the others of his generation who left behind greater reputations than he. Since that summer, when I got to know Liessin the whole man, I knew that he had a great deal of Jewish and secular knowledge, a phenomenal memory, a keen mind, and a big heart that understood and responded deeply to the difficult fate of his people and to the great hopes of humanity for a better and more just world order.

But the fate of the Jews mattered more to him than the fate of humanity. That summer in Eretz Israel, there were Arab attacks on Jews and pitched battles between the Arab attackers and the Jewish defense groups. And that summer Hitler threatened Czechoslovakia and English diplomats were sent to Prague, ostensibly to find out if Hitler's complaints about the Sudetenland had some basis, but really to pressure the Czech government to give in to Hitler's demands and give up the Sudetenland to Germany. The newspapers, then, were full of news about both places. Liessin and I both subscribed to the *New York Times*. Every morning, the people in the colony went to the gate and waited for the mail that always came exactly at the appointed time. When I got the *Times*, I read, first of all, the news about Czechoslovakia. When Liessin got the *Times*, he read, first of all, the news about Israel. Liessin noticed that I went right to the news about Czechoslovakia, and apparently it annoyed him. Several mornings he said nothing. Once, though, he could no longer hold himself back, and he said to me, "You're no Jew, Iceland. Does it matter nothing to you what is happening in Israel?"

I assured him that it concerned me a great deal. Of course! I went first to read the news about Czechoslovakia because England's behavior there showed how she would behave toward us in Israel and how she was already behaving there. But Liessin shook his head. My answer did not satisfy him.

Most of those who visited Liessin looked up to him with great respect and hung on his every word even though he was not a good speaker and even though he spoke almost exclusively about himself and, like all of us when we talk about ourselves, there was in what he said more than a little bragging. When now I try to explain to myself why everyone was so keen to hear what Liessin said, I think it was because he was speaking about intellectual developments, and because of that his listeners saw a man who had had to struggle with himself in his transition from a deeply religious, rooted, traditional Jewish life, to a free secularism; from Talmudic brilliance, to great universal knowledge; from a narrow rabbinic and Talmudic background, to becoming an ardent Socialist fighter for the masses and for a new, better, and more beautiful world.

What was most interesting, however, was that with all the metamorphoses that he went through in his spiritual development, he never could forget his Talmudic and rabbinic background. His lineage stretched from generations and generations of rabbis, back to the seventeenth and sixteenth centuries, and he was very proud of it. Because of that, a rather comical scene took place. Menasha Unger was among the writers who were in the area that summer. He spent several weeks about a mile and a half from the colony. Like all the other writers and artists there, he also visited Liessin. One day, in conversation, the subject of ancestry arose. And it turned out that Liessin and Unger both descended from the same rabbis and prominent men who lived and were active in various Jewish communities in Germany, Bohemia, and Poland several hundred years ago.

Liessin, for a while, was beside himself. In no way did he want to believe that he, the grandson and great-grandson of great Lithuanian rabbis and *Misnagdim*, would have the same pedigree as Unger, the son, grandson, and great-grandson of Hasidic rabbis in Galicia. It was as if Liessin had been robbed, and he kept saying, "It can't be!"

Liessin, true to the strict *Misnagdish*, scholarly, and rabbinic atmosphere in which he grew up, did not like Hasidism. He also couldn't understand Hasidism as it was supposed to be. One can see it best when one tries to compare his poem "Der bahelfer" (The assistant), in which he glorified the father of Hasidism, the Baal Shem Tov,[2] with his poem "Frantsisk fun Asisi" (Francis of Assisi). In the latter, he relates only what can be found in books about the great Catholic mystic, and he writes in such an economical way that you get only a tiny scrap of the stories that are told about him. Yet you feel that Liessin had great respect for him. In the former, on the contrary, the poet doesn't scrimp on the creation and shows us the wonderful assistant as he goes out on a summer morning and gathers together Jewish children. But instead of taking them to *kheyder*, he takes them to the woods. And the forest looms with its huge gold-tipped, red-trunked pines. And one feels a loneliness, "full of mournfulness." But the

2. Rabbi Israel ben Eliezer (1698–1790), the founder of Hasidism.

Jewish children are not afraid, because they sense that "with every step they, like Enoch, are walking with God."[3] And they don't see fear in the thick forest, but only "God's mercy and God's grace." The assistant sings and the children sing and there is "singing through seven heavens high, a synagogue with *tsadikim* wrapped in *taleysim*." And with them, the whole forest sings and "the great 'Perek *Shire*'[4] resounds" from all the animals, all the fowl, all the worms, all the rocks, and all the plants. But the wizard and his master Ashmodai stand in sorrow. Because they "see the assistant as he goes, and a new, wonderful joy in the people of Israel goes with him, and the cosmos sings with his voice. Both stand back and roar, 'The Baal Shem Tov has come! The Baal Shem Tov has come!'"

Yet one feels precisely in the suffocation and exaggeration that the poet is cold to the Baal Shem Tov and is cold to the whole subject and that "Der bahelfer" was, for him, no more than a good theme that he botched and that he had to botch because, in essence, the Baal Shem Tov, for Liessin, could not be more than a theme.

In conversations I had with him, I told him that when I heard him speaking and when I heard his poetry, I knew why the Vilner Gaon[5] took such a hostile position against Hasidism. Because he was, in the end, a child of the Lithuanian, scholarly doctrine that didn't accept insight without erudition and for which insight was, in essence, no more than erudition. Genius, according to this doctrine, consists mainly of extraordinary memory. And one can remember only what has already been written and accepted. And so one looks with suspicion on everything that is new and that was not written earlier. When one approaches a subject, one must know it thoroughly from A to Z. And if one writes about a subject, one must include everything that one knows about it and how it was interpreted before. One can and may interpret a subject differently. For a

3. "And Enoch walked with God . . ." (Genesis 5:24).

4. Literally, "Chapter of Song." It is an ancient Hebrew text of unknown authorship. It lists eighty-four natural elements, attaching a verse from the Bible, Talmud, or Zohar to each in order to show that everything in the natural world has something to teach us.

5. Rabbi Elijah ben Shlomo Zalman (1720–1797), one of the greatest Talmudists and the foremost leader of non-Hasidic Jewry in Europe.

scholar of that school of thought, that is laudable, for the poet—a duty. Because otherwise, how can the poet innovate? But to come up with something absolutely new—that the doctrine cannot abide.

To be satisfied with a spark and depend on it to illuminate the heart and mind, and through that sense the whole fire, that, of course, one must not do. Hasidism was satisfied with sparks and used them to try to illuminate the path of the chosen individual, the saint who strives to achieve high levels of spirituality and the masses that cleave to him and live in the illumination of his brilliance.

The modern poet is often satisfied with a spark, with a hint or suggestion. But Liessin couldn't do this. It was alien to his nature. For each subject that Liessin treated in his poem, he cited every detail he knew. Sometimes the details were simply cited briefly and sometimes he elaborated on all or some of them. To grasp one trait of a person and, through it, give an inkling of his whole character—that he couldn't do in his poetry.

Also alien to him was the mood of a moment that can sometimes illuminate the course of an entire life. When one reads Hasidic books, one notices how close Hasidism was, in such things, to modern poetry.

Rokhl

From Liessin's cottage to the colony's gate there ran a wooden walkway. Aaron Rappaport had it built at Liessin's request for Rokhl's sake. As I noted, she could not walk on her own. And so someone had to go with her. And one could not walk with her on the grass because her crippled feet could not make even one step in the grass, even with help.

On this walkway, which was two hundred feet long, Liessin took his daughter strolling twice a day. Part of the time it wasn't he, but his sister-in-law, Beyle, who went with her. The doctors said that Rokhl needed to have exercise. But leading Rokhl was not at all an easy thing to do. In fact, one could not lead her, one had to drag her. Liessin, or Beyle, would take her by the arm, and short as she was, she would hang onto the arm like a dead weight. After such a stroll, Liessin was often completely covered with sweat. Once, Rokhl fell during a walk and pulled her father down with her. Liessin, by then, had a weak heart, and getting up from the fall and then lifting up Rokhl was too much for him. He had to immediately lie down in bed and remained there for several days.

Beyle at one time must have been very pretty. How old she was that summer in the colony, I don't know. How old she was when her sister died of tuberculosis and left behind the poor orphan, I don't know either. But I do know that the one and only time I was in Liessin's house, two or three years after her sister's death, the cripple was already on her hands and she also had to tend to her brother-in-law and the house work. When, in the company of a lady, I entered Liessin's house, Beyle was wearing a wide apron and her head was wrapped in a scarf, because she happened to be busy cleaning house. She probably was not happy to be seen this way by a strange man. And I was not happy to be in the house when she was dressed that way. The result was that we avoided each other's glances, so that in the short time I spent there, I wasn't able to form even an idea of what she looked like. Some thirty years later, the poor orphan still was on her hands and she still was taking care of her brother-in-law and the housework.

These two burdens and the burden of years, naturally, took their toll. But traces of the old beauty were still on her face. Her figure was straight, and her gait was light, not at all in keeping with her years. If a stranger saw her sitting on the porch with Liessin and Rokhl, he would never have known that the man she was sitting next to was only her brother-in-law, because her manner was comfortable and intimate.

But there were also days when Beyle sat on the porch sad and depressed. On such days, one could hear among the women in the colony remarks that showed that they blamed Liessin. To say openly what was bothering them, that they could not do. It was, after all, Liessin, and they all had great respect for him. But sometimes they couldn't help whispering to one another. With a word here and a word there, one could deduce that the women were angry that Liessin didn't marry his sister-in-law after his wife died.

Why he did not marry Beyle, no one knew. Some tried to guess, and two opinions were expressed. One was the refusal was not on his part, but on hers. Beyle, the daughter of the Smargoner Rabbi, remained her whole life, except for her revolutionary past, a rabbi's daughter, with the ethical precepts of a rabbi's daughter in addition to her own, emphatic moral code. She could not marry Liessin after her sister's death any more than she could have taken him from her while she was alive.

"Bullshit," said a woman when she heard the opinion.

"Bullshit!" said the same woman when she heard the other opinion, that the memory of Liessin's wife was so holy for him that he did not want too marry anyone else.

So the mystery remained.

In the several days that Liessin lay in bed, Beyle, naturally, had to take Rokhl for walks on the walkway both morning and afternoon, and since the yoke of the housework also lay on her shoulders, and besides taking care of Rokhl she also had to take care of Liessin, she looked very tired, and with the fatigue there was also an expression of terrible depression. One evening, she was sitting on the porch, resting by herself. Liessin and Rokhl remained inside. Suddenly, her straight figure bent forward as if she was deep in thought, and she began to slowly rock from side to side. My impression was that everything in her had suddenly screamed, "What have I wasted my life on?"

When I told Anna Margolin about it, she became angry with me. "And what have we all wasted our lives on?" she asked.

After those several days, Liessin was not the same. From then on, he was not seen as often on the porch, and when one did see him, he seldom smiled. Rokhl, apparently, felt that her fall that had dragged her father down had hurt him. And she became sick over it.

But her distress also hurt him. It came to the point that Liessin complained about it, which was not in his nature. Apparently he had to get it off his chest and it didn't matter with whom he did it. One morning, when we were standing in the road in front of the gate to the colony, after getting the mail, Liessin told me that Rokhl couldn't sleep the night before. So great was her physical suffering that she threatened to do something to herself, kill herself, and he, her father, thought with pain: "You are so depressed that you cannot even do that." Hardly had Liessin said that when he became frightened by his own words and waved his hand as if to say: "The things a person can say!" He turned from me and quickly returned to his cottage.

Not until the middle of August was Liessin finally a little more like his old self. That was after his secretary, Krepliak, called him from New York and told him that the new issue of *Tsukunft* couldn't be finished without Liessin's editorial and without Liessin's poem, and Liessin did not sit down to write either until the last minute. It was very hard for him to sit down and write. But once he sat down, he did not stand up again until he had the editorial or the poem finished—often, both at once. Mostly, this was at night.

One of Liessin's greatest weaknesses was reading poems to others. Whatever was being talked about, he would remember that he had at one time written a poem, or even a whole series of poems, about that very topic, and soon he would begin to recite from memory the poem or poems. At that time, he already had all three books of his collected poems bound, but still without covers, and at the least opportunity he would stop, on the road or in the field, any of the writers who were in the vicinity of the colony and read for them entire series of poems from his books. These were poems that were already published. I don't remember, though, if he would read an unpublished poem that he had just written to strangers in the colony. Hardly had he written a poem than he immediately read it to his sister-in-law and his daughter. They, of course, liked everything he wrote. But like all poets, he immediately sensed whether they truly liked it.

The poem he wrote for that issue of *Tsukunft* was, apparently, very much liked by both Beyle and Rokhl, because the next day, Liessin went around the whole day with a happy smile on his face, like a child. For several days, he felt very good. And as always when he felt good, he liked to brag about his physical strength and would demonstrate it with a handshake that could make you see your great-grandmother, so strong was his grip. But that strong grip fooled him. Because Liessin was already, then, a very sick man.

Soon afterward, he suddenly became very uneasy. What was the matter? He had heard all kinds of rumors about *Tsukunft*. He had known for a long time that in the Forward Association, which published *Tsukunft*, there was a large faction that wanted to discontinue the journal in which they had invested thousands of dollars for years. Among those who wanted to give up on *Tsukunft* was Abe Kahan, the editor of *Forverts*, whom Liessin considered a personal enemy. B. Vladek, then the business manager of *Forverts* and a very close friend and admirer of Liessin, would not allow *Tsukunft* to be abandoned. In those days, Liessin heard a rumor that the Forward Association had decided to severely cut the budget of *Tsukunft*, and a second rumor—that Vladek's position notwithstanding, the association had decided to shut down the journal immediately. Both rumors turned out to be false. Neither of the decisions was accepted by the Association. Liessin, however, deduced from the rumors that had reached him that the faction that wanted to close the journal was becoming stronger, and Vladek's side was becoming weaker. That made him nervous and depressed. Everyone knows that stress is like poison to someone with a bad heart.

Liessin now began to complain bitterly about his heart. Those days were the most beautiful in the colony. At dawn and early morning, heavy mists hung over it. But the days were brilliant. The first red leaves on the sumac bushes and ivy plants emphasized the verdant green interspersed with white over the whole semicircular valley, above which the Catskills towered higher and bluer than ever. There were also unusual sunsets in the evenings. But the days became shorter and shorter and the nights, longer. And as the nights became longer, so did Liessin's sleeplessness, despite heavy doses of sleeping pills. Because of the sleeping pills, he went around for half the day like a drunkard. With each day that passed, he became more uneasy and began to count the days he had left to stay in the colony. And in fact, he was among the first to leave.

That was in the first days of September. About two weeks later, he telephoned me at *Der tog* that he wanted to see me. When? Right now, if that wouldn't be a burden. He was in the *Tsukunft* editorial office and would wait for me downstairs on the steps to the entrance of the *Forverts* building. A few minutes later I was at his side. Why did he need to see me? Over a trifle. In the middle of the summer I had told him I lived in Knickerbocker village, where I had a penthouse apartment with a large terrace. He, too, wanted to rent such an apartment if he could get a suitable one. Rokhl was becoming sicker and more nervous. With every day, it was becoming more difficult for him and Beyle to take Rokhl for her walks. If he could rent such an apartment with a terrace like the one I had told him about, it would solve two problems at once. First, they wouldn't have to drag Rokhl downstairs to the street because they could walk with her on the terrace, and second, he would be closer to the *Tsukunft* office and to the *Forverts* building. The enemies of *Tsukunft* were increasing and he felt that if he were close and if he were seen more often, those enemies wouldn't be able to do what they wanted.

I told him that the best thing would be for him to go with me several blocks to 10 Monroe Street, go to the management office, and see if they had an empty penthouse apartment to rent. When could this be done? For my part, right away. And we immediately went to the office, and found out that there was a penthouse apartment to rent and that it could be seen immediately. We went to look at the apartment, but as it turned out, it was not for Liessin. It was too small, and the terrace was very narrow. They wouldn't be able to walk it with Rokhl.

I never saw him again. About five weeks later, B. Vladek had a heart attack and died. Liessin wrote a beautiful poem about Vladek's death, and after his friend's funeral he himself had a heart attack. On the morning of the fifth of November, he too was gone.

Rokhl remained entirely on Beyle's hands. Ten years later, when Beyle was old and broken, Rokhl was still on her hands. Beyle had to dress her and had to drag her from place to place. How Beyle managed it, only those in whom she confided knew—that is, if she confided in anyone. She had taken upon herself a yoke, her own flesh and blood, and with love and patience she wore that yoke faithfully and patiently for many years. But that year I happened to be living for six months in the same house with a woman who had on her hands exactly such a burden as Beyle. She was a wonderful old woman—the goodness and patience alone! And her burden, too, was her own flesh and blood: a wonderfully beautiful daughter, about thirty years old, who had been run over by a truck when she was eighteen. It had paralyzed her body. Both her feet and one hand were entirely crippled. The other hand, though it was not paralyzed, was now limp. Her speech was also paralyzed so that one could hardly understand what she wanted to say. Even so, she wanted to take part in conversations because she was very intelligent and had her own opinion about things. She, too, had to be dragged around because she couldn't walk by herself.

And she had the face of a beautiful young woman, and also, no doubt, the desires of a young woman. The desires of a young woman were also noticeable in Rokhl in that summer colony, especially when a man came to her father dressed for the summer in shorts. There were also outbreaks of hysteria, and who knows if they were not caused by her desires?

But there were days when her wonderful mother could not stand the burden that fate had laid upon her. There were days when she wanted to escape her fate, even for a half hour—run away. She once confided in me: "There are days when I can't go on; there are days when I feel that there has to be an end to this; there are days when I want to run and scream like a wild animal. On such days, I bite my lips and beg: 'Merciful god, strengthen me so I don't lose my patience and do something foolish.'"

Did Beyle, too, have such days? Who knows?

One day there appeared a short notice in the New York English newspapers: "An elderly woman, Beyle Toyzner, fell or threw herself from the window of her apartment, and she died on the spot." The Yiddish newspapers revealed a little more about it, but not much. In the Yiddish newspapers, it was told that Beyle Toyzner, the sister-in-law of the beloved poet and journalist A. Liessin, was in the habit of feeding the birds every morning right after getting up. When, a day earlier, she went to the window, opened it, and wanted to give the birds food, she lost her footing and fell out. When neighbors heard the sound and ran to see what happened, they found her dead.

That, in short, was the announcement in the Yiddish newspapers. But those who lived in the same house with her and who knew her, knew the truth: that Beyle Toyzner, the sister-in-law of A. Liessin, did not fall out the window, she threw herself out.

Rokhl, who outlived both her mother and her aunt, was taken to a home for the incurably ill, and this past winter she too was gathered to her people.

The only thing of A. Liessin's that remained was his collected poems in three volumes, which lie where he, in sorrow, predicted, in a cellar gathering dust.

Perhaps these notes of mine will cause at least some of his former admirers and followers to remember his poetic legacy and see to it that his books are cleaned of their dust, carried up from the cellar, and brought to the public. Perhaps willing readers will be found for them. Perhaps they will feel ashamed that his legacy has been left to gather dust. And it would be worthwhile. For all of us, it would be worthwhile. Because we would get to know one of the most important poets and one of the most interesting personalities we have ever had.

12. Reuben in Miami Beach, ca. 1952.

❀ Afterword

Twenty-Five Years and a Century Afterward

KEN FRIEDEN

THIS YEAR MUST BE a Reuben Iceland landmark of some kind, as 1912 was the heyday of the poetic movement Di Yunge (The young), which he helped to found. If it is not a centennial, then at least for me it marks a quarter centennial, because I vividly remember reading his memoir *Fun unzer friling* (*From Our Springtime*) twenty-five years ago, while giving lectures and writing about American Yiddish poetry. Although I came to prefer the poetry of Jacob Glatshteyn, Y. L. Teller, and the group called the Inzikhistn (the Introspectivist Poets)—who were successors and rivals to the authors who formed Di Yunge—Iceland's book made a deep impression on me.

In retrospect, I realize that *From Our Springtime* is one of the most successful literary memoirs of a movement I have ever encountered. This reaction is unexpected now, in light of the astonishing discrepancy between the significance of the New York Yiddish authors and the relative oblivion into which most of their names have fallen. How many among American literati today know the luminous verses of Mani Leyb, Moyshe Leyb Halpern, Zishe Landau, Reuben Iceland, or Anna Margolin? We can only hope that the outstanding book you are reading, in a fine English translation by Gerald Marcus, will help to remedy this neglect. Reuben Iceland's volume adds the needed insight and perspective, giving us a graphic picture of the Yiddish literary scene in New York in the early twentieth century.

206

A small measure of recognition came to the New York Yiddish poets in 1969, when Irving Howe and Eliezer Greenberg included them in a groundbreaking anthology.[1] To that collection they brought the talent of some remarkable translators, including John Hollander and Cynthia Ozick, who themselves achieved renown for their poetry and prose. But not until 1986 did a group of New York Yiddish poets (Leyeles, Glatshteyn, Halpern, Teller, Heifetz-Tussman, and Vaynshteyn) receive extensive representation in Benjamin and Barbara Harshav's landmark bilingual anthology.[2] Since the mid-1980s, scattered other volumes have brought attention to individual authors, especially the women writers who had previously been neglected, such as Rachel Korn, Malka Heifetz-Tussman, Rokhl Fishman, and Kadya Molodowsky.[3] Among the many authors discussed in depth by Iceland, Anna Margolin (Roza Lebensboym)—with whom he lived for decades—produced some of the most memorable, enduring Yiddish poetry.[4] Iceland provides the fullest account of her

1. Irving Howe and Eliezer Greenberg, *A Treasury of Yiddish Poetry* (New York: Schocken, 1969).

2. Benjamin and Barbara Harshav, *American Yiddish Poetry* (Berkeley and Los Angeles: University of California Press, 1986), with translations by the Harshavs and by Kathryn Hellerstein, Brian McHale, and Anita Norich.

3. See, for example: *Paper Roses (Papirene royzn): Selected Poems of Rachel Korn*, trans. Seymour Levitan (Toronto: Aya Press, 1985); *With Teeth in the Earth: Selected Poems of Malka Heifetz Tussman*, trans. and ed. Marcia Falk (Detroit: Wayne State University Press, 1992); *I Want to Fall Like This: Selected Poems of Rukhl Fishman*, trans. Seymour Levitan (Detroit: Wayne State University Press, 1994); *Paper Bridges: Selected Poems of Kadya Molodowsky*, trans. and ed., Kathryn Hellerstein (Detroit: Wayne State University Press, 1999). In prose, see the groundbreaking *Found Treasures: Stories by Yiddish Women Writers*, ed. Frieda Forman et al., introduction by Irena Klepfisz (Toronto: Second Story Press, 1994), and the impressive volume by Kadya Molodowsky, *A House with Seven Windows: Short Stories*, trans. Leah Schoolnik (Syracuse: Syracuse University Press, 2006). Thanks go to Kathryn Hellerstein for her help in compiling this list. We can look forward to her forthcoming anthology *Women Yiddish Poets*, to be published by Stanford University Press.

4. For a concise overview of her biography in English, see Faith Jones, "Anna Margolin (Rosa Lebensbaum [Roza Lebensboym])," in *Dictionary of Literary Biography*, vol. 333, *Writers in Yiddish*, ed. Joseph Sherman, (Detroit: Thomson Gale, 2007), 163–73. This volume also

fascinating life; an English translation of her impressive poems is now available in book form.[5]

For readers who lack prior exposure to the Yiddish literary tradition, it is worth noting that modern Yiddish writing began only a few decades before Iceland and his friends appeared on the New York scene. Most scholars trace the origins back to the early novels of S. Y. Abramovitsh (Mendele Moykher Sforim), which he published in Russia between 1864 and 1878.[6] In the nineteenth-century realist tradition of European fiction, Abramovitsh's works influenced Sholem Aleichem's voluminous output of stories, novels, and plays (1883–1916). Contemporaneous with both of them was I. L. Peretz, the father of another Yiddish literary family. Peretz became the mentor to a generation of modernist writers who arrived in Warsaw in the years 1900–1915.[7] Reconsidering classic Yiddish writing from 1864 to 1920, we should be surprised that it was possible for a literary tradition to evolve so fast. In less than sixty years, Yiddish writing developed from nineteenth-century realist and satiric fiction to modernist twentieth-century experimentation.

---

contains pertinent literary biographies of Jacob Glatshteyn, Moyshe Leyb Halpern, Rachel Korn, Mani Leyb, and Kadya Molodowsky.

5. *Drunk from the Bitter Truth: The Poems of Anna Margolin*, trans. and ed., Shirley Kumove (Albany: State University of New York Press, 2005).

6. An account of Abramovitsh's seminal period of creativity—starting in the time of the reforms instituted by Alexander II—is contained in Ken Frieden, *Classic Yiddish Fiction: Abramovitsh, Sholem Aleichem, and Peretz* (Albany: State University of New York Press, 1995), chapters 1–3. Regarding Sholem Aleichem, see chapters 4–8; I. L. Peretz is the subject of chapters 9–11.

7. A short generation later, in Vilna (Vilnius), Yiddish creativity burst into the poetry of a group that came to be known as *Yung Vilna*, or "Young Vilna." It is perhaps surprising that Iceland never mentions the later, Vilna-based group whose name echoes Di Yunge; nor does he write much about his talented rivals among the Inzikhistn. But he himself explains this in his foreword: "I will be writing only about those with whom I was intimate and whom I knew well enough that I could do right by them and their writing. If I was not close to someone during those years, I must not write about him, no matter who it was." For a discussion of *Yung Vilna*, see Justin Cammy, *Young Vilna: Yiddish Culture of the Last Generation* (Bloomington: Indiana University Press, forthcoming).

The American Yiddish scene began awkwardly, with the politically engaged poetry of the so-called Sweatshop Poets. In "My Little Son," Morris Rosenfeld (1862–1923) wrote with pathos about the hardship of working long hours and seldom seeing his child:

> I have a son, a little son,
> a youngster very fine!
> and when I look at him I feel
> that all the world is mine.
>
> But seldom do I see him when
> he's wide awake and bright.
> I always find him sound asleep;
> I see him late at night.[8]

> Ikh hob a kleynem yingele,
> a zunele gor feyn!
> Ven ikh derzey im dakht zikh mir,
> di gantse velt iz mayn.
>
> Nor zeltn, zeltn zey ikh im,
> mayn sheynem, ven er vakht,
> ikh tref im imer shlofndik,
> ikh zey im nor bay nakht.[9]

The cadences and rhyme schemes have become so outmoded as to make successful translation difficult. In a more dogmatic mode, Rosenfeld wrote in his allegorical poem "The Sweatshop":

> Corner of Pain and Anguish, there's a worn old house:
> tavern on the street floor, Bible room upstairs.

8. Translation by Aaron Kramer, in *A Treasury of Yiddish Poetry*, ed. Irving Howe and Eliezer Greenberg (New York: Schocken, 1969), 79.

9. "Mayn yingele" was reprinted in *Antologiye finf hundert yor yidishe poeziye*, ed. M. Bassin (New York: Dos Bukh, 1917), 8.

Scoundrels sit below, and all day long they souse.
On the floor above them, Jews sob out their prayers.[10]

Korner vey un elent shteyt an alte hayzl,
untn iz a shenkl, oybn iz a klayzl.
Untn kumen lumpn oyfton nor neveyles,
oybn kumen yidn, klogn afn goles.

Presumably it was verses like these that led Zishe Landau, Reuben Iceland, and their peers to see the need for a change. Trying to set a new course for Yiddish writing in America, Zishe Landau referred to the Sweatshop Poets as "the rhyme department of the labor movement."[11]

American Yiddish poetry quickly came into its own with the help of several newly arrived poets, in particular the leaders of Di Yunge: Mani Leyb, Zishe Landau, Reuben Iceland, and Moyshe Leyb Halpern. The great accomplishment of these writers was their somewhat exaggerated separation from the mundane (and often impoverished) world of immigrant life. Following Di Yunge, the Inzikhistin continued this impractical bent with exotic lines like the opening of A. Leyeles's poem "Bay dem Ganges":

By the Ganges, by the Ganges,
Lotus flowers blossom. . . .

Bay dem Ganges, bay dem Ganges,
blihen lotus-blumen. . . . [12]

---

10. Translation by Aaron Kramer, in Howe and Greenberg, *A Treasury of Yiddish Poetry*, 78. Reprinted bilingually in *The Penguin Book of Modern Yiddish Verse*, ed. Ruth Wisse et al. (New York: Viking, 1987), 84–85.

11. For samples of early American Yiddish poetry, see the selections in *Jewish American Literature: A Norton Anthology*, ed. Kathryn Hellerstein et al. (New York: Norton, 2000). Additional information about American Yiddish poetry may be found in many sources, including Irving Howe's *World of Our Fathers*, Ruth Wisse's *A Little Love in Big Manhattan*, and in the Yiddish entry of the *Encyclopedia Britannica*.

12. Printed in the journal *Inzikh: A zamlung introspective lider* (New York: M. N. Maisel, 1920), 95.

After Iceland's circle enabled the next group of rebels to take aestheticism one step further, Jacob Glatshteyn made an indelible mark with his volumes of poetry. One unforgettable aspect of his originality was the use of exotic or fantastical motifs, as in the poem "Sesame," which dramatizes the story of Ali Baba and the Forty Thieves—from the perspective of the doomed brother-in-law who is trapped inside the cave of treasure:

> Open, sesame.
> It darkens in the cave.
> And I, weakened under the weight
> Of the sacks of gold, silver, and diamonds,
> whisper without strength:
> Open, sesame.
>
> Efn zikh sesame.
> S'tunkelt in heyl.
> Un ikh
> farkhalesht unter dem yokh
> fun di zek mit gold, zilber un brilyantn,
> sheptshe on koykhes:
> Efn zikh sesame.[13]

Pure poetry and art for art's sake were seldom the domain of Jewish writing before the twentieth century. Under the pressure of social, historical, economic, and religious circumstances, Jews more often took refuge in the timeless study of Torah, *di beste skhoyre* (the best merchandise); or, when Jews secularized, they usually turned to immediate educational, financial, or political concerns.

Reuben Iceland's longtime companion Anna Margolin, as mentioned above, wrote some of the most remarkable modernist Yiddish poetry. "Shlanke shifn" (Slender ships, 1921), for instance, presents an unforgettable moment in time, the calm before a storm as reflected in the poet's consciousness. It embodies T. S. Eliot's notion of an "objective

---

13. My translation; for the original Yiddish, see Jacob Glatshteyn, *Yankev Glatshteyn* (New York: Kultur, 1921), 60.

correlative,"[14] an external object that represents unspoken emotion. This is the entire miniature poem:

Slender ships drowse on the swelling green water;
black shadows sleep on the cold heart of the water.
All the winds are still.
Clouds pass by like ghosts in the muted night.
Pale and calm, the earth waits for storm and thunder.
I shall be still.

Shlanke shifn drimlen afn geshvoln grinem vaser,
shvartse shotns shlofn afn kaltn harts fun vaser.
Ale vintn zaynen shtil.
Khmares rukn zikh geshpenstik in der nakht der shtumer.
Bleykh un ruik vart di erd af blits un duner.
Ikh vel zayn shtil.[15]

The years from 1905 to 1933 were a golden period of creativity in which Yiddish poetry generated original modernist verses, at the same time as Dovid Bergelson and several other prose writers published world-class modernist fiction. When the Nazis entered Vienna in March 1938, however, the end was in sight. Immediately following the *Anschluß*, Glatsteyn saw this quickly and wrote one of the angriest poems in the Yiddish canon, calling it "Good Night, World":

Good night, wide world.
Big, stinking world.

14. T. S. Eliot, "Hamlet and His Problems," in *The Sacred Wood: Essays on Poetry and Criticism* (London: Methuen, 1920): "The only way of expressing emotion in the form of art is by finding an 'objective correlative'; in other words, a set of objects, a situation, a chain of events which shall be the formula of that *particular* emotion; such that when the external facts, which must terminate in sensory experience, are given, the emotion is immediately evoked" (100).

15. My translation. For a reprint of the original Yiddish poem, see Anna Margolin, *Lider*, ed. Avrom Novershtern (Jerusalem: Magnes Press, 1991), 48. Setting Margolin's lyrics, two decades ago I composed a piece called "Shlanke shifn" for voice, clarinet, and piano, which was performed—in an arrangement for soprano, clarinet, and guitar at the School of Music, Syracuse University, in December 1993.

Not you, but I, slam the gate.
In my long robe,
With my flaming, yellow patch. . . . [16]
A gute nakht, breyte velt.
groyse, shtinkendike velt.
Nisht du, nor ikh farhak dem toyer.
Mit dem langn khalat,
Mit der fayerdiker, geler lat. . . .

In these years, when one author wrote powerful "news poems" about Sigmund Freud and the fall of Vienna, it appeared that Jewish writers could never again set aside historical concerns.[17] Cynthia Ozick says it well in her masterful story "Envy; or, Yiddish in America."[18] The narrator empathizes with aging Yiddish writers in New York after the Holocaust (*khurbn*), who—having lost their Yiddish-speaking audience—are reduced to silence or an anguished cry over the doom of their artistic medium and the *mame-loshn* (mother tongue) of Eastern European Jews for centuries. Some scholars believe that the future lies with Yiddish among the Hasidim, but since the 1870s they have produced little original literature.

Reuben Iceland was one of the last Yiddish poets in New York who could have confidence that our new literature was thriving. And he was not necessarily wrong, because if it had not been overwhelmed by the fickle, unmasterable storms of history, Yiddish writing could still be vibrant today. Iceland's memoir shows us how alive Yiddish was at the beginning of the twentieth century and reminds us that in some alternate

16. Benjamin and Barbara Harshav, *American Yiddish Poetry*, 305. The original Yiddish poem was first published in the journal *In zikh* and in the newspaper *Der morgen zhurnal*, April 1938. There is a recording of Jacob Glatstein reading his poem in a strikingly unemotional voice, included on the audio CD *The Golden Peacock: The Voice of the Yiddish Writer (Di goldene pave: Dos kol fun dem yidishn shrayber)*, edited and produced by Sheva Zucker in 2001.

17. For a detailed study of this trend, centering on the work of Yehuda Leyb Teller, see Ken Frieden, "New(s) Poems: Y. L. Teller's *Lider fun der tsayt(ung)*," *AJS Review: The Journal of the Association for Jewish Studies* 15 (1990): 269–89.

18. Cynthia Ozick, "Envy; or, Yiddish in America," in *The Pagan Rabbi and Other Stories* (1971) (Syracuse: Syracuse University Press, 1995), 39–100.

history it could have become the Jewish language of the future. Yet in the face of the Nazi genocide, Zionist intolerance of Yiddish, Soviet oppression, and American assimilation, the decline of Yiddish as a literary language became inevitable.

And yet, as Jeffrey Shandler argues, we have entered a period of "postvernacular Yiddish." In the academic world and on the grassroots level, there is growing interest in Yiddish literature and culture. This ranges from popular study of the Yiddish language, university courses on Yiddish literature in translation, the performance of Yiddish song repertoire, and the revival of Klezmer music. While Yiddish is being spoken less than in the past, and its "primary level of signification" is shrinking, Shandler points out that "its secondary, or meta-level of signification—the symbolic value invested in the language apart from the semantic value of any given utterance in it—is expanding." Hence he introduced the term "postvernacular Yiddish" to indicate the situation in which "familiar cultural practices—reading, performing, studying, even speaking—are profoundly altered."[19]

Instead of looking back in anger and endlessly recalling the destruction of Eastern European culture, we can gain strength from what remains behind. As a viable alternative to both narrow-minded Zionist thinking and insular Orthodox Judaism, we can reappropriate the vast civilization that was Ashkenazic Jewish life and reincorporate it into our lives. Much as Jews traditionally relive the exodus from Egypt every year at Passover, so in American Jewish life we can relive some aspects of Yiddish culture. Continuing Yiddish culture, and playing a part in its survival, may be the most fitting memorial we can construct to honor our ancestors' accomplishments. Gerald Marcus's translation of Reuben Iceland's *Fun unzer friling* is a good place to start.

19. Jeffrey Shandler, *Adventures in Yiddishland: Postvernacular Literature and Culture* (Berkeley and Los Angeles: University of California Press, 2006), 4.

Guide to Pronunciation
of Transliterated Words

Biographies

Glossary

Index

Guide to Pronunciation of Transliterated Words

This guide follows the standard YIVO orthography.

a: sounds like w*a*nd

ay: sounds like s*i*de

dzh: sounds like fu*dge*

e: at the end of a word is pronounced like a short English "e." For example, "shtime" is pronounced shtim-*eh*

ey: sounds like d*a*te

g: sounds like *g*ive

i: sounds like str*i*ct

kh: sounds like lo*ch*

o: sounds like *aw*

tsh: sounds like *ch*eer

u: sounds like tr*oo*p

zh: sounds like trea*s*ure

 Biographies

Menakhem Boraisha (Goldberg), also known as Menakhem, b. 1888, Brest-Litovsk, Polish Lithuania, d. 1949, New York. The son of a Hebrew teacher, he received his Jewish education at home and later attended the local Russian school. In 1905 he moved to Warsaw and joined I. L. Peretz's literary circle. He published his first poems in *Der veg* in 1906. He published a cycle of poems and essays in the anthology *Nay tsayt* as well as in *Di yudishe yugend* and other journals; in the anthology *Yudish* he published the beginning of a longer poem, "Shloyme," and he wrote poems and drama reviews for the daily *Haynt*. He also wrote articles about the theater for the *Yidishn vokhenblat* and *Literarishe monatshriftn*. He served in the Russian army from 1909 to 1911 and wrote about his experiences in *Haynt* and *Fraynd*. During the boycott of Jewish businesses in Poland, he published the poem "Poyln," expressing his feelings of bitterness and protest. At the outbreak of World War I he went to Switzerland and then Paris and London. In 1914 he arrived in New York and wrote regularly for *Der tog, Firer,* and *Haynt*.

In New York he contributed to the monthly *Literatur un lebn,* and in 1916 he edited with Moyshe Leyb Halpern the anthology *Ist brodvey*. In 1918 he joined the editorial board of *Der tog*. His book of poems *A ring in der keyt* was published by The Yiddish Literary Publishing Company in 1916. After a trip to the USSR in 1926, he contributed to the Communist daily *Frayhayt,* but parted company with it in 1929 when it justified Arab attacks on Jews in Palestine. He then wrote for the newspapers *Vokh* and *Yidish* and became press officer of the American Jewish Joint Distribution Committee. Later he worked with the American Jewish Congress and edited the "Congress Weekly" in English. Other major works include *Zamd* (New York: Yidish, 1920); *Zavl Rimer* (Warsaw: Kultur Lige, 1923); *Der geyer,* (New York: Matones, 1943); a collection of poems, *A dor* (New York: Matones, 1943); and *Durkh Doyres* (New York: Matones, 1950).

Avrahm Moyshe Dilon (A. Zhukhovitski), b. 1883, Zhetl, Belarus, d. 1934, New York. He was educated by private tutors and later in Slonim. He immigrated to the United States with his parents in 1904. His first poem was published in *Literatur* in 1910; he also published works in various journals and anthologies such as *Dos naye lebn, Shriftn, Di feder, Der onhoyb, Tsukunft,* and others. A book of his poetry, *Gele bleter,* was published by Farlag Amerike (New York, 1919). A posthumous volume of poems, *Di lider,* was published by his friends in New York in 1925.

A. M. Fuks, b. 1890, Yezyerno, East Galicia, d. 1974, Tel Aviv. His father traded in flax, wheat, and fur in the surrounding villages and also owned an orchard. He attended the local *kheyder* and Baron Hirsh School. When he was sixteen, he went to Lemberg and joined the Galician Bund, then lived for a while in Tarnopol. In 1911 he published several stories and sketches in *Folksfraynd, Yidishn arbeter,* and the Lemberg *Togblat.* His first collection of stories was published in 1912 by Farlag Sh. Levin, Lemberg. He came to the United States in 1912 and published stories in *Dos naye land* and other publications. He returned to Europe in 1914 and settled in Vienna. In 1917 he began to work for *Viener morgentsaytung* and later for the *Morgenpost.* He wrote articles for the monthly *Kritik* about Mani Leyb, Zishe landau, Reuben Iceland, Fradl Shtok, and Noah Steinberg. His work appeared in the United States in *Shriftn, Inzl,* and other journals. In 1920 he became a correspondent for the *Forverts* for Austria and Hungary. He settled in Israel in the 1950s.

Herman Gold (Hillel Gurney), b. 1888, Brest-Litovsk, Polish Lithuania, d. 1953, New York. He was taught at home until age twelve and then studied at the Pinsker Yeshiva. He lived in Vilna and Warsaw and immigrated to the United States around 1905. He worked in factories, as a correspondent for *Fraye arbeter shtime,* and became a bookseller of Yiddish and English books. His first story published in the United States was "Lilis," in *Tsukunft* (1907); he published the first story of the series *Shloyme hamelekh* in the anthology *Ist brodvey* in 1916 and was highly praised by the critic Bal Makhshoves. Major books include *In vald* (New York: Yidish, 1919), *In mayn shtot Brisk* (New York: Yidish lebn, 1920), *Dos eyntsike* (New York, 1922), *Mayselekh* (New York: Yidish lebn, 1928), and the monograph *Zishe landau* (New York: Aldine, 1946).

Moyshe Leyb Halpern, b. 1886, Zlotchev, East Galicia, d. 1932, New York. He attended *kheyder* and the Baron Hirsh School in Zlotchev. At age eleven he was sent to Vienna to be apprenticed to a sign painter and remained there for ten years. His first poems were in German, but when he returned to Zlotchev and met S. J. Imber and Jacob Mestet, he began writing in Yiddish. He published poems in the *Togblat* and *Der yidisher arbeter*. He came to New York in 1908 and became one of the most important poets of Di Yunge. He published poems in *Yidisher kemfer*, *Yidishe folk*, *Fraye arbeter shtime*, *Literatur un lebn*, and in *Literatur* and *Shriftn*. He published humorous pieces in *Der gazlen*, *Der kibitzer*, and *Der groyser kundes*. He published the anthology *Fun mentsh tsu mentsh* with Moyshe Nadir in 1915, *Ist brodvey* with Menakhem Boraisha in 1916, and the monthly journal *Otem* with B. Grobard and V. Veynper in 1923. When the Communist newspaper *Frayheyt* was founded he became a regular contributor. His book-length poem *Nyu york* was published in 1919 by Farlag Vinkel (New York). *Di goldene pave* was published by Farlag Nyu York in 1924.

Reuben Iceland, b. 1884, Radomysl, Galicia, d. 1955, Miami Beach, Florida. He attended *kheyder* and was taught by private teachers in German, Polish, and Hebrew. He came to New York in 1903. He published poetry and essays in such journals and anthologies as *Tsukunft*, *Fraye arbeter shtime*, *Dos naye land*, and others. He was a central figure in Di Yunge and took part in their publications *Literatur*, *Shriftn*, *Velt ayn velt oys*, and *Fun mentsh tsu mentsh*. He was coeditor with Mani Leyb of *Literatur un lebn*. A collection of his poetry *Fun mayn zumer* was published in 1922 by Farlag Unzer shayer (Vienna). He was a writer and editor for many years for *Der tog*. His long poem *Gezang fun hirsh* was published in 1944 by Inzl. His memoir *Fun unzer friling* was published in 1954 by Inzl. Among other translations, he participated with poets in the translation of *Heinrich Heine: Zayn lebn un zayne verk*, 8 vols. (Farlag Yidish, 1918).

David Ignatoff, (Ignatovski) b. 1885, Brusilov, Ukraine, d. 1954, New York. He was born into a poor Hasidic family and often heard his father tell stories of the Bal Shem Tov and his mother's stories from the *Tsene-rene*. He went to Kiev in 1903, where he was arrested for revolutionary activities. He came to New York in 1906, working in factories in various cities and becoming active in union organizing. He published his first story, "Ervachung," in *Der yugend* in 1907. His novel *Tsvey kreftn* was published in 1908 by Farlag Yidish. In 1910 he edited the Di Yunge anthology *Literatur* with I. J. Schwartz; he edited *Shriftn* beginning in 1912, and published work in other anthologies. He edited the anthology *Velt ayn velt oys* in 1916. Major works include *In kesl grub* (New York: Frayheyt, 1928), the trilogy *Af* *vayte vegn* (New York: Farlag Amerike, 1932), *Dos vos kumt for* (New York, 1932), and *Far a nayer velt* (New York: Farlag Amerike, 1939).

David Kazanski, b. 1880, Piratin, Ukraine, d. 1945, New York. He immigrated to America in 1908 and worked as a launderer, merchant, and sales agent for the newspaper *Der tog.* His first story was published in Khaym Zhitlovski's publication *Dos naye lebn.* He was part of the group with Mani Leyb, Zishe Landau, and Reuben Iceland that published the journal *Inzl,* and he also contributed to the journal *Literatur un lebn.* He wrote a novel, *Arum un arum* (New York: Inzl), that was planned as five volumes, but only three were published: *Blinder mazl,* 1930; *Treyfene blut,* 1930; and *In yokh,* 1935. He also published the anthology *Zishe Landoy zamelbukh* (New York: Inzl, 1938.)

Moyshe Yoyne Khaymovitch, b. 1881, Mir, Belarus, d. 1958, New York. Born into a poor family, he attended *kheyder,* the Talmud Torah, and the Mirer Yeshiva. He immigrated to the United States in 1902 and worked as a tailor. He published his first story, "Farblondzhndik," in the *Fraye arbeter shtime* in 1905. He coedited *Di yugend* and *Literatur* and wrote over two hundred short stories for *Der tog.* Major works include *Tsvey dersteylungen* (New York: Greyzel and Komp, 1911); *Ofyn veg,* a novel published in the anthology *Di heym* (1914); *Arum dem man fun notseres* (New York: Kultur, 1924); and *Karosel* (New York, 1946).

I. Kisin (I. Garnitski), b. 1886, Kovne, d. 1950, Dayton, Ohio. His father was a preacher. He studied secular subjects with private tutors, became well versed in Russian literature, and began writing at an early age. He came to the United States in 1904, and beginning in 1916 he published stories, poems, critical articles, and translations. They appeared in *Literatur un lebn, Der tog, Tsukunft, Fraye arbeter shtime, Di naye velt,* and other journals. He was a writer for the *Forverts* for twenty-four years. His books include *Lider fun der milkhome* (New York: Bibliotek fun poezye un eseyen, 1933) and *Lid un esey* (New York, 1953).

Zishe Landau, b. 1889, Plotsk, Poland, d. 1937, New York. He was the grandson and great-grandson of the renowned rabbis Wolf Strickover and Abraham Landau. He had a traditional Jewish education and also studied Polish, Russian, German, French, and modern Hebrew. He became active in the Bund before immigrating to the United States in 1906. He was a central figure of Di Yunge, and published poems and essays in *Tsayt gayst, Dos naye land, Dos naye lebn, Shriftn, Velt ayn velt* *oys, Der tog,* the *Forverts,* and other journals, as well as in the monthly journal *Inzl* that he helped found. His only collection of poems in book form, *Zishe Landoy* (New York: Inzl, 1938), was published by his friends after his death.

Berl Lapin, b. 1889 in a village near Volkovisk, Belarus, d. 1952, New York. His father was a wealthy miller. When he was six they moved to Argentina but four years later returned to Galicia and Lithuania. Because of the frequent moves, *kheyder* was his only formal education. In 1908 he published three stories, "Umetike vegn," "Di velt," and "Vilne," in a collection that brought him renown in Vilna literary circles. He immigrated to the United States in 1909 and published works in Zhitlovski's *Dos naye lebn.* In 1913 he returned to Argentina for several years before coming back to New York. He published poems in several issues of *Shriftn* from 1925 to 1928, as well as in *Der tog, Yidisher kemfer, Yidishe kultur, Zamlbikher,* and other journals. He translated the poetry of many Russian poets and published an anthology, *Rusishe lyrik* (New York: Naye tsayt, 1919). Collections of his poems in book form include *Tseykhns, lider un poemes* (New York: Khaveyrim, 1934), *Naye lider* (New York: Atlantik, 1940), and *Der fuler krug* (New York: Ikuf, 1950).

Malke Lee (Malka Leopold), b. 1904, Monastrikh, Galicia, d. 1976, New York. She was born into a Hasidic family and spent part of her youth in Vienna, where she fled with her family during World War I. After the war she returned to Poland, and then immigrated to New York in 1921. In New York she attended Hunter College and the Jewish Teachers Seminary. Lee and her first husband, Aaron Rappaport, owned and managed a bungalow colony in High Falls, New York, which became a gathering place for Yiddish intellectuals. Her collections of poems include *Lider* (New York: Farlag Nyu York, 1932), *Gezangen* (New York: Farlag Nyu York, 1940), *Kines fun undzer tsayt* (New York: Ikuf, 1945), *Durkh loytere kvaln* (New York: Ikuf, 1950), *Durkh kindershe oygn* (Buenos Aires: Yidbukh, 1955), *In likht fun doyres* (Tel Aviv: Y. L. Perets, 1961), *Untern nusnboym* (Tel Aviv: Y. L. Perets, 1969), and *Mayselekh far Yoselen* (Tel Aviv: Y. L. Perets, 1969).

H. Leivick (Leivick Halpern), b. 1888, Igumen, Belarus, d. 1962, New York. His father was a private tutor for girls. Leivick attended the local *kheyder* and the yeshiva at Berezine. He then attended the yeshiva in Minsk, where he prepared to become a rabbi but was expelled for reading secular books. He joined the revolutionary movement and worked for the Bund for two years, for which he was arrested and sentenced to prison for four years. From prison he published his first poems in *Tsayt gayst* (New York). He was then exiled to Siberia for life. In 1913 he escaped and made his way to New York. He was close to the poets of Di Yunge and his poetry appeared in their publications. He also wrote for *Der tog, Tsukunft, Forverts, Frayheyt,* and *Fraye Arbeter Shtime,* and became a major figure in Yiddish literature. His major works include the play *Der goylem* (New York: Farlag Amerike, 1921), based on the legend of the Maharal of Prague, for which he became famous in Europe and the United States. Other publications include his lyric poem series *In keynem's land* (Warsaw: Kultur lige, 1923) and *Geklibene verk,* 5 vols. (Vilna: B. Kletskin, 1925, 1927).

Mani Leyb (Mani Leyb Brahinsky), b. 1883, Niezhin, Ukraine, d. 1953, New York. Mani Leyb's father was a fur merchant; his mother was a great lover of idiomatic expressions and folk songs. He attended *kheyder* until he was eleven and was apprenticed to a bootmaker; after six years he opened his own business. He took part in various revolutionary movements including the Bolshevik Revolution and was arrested in 1904. After a second arrest in 1905 he escaped and came to the United States. His first poem was published in the *Forverts;* he also published in the *Fraye arbeter shtime, Tsukunft, Yidisher kemfer,* and other journals, as well as in Di Yunge publications, *Shriftn, Literatur,* and *Fun mentsh tsu mentsh.* He coedited the anthology *Inzl* with David Kazanski in 1918. He coedited for a time the journal *Literatur* with Reuben Iceland and in 1925 founded the monthly journal *Inzl* with Reuben Iceland and Zishe Landau. He contributed regularly to the *Forverts.* One of his most popular books was his book-length children's poem, *Yingl tsingl khvat* (Warsaw: Kultur lige, 1918). Other books include *Blimelekh krentselekh* (Inzl, 1918), *Vunder iber vunder, lider, baladn, mayselekh* (New York: Arbeter ring, 1930), *Sonetn* (Paris: Di goldene pave, 1962), and *Lider un baladn* (Tel Aviv: Y. L. Peretz, 1977).

Abraham Liessin (Valt), b. 1872, Minsk, Belarus, d. 1938, New York. His father, who came from a long line of rabbis and scholars, was a follower of Rabbi Israel Salanter, founder of the Musar movement. His mother, too, came from a family of renowned rabbis. Liessin was a prodigious child with an amazing memory and ability to read. He began studying the Talmud when he was seven and at age nine began writing *shirim* and religious commentaries. When he was twelve he ran away to Slobodke and became a passionate follower of the Musar movement. He attended the Volozhiner Yeshiva for a while but became rebellious, and when he was found smoking on the Sabbath he was expelled and had to leave town. He went to Vilna, where he became an expert in Russian, memorizing the Hebrew-Russian dictionary in just a few weeks. He moved to Minsk, where he became involved in spreading Socialist propaganda among the workers. He immigrated to the United States in 1896 and became one of the first writers for the *Forverts*, but left after a falling out with the editor, Abe Kahan. He was the editor of *Tsukunft* for many years. Anthologies include *Blumen un funken, lider*, vol. 2 (Vilna: Di velt, 1906) and *Pionern fun yidishn poezye in America, sotsyale lid*, vol. 2 (New York: Di velt, 1956). His collected poems *Lider un poemen* were published in 1938 in three volumes, with illustrations by Marc Chagall, by the Forverts Association, New York.

Joseph Opatoshu (Opatovsky), b. 1886 in the forest near Mlawe, Poland, d. 1954, New York. His father was a forest merchant from an old Hasidic family, a very learned man and one of the first Maskilim in Poland. He wrote *shirim* that appeared in many of Opatoshu's stories. His mother grew up in the forest and knew many Polish legends. He studied at home with his father until he was twelve, when he left to attend school in Mlawe. At age fourteen he attended a commercial school in Warsaw, but when the school was shut by the czarist regime, he went to Nancy, France, to attend the polytechnic there. He was forced to return home when the czar forbade the cutting of forests in Poland. He came to New York and worked in a factory until he found a job as a Hebrew teacher. In 1914 he completed his studies to be a civil engineer, but worked in that profession only a short time. The first story he published was "Af yener zayt brik" (1910) in *Literatur*. In 1912 he cofounded *Shriftn* with David Ignatoff. He published two novels in that journal, *Roman fun a ferd ganev* and *Moris un zayn zun Filip*. After disagreements with Ignatoff, he withdrew and founded *Di naye heym* with a group of other young writers; he published several of his longer stories there. He also published over three hundred stories in *Der tog*. His major books include *Aleyn* (New York: Naye tsayt, 1918), *Hebru* (New York: M. N. Mayzel, 1920), *In poylishe velder* (New York: M. N. Mayzel, 1921), *Arum dem khurves* (Vilna, 1925), *A tog in regensburg un elyahu bokher* (New York: E. Malino, 1933), *Ven poyln iz gefaln* (New York: CYCO, 1943), *Di letste oyfshtand* (New York: CYCO, 1948), and *Yidn legende un andere dertseylungen* (New York: CYCO, 1951).

Isaac Raboy, b. 1882, Zavalye, Ukraine, d. 1944, Los Angeles. He was born into a traditional Hasidic family and studied with the finest teachers his father could find, but he became interested in the Haskalah and was expelled from the local synagogue when he was fifteen for reading secular literature and cutting off his *peyes*. He began writing in Russian, Hebrew, and Yiddish but did not publish anything. He came to the United States in 1904 and in 1906 published several pieces in the weekly *Der arbeter*. His short story "Di royte blum" was published in the *Yugend*. Around 1908 he left New York to become a farmer, studying in an agricultural school before getting a job on a horse farm in North Dakota. In 1913 he returned to New York and published his first novel, *Her Goldenberg*, in *Shriftn*; it was received enthusiastically as the first description of Jewish life in rural America. His second novel, *Der pas fun yam*, published in 1917 in the anthology *Inzl*, was also well received, as was *Dos vilde land* published in 1919 in *Shriftn*. In 1928 he became a regular writer for the *Frayheyt*. His major books include *Nayn brider* (New York: Internatsyonaler order, 1936), *Der yidisher kauboy* (New York: Ikuf, 1932), *A dorf fun kinder* (New York: Ikuf, 1953), *Iz gekumen a yid keyn amerike* (New York: Ikuf, 1944), and Mayn lebn (New York: Ikuf, 1945).

Joseph Rolnik, b. 1845, Zhukhovitch, Belarus, d. 1955, New York. His father owned a mill; his mother came from a family of farmers. He was taught by private tutors and later attended the Mirer Yeshiva. He wrote poetry in Russian, Hebrew, and Yiddish. He came to the United States in 1899, then moved to England and Russia, returning to New York in 1906. He was often in poor health. He worked for *Der tog* for many years as a proofreader. He published poems in *Fraye arbeter shtime, Di yugend, Dos yidishe folk, Der yidisher kemfer, Dos naye lebn, Tsukunft,* and other journals. His memoir, *Zikhroynes,* was published in 1954 in New York with the help of the David Ignatoff literature fund.

I. J. Schwartz, b. 1885, Petrushany, Lithuania, d. 1971, New York. His father was the local rabbi. He received a strict Orthodox upbringing and studied at the Kovner Yeshiva. His first poem was published in *Dos yidishe folk* in 1906. He came to the United States in 1906 and published poems and translations in *Tsukunft* and *Der yidisher kemfer*; he translated Bialik, Yehuda haLevi, Walt Whitman, Shakespeare, and Milton. He published work in *Shriftn, Literatur, Di naye heym,* and *Velt ayn velt oys*. In 1918 he moved to Lexington, Kentucky, where he and his family opened a store. His epic poem *Kentoki* was published in 1923 by Sh. Rabinovitch (New York) and was hailed by critics as an authentic American epic and one of the most important American works concerning Jewish life in America. In 1928 he returned to New York. Other major works include *Geklibene lider* (New York: Ikuf, 1961), and *Lider un poemen,* in the journal *Goldene Keyt* (Tel Aviv, 1968).

Abba Stoltsenberg, b. 1905, Gline, Poland, d. 1941, New York. His father had a flour business; he attended the local *kheyder,* the Baron Hirsh School, and the Torner Gymnasium. He came to the United States with his parents in 1923. He published poems in *Inzl, Tsukunft, Yunge kuzine,* and other journals. He wrote poetry over a period of many years, but with frequent interruptions. His first book of poems, *Lider,* was published after his death (New York: M. N. Mayzel, 1941).

Moyshe Warshaw, b. 1887, Antopol, Belarus, d. 1912, New York. His father was an impoverished teacher. He was influenced by Zionism but went over to the Bund and was arrested for his activities. He came to New York in 1906 and worked in factories and sold newspapers. He translated quite a lot, including plays of Chekhov. He committed suicide by jumping off an upper story of an unfinished building where he was working as a watchman. His diary was published by K. Tepler and Zishe Landau under the title *Vegn fun a neshome* (New York: Nyu York, 1913).

 Glossary

alrightnik: someone who is smug and self-satisfied; used contemptuously.

Ashmodai: king of demons.

avoda: worship; religious service.

bentshing: grace after meals.

daytshmerish: a mixture of Yiddish and High German, once considered elegant and sophisticated in some intellectual and artistic circles, but disapproved of by Di Yunge and in modern Yiddish circles as a foreign and inauthentic intrusion.

faynshmeker: someone overly refined or sensitive; used ironically or contemptuously.

gaon: an exceptionally learned religious scholar; a genius.

Gemore (Gemara): the main body of the Talmud, it consists of a record of ancient rabbinical debates about the interpretation of the Mishna and is the primary source of Jewish religious law.

Haskole (Haskalah): a movement in eighteenth- and nineteenth-century Europe, sometimes called the Jewish Enlightenment. It favored the teaching of secular subjects as part of Jewish education as well as the secularization of Jewish life to various degrees.

HIAS: Hebrew Immigrant Aid Society; founded in 1881 to assist Jewish immigrants and refugees in the United States and other countries.

high holidays: Rosh Hashona and Yom Kiper (Yom Kippur).

kheyder: traditional religious school for young boys.

Khumesh (Khumoshim): the Torah, divided into weekly portions along with associated readings from Prophets and other writings that are read in the synagogue on the Sabbath.

kibitzarnia: from the word kibitz, meaning to banter, gossip, or offer unwanted advice.

klutz: someone who is clumsy or not overly bright.

lamed: Hebrew letter equivalent to "L."

Litvak: literally, a Jew from Lithuania; idiomatically it connotes someone who is stubborn, rigid, or overly zealous.

Maskil (Maskilim): follower(s) of the Haskalah movement.

mikve: Jewish ritual bath.

Minkhe: afternoon prayer service.

Misnagdim: Orthodox Jews in Europe who opposed Hasidism.

mume: aunt.

peyes: side locks worn by traditional Orthodox and Hasidic boys and men.

rubashke: a type of Russian shirt.

shabes-yontevdik: in this context, nostalgic, celebratory, or uplifting.

shatnez: cloth that contains both wool and linen; Jews are forbidden by the Torah to wear such cloth; by extension, two things that don't go together.

shire (shirim): religious song(s) of praise.

shloshim: the first thirty days following a person's burial.

sholem aleykhem: peace unto you, a common greeting.

shund: trashy or vulgar literature or theater.

Shvues (Shavuoth): Feast of Weeks, celebrates the spring harvest season in Israel; it also commemorates the giving of the Torah to Moses and the Israelites at Mount Sinai.

sikkhe: stalks left behind in a field after the harvest is completed; according to Jewish law, they belong to the poor and may not be used by the farmer. The law applied to the Land of Israel during the First Temple period.

Sukes (Succoth): Festival of the Tabernacles. Celebrates the fall harvest season in Israel; also commemorates the Israelites' journey through the wilderness after their exodus from Egypt.

tahores shtibl: small building in a cemetery used for the preparation of corpses for burial.

takhles mentsh: someone concerned above all with results.

tales (taleysim): prayer shawl(s).

taytsh khumesh: the Hebrew Bible translated into Yiddish with commentaries and legends; intended for use by women.

tkhines: prayers in Yiddish intended for use by women; first compiled in the seventeenth century.

tsadik: a very pious, righteous person.

Tsene-rene: the most popular and beloved Yiddish adaptation of the Bible, published by Yacov ben Yitzhak Ashenazi late in the sixteenth century.

tsholent: a type of stew traditionally eaten on the Sabbath.

yontev: religious holiday; a celebration or joyous time.

yortsayt: anniversary of a person's death.

Zionist: an adherent of Zionism, the Jewish nationalist movement advocating the migration of Jews to Palestine to establish a Jewish state; someone who supports the establishment of the State of Israel.

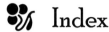

Index

Other titles from Judaic Traditions in Literature, Music, and Arts

American Hebrew Literature: Writing Jewish National Identity in the United States
   Michael Weingrad

Classic Yiddish Stories of S. Y. Abramovitsh, Sholem Aleichem, and I. L. Peretz
   Ken Frieden, ed.

Finding the Jewish Shakespeare: The Life and Legacy of Jacob Gordin
   Beth Kaplan

Here and Now: History, Nationalism, and Realism in Modern Hebrew Fiction
   Todd Hasak-Lowy

The Image of the Shtetl and Other Studies of Modern Jewish Literary Imagination
   Dan Miron

Intimations of Difference: Dvora Baron in the Modern Hebrew Renaissance
   Sheila E. Jelen

Missing a Beat: The Rants and Regrets of Seymour Krim
   Mark Cohen

The New Country: Stories from the Yiddish about Life in America
   Henry Goodman, trans. and ed.

The Passing Game: Queering Jewish American Culture
   Warren Hoffman

Translating Israel: Contemporary Hebrew Literature and Its Reception in America
   Alan L. Mintz